HERITAGE TRA
GREAT SOUTH EAST

Queensland Environmental Protection Agency

Brisbane, 2000

GW00832761

Queensland
Government
Environmental
Protection Agency

The
Great
South
East

CONTENTS

Etheridge's Garage, Eumundi. c1936 (John Oxley Library)

Moreton Bay

In 1770 Lieutenant James Cook, in the *Endeavour*, charted the east coast of Australia, naming 'Morton Bay' after the president of the Royal Society in London. Cook's voyage was the catalyst for the British colonisation of New South Wales as a penal colony in 1788. In 1799, Lieutenant Matthew Flinders explored Moreton Bay and Pumicestone Passage and journeyed inland to the Glass House Mountains, ascending Mount Beerburrum. A recommendation was made for the establishment of a penal settlement at Moreton Bay, and in 1823 exploration by Surveyor-General John Oxley located the entrance to the Brisbane River.

Oxley's recommendations to Governor Brisbane led to the formation of the Moreton Bay penal settlement in 1824, providing a focus for further exploration of the coast and hinterland. In 1825 Major Edmund Lockyer followed the Brisbane River upstream to the present vicinity of Esk. Commandant Patrick Logan explored the Logan River district in 1826, and the Fassifern Valley and Beaudesert districts in the following year. In 1827 and 1828 the botanist Allan Cunningham reported on the fine pastoral country of the Darling Downs on the inland side of the Dividing Range, a region previously unknown to Europeans.

The squatters

The rush to occupy south-east Queensland, still part of New South Wales, began in 1840. It was spearheaded by the Leslie brothers, who knew of Cunningham's exploration of the Downs. The would-be squatters, the first to reach the Downs from the New England district, established a pattern of pastoral expansion into south-east Queensland by way of the interior. The Leslies explored the southern Downs and took up Canning Downs run, a vast expanse of grazing country along the Condamine River that included the future site of Warwick. Other pastoralists soon followed, taking up runs regardless of Aboriginal resistance.

In late 1840 Hodgson and Elliott, who had followed the Leslies to the Downs to take up Eton Vale run, passed through Cunningham's Gap to Ipswich, then on to Brisbane, where they purchased supplies despite a ban on settlers entering the penal settlement. Their journey marked the beginning of trade and traffic between the Downs and Brisbane. From 1841 pastoralists spilled over from the Darling Downs into the Lockyer Creek and Brisbane River valleys. The Moreton Bay district was thrown open to free settlement in February 1842. The speed with which huge tracts of land were occupied by pastoralists was staggering. By the time Queensland was formally separated from the colony of New South Wales in December 1859, pastoralists had occupied most of south-east Queensland from the Tweed to the Fitzroy, and from the coast to the western Darling Downs.

Timber-getters

Timber was the first natural resource exploited by Europeans in south-east Queensland. Logging and rafting of timber for local consumption or for shipping to southern settlements began in the convict period along the banks of the Brisbane and Logan rivers and accelerated under free settlement, a pattern repeated throughout the timbered districts from the Tweed to the Noosa River. Timber-getting intensified with the introduction of the first steam sawmills during the 1850s at Brisbane, Warwick, Toowoomba and Crows Nest. Timber-getters and gold seekers, often the first Europeans to enter the dense scrubs of the south-east, paved the way for closer settlement. Selectors followed, clearing land for farms where before there had been thick scrub.

Gold-diggers

During the 1860s nothing had a greater impact on settlement than the shout 'Gold!' Queensland's coffers were almost empty as a result of a slump in the price of wool and a severe financial depression when, early in 1867, the government offered rewards for the discovery of a mineral field in the colony capable of supporting a population of 3000. By August that year a prospector named James Nash had discovered gold at Gympie. Within months, over 15,000 diggers had arrived on the field, coming first through the ports of Maryborough and Tewantin then by new tracks from the Brisbane district. The Gympie gold rush revived the new colony's fortunes. A better route to the goldfield was needed, however, and by 1868 a new Cobb and Co. coach road had been established from Brisbane through Caboolture, Glass House Mountains, Mellum Creek (Landsborough), Petrie's Creek (Nambour) and Yandina, opening up the north coast to logging and farm selection.

❶ *Canning Downs Homestead (John Oxley Library)*
❷ *Shearing at Talgai West (John Oxley Library)*
❸ *Gympie gold diggings 1868 (John Oxley Library)*

Closer settlement

Pastoralism remained the dominant economic activity in Queensland until the colony separated from New South Wales in 1859. Between 1860 and 1894 the Queensland Parliament passed a series of bills aimed at opening up the land for closer settlement and agricultural development, in the process challenging the squatters' hold. The objective was to create an economic basis for the future development of the colony by a combination of land reform, development of transport infrastructure and encouragement of immigration. The effect of the first of the 1860 Land Acts on the southern Darling Downs, with its well-watered blacksoil plains, was immediate. Over the next three decades, more and more pastoral land was resumed for farming and settlement.

Dairying

Closer settlement in the south-east promoted the establishment of dairying as a commercial activity, and caused significant changes to the landscape as land was cleared, roads and railways were built and settlements expanded. New legislation in 1906 encouraged further opening of land for dairying in the heavily timbered ranges of the coastal hinterland. Dairying became a staple economic activity with the introduction of pasteurisation, construction of local dairy factories and production of export-quality butter. The expanding network of railway branch lines throughout the south-east during the early 1900s encouraged the establishment of centralised butter factories, nearly all operated as co-operatives by local dairy farmers by the 1920s. Despite drought in the mid-1920s, dairy cattle numbers increased and dairying was the most widespread agricultural activity in south-east Queensland during the Depression.

❹ *Butter factory, c1900s (John Oxley Library)*
❺ *Grandchester Railway Station*
❻ *Toowoomba's first town hall (John Oxley Library)*

Railway expansion

Following Separation in 1859, Darling Downs squatters persuaded the new colonial government to borrow overseas to establish a rail link from Ipswich, the squatters' capital, west to Toowoomba and ultimately south to Warwick. Work on the Main Line section of the Southern and Western Railway from Ipswich to the Darling Downs started in 1864. In 1881 work started on the North Coast Railway to link Brisbane with the regional centres of Gympie, Maryborough, Bundaberg and Rockhampton.

Railways became one of the most politically sensitive issues in 19th century Queensland. Wherever the railway went, rapid development followed. New settlements emerged around rail sidings, while towns bypassed by the railway declined.

The expansion of railways was fundamental to Queensland's economic boom in the 1880s, but carried a heavy price. Construction absorbed the colony's financial and engineering resources and the government's borrowings to finance railway expansion nearly bankrupted Queensland when the Depression struck in the early 1890s. Many of the branch lines established in the south-east in the early 20th century were closed from the 1960s, reflecting changes in the rural economy and the increasing reliance on road transport.

Small towns

Rural south-east Queensland is serviced by a network of small townships established along the region's principal road and rail systems and by a handful of larger towns at the junctions of these systems. Some rural towns were purpose-built, while others evolved in consequence of land use, demographic patterns and transport routes. Townships established in the 1840s and 1850s developed to serve the pastoral industry. After Separation in 1859 and the introduction of closer settlement, new townships developed to service the developing farming districts. With the expansion of railways from the 1860s, many railheads and sidings evolved into permanent settlements.

By the 1870s the government's closer settlement schemes were beginning to have an impact on the pattern of settlement in the south-east. On the plains of the Lockyer Valley, Laidley, which had been growing in importance, was overshadowed by Gatton. Meanwhile, Helidon was emerging as the service centre for communities at the foot of the Main Range. On the Range itself, Toowoomba had supplanted Drayton during the 1860s and had become a well-established municipality, increasing in importance as the main centre for transport and heavy industry beyond Brisbane.

Warwick, established in 1849 as the administrative centre of the Darling Downs, continued to grow in importance as the hub of the southern Downs. On the northern Downs, a shanty known as Goode's Inn, established in 1847 at a teamsters' camp, became the township of Nanango in 1861. To the south, Crows Nest had developed as the centre for logging and timber-milling in the district by the late 1850s.

South of the Logan River, the town of Beenleigh had become an important centre for sugar and arrowroot milling. On the south coast, Southport was surveyed in 1874 and by 1880 had become a popular seaside resort for Brisbane families. Further south, the beach settlement of Coolangatta gained its first hotel in 1884. The river port of Nerang, surveyed in 1865, was the earliest settlement to develop as a service centre for the south coast. By the 1870s Nerang had become the centre for timber-getting and cotton, sugarcane and tobacco growing in the district. Development of Elston quickened during the 1930s, and in 1933 residents asked for the town's name to be changed — Surfers Paradise was the new name, inspired by the name of the local hotel built in 1925.

In the Fassifern Valley, small settlements such as Boonah, Kalbar, Harrisville and Peak Crossing serviced the needs of local selectors. Ipswich was regarded as the municipal centre of the Fassifern until Boonah and Kalbar grew in the 1880s. To the east, the township of Beaudesert had been subdivided from the pastoral run in the 1860s, yet until the 1880s its growth was slow as it continued to be regarded as a 'private town' in the hands of the local squatters.

On the Sunshine Coast, Gympie gold established Tewantin on the Noosa River as an alternative port to Maryborough.

Tewantin, where ships could land gold-diggers and supplies and load timber, was proclaimed a town in 1871. Sawmilling towns developed nearby at Eumundi and Mill Point on Lake Cootharaba. By the 1890s Nambour had emerged as the main centre for the north coast hinterland, replacing Yandina. The scenic beauty of the Blackall Range had attracted visitors from the 1890s, and guesthouses became popular as holiday accommodation from the early 1900s at places such as Maleny and Montville. Buderim became a favourite destination for excursions from Brisbane in the 1910s after a tramway was constructed through the rainforest from the railway at Palmwoods. Tourism increased at Caloundra, Maroochydore and Noosa Heads in the 1920s, as new roads linked them to the north coast highway.

Soldier settlers

Even before the end of World War I, the Queensland Government had introduced a soldier settlement scheme through which returned servicemen could acquire low-cost scrub land for farming. The soldier settlement at Beerburrum, established in 1916, became one of the largest in Australia. The new farmers were encouraged to plant pineapples and other tropical crops and the township of Beerburrum developed to service their farms. Other soldier settlements were established in the Coominya and Mount Mee areas, where pineapples and bananas were cultivated, and in the Stanthorpe district, where fruit orchards were planted at new settlements named after the battlefields in France where Australian troops had fought. By the early 1930s most of these farms had been abandoned and the government later resumed the cleared blocks for state forest development.

Natural values

By 1890 the view that native forests were inexhaustible was being replaced by concern about their rapid depletion and the need for their conservation, particularly in the south-east. In 1900 the government formed the State Forestry branch to establish timber reserves for conservation and plant forests to meet future needs. The introduction in 1906 of the State Forests and National Parks Act supported a concept of land use that was new in Australia — the creation of national parks with areas set aside for public recreation and the conservation of important natural values. Witches Falls on Tamborine Mountain was set aside as Queensland's first national park in 1908. Bunya Mountains National Park was gazetted in the same year, followed by Cunningham's Gap in 1909. Lamington National Park was created in 1915.

7 *Gympie grocery store, c1870s (John Oxley Library)*
8 *Boonah blacksmiths, c1880s (John Oxley Library)*
9 *Soldier-settler family at Amiens, c1920 (John Oxley Library)*

Declaration of state forest reserves in south-east Queensland at Beerburrum–Beerwah, Kenilworth and Imbil in the early 1900s was followed by the experimental planting of stands of hoop and bunya pine. During the 1920s and 1930s more land was acquired for state forest development as abandoned soldier settler farms were resumed in the Stanthorpe, Mount Mee and Beerburrum–Beerwah districts. Government reforestation programs increased in the late 1940s, assisted by an employment pool of displaced persons from Europe; these programs peaked in the 1970s after loans from the Commonwealth under a softwood forestry agreement provided even greater incentives for the establishment of more pine plantations in the region.

Road improvement

An efficient transport system was essential to effective economic growth. From the 1820s to the 1860s much use was made of waterways and existing Aboriginal pathways — for example, the Leslies' road from Canning Downs to Drayton followed an Aboriginal track. Corduroy and stone-pitched surfaces were laid on difficult sections of teamster routes from the 1860s and can still be seen on some early roads such as the Spicers Gap track. From the 1860s, the government spent large sums on improving tracks and constructing bridges. Road development became the responsibility of the newly created divisional boards from 1880 and lagged behind the expansion of railways until the introduction of Main Roads legislation in 1920. During the 1930s Depression, local councils used government subsidies to fund road improvements, made by unemployed workers. From the mid-1920s many state highways were sealed, main roads macadamised, and other roads made permanently passable. Much of this work was carried out during emergency wartime programs in the 1940s.

Tourism

Continuing growth of Brisbane's population and the expansion of the railway network into the south and north coast hinterlands from the 1880s contributed greatly to the development of tourism in south-east Queensland. By the early 1900s, Caloundra and Noosa Heads were already seaside resorts. The scenic beauty of the Blackall Range had attracted tourists from the 1890s, and by the 1920s guesthouses were accommodating holiday visitors on the tablelands from Maleny to Mapleton. Guesthouses were also operating in the south coast hinterland at the entrances to new national parks at Springbrook and on the Lamington Plateau. The lodging of tourists helped sustain family dairy farms in many districts during the Depression years in the 1930s.

Development of south-east Queensland as a major tourism destination took off during the 1950s, spurred by the growth in air travel and car ownership and the relaxation of building restrictions, which allowed the first high-rise development on the Gold Coast. Meanwhile, by 1960 a coastal road had been constructed on the Sunshine Coast, linking Caloundra, Maroochydore and Noosa. Queensland's Great South East is now Australia's premier tourism destination.

7

🔟 *Pineapple crop near Woombye, c1908 (John Oxley Library)*
⓫ *Early cabin at Binna Burra Lodge*
⓬ *Constructing the Jimna Range road (John Oxley Library)*
⓭ *Majestic Theatre at Pomona, 1927 (John Oxley Library)*

HOW TO USE THIS GUIDE

Rural heartland

The Great South East is Queensland's heartland — here European settlement of the State began. The course of history can be charted in the green rolling hills, bountiful forests, flowing streams and rich soil that offered ample resources for growth. This guide is about rural south-east Queensland, the region beyond the high-rise buildings and dense housing of greater Brisbane and its satellites, the Gold and Sunshine Coasts.

The Great South East has been shaped by European land use since the 1840s. Its historic cities — Toowoomba, Warwick, Stanthorpe and Gympie — are the product of pastoralism, timber-getting, mining and farming. The eight heritage trails of Queensland's Great South East reflect these themes.

Heritage Trails of the Great South East has simplified route maps of eight colour-coded heritage trails. Each site in the guide is numbered and colour-coded so you can find it on the relevant map. The maps are intended as trail guides only and do not show all roads and townships. **You are advised to use the route maps in the guide in conjunction with detailed road maps of the region (available through Sunmap).**

1. Gold Coast Hinterland Heritage Trail

Inland from the Gold Coast, discover dramatic green ranges, rainforests and mountain pools. The trail links Tamborine Mountain, Mundoolun, Canungra, Lamington National Park, Beechmont, Numinbah, Springbrook National Park and Mudgeeraba.

2. Fassifern Valley Heritage Trail

Experience the richness of the fertile Fassifern Valley and the rugged grandeur of the Main Range. Visit Beaudesert, Rathdowney, Mount Barney, Mount Maroon and Moogerah Peaks national parks, Spicers Gap, Kalbar, Boonah and Harrisville.

3. Brisbane River Valley Heritage Trail

Explore the 'Valley of the Lakes' and the hills and ranges of the Brisbane River watershed. Travel through Coominya, Esk, Somerset Dam, Blackbutt, Yarraman, Cooyar, Crows Nest, Murphys Creek, Helidon, Gatton, Laidley, Rosewood and Marburg.

4. Toowoomba Heritage Trail

Nestled on the edge of the Main Range and renowned for its magnificent views, Toowoomba is Queensland's largest inland city. The trail links Ruthven Street, Russell Street, Neil Street, Margaret Street, Queens Park and Drayton.

5. Southern Downs Heritage Trail

Discover one of Queensland's most historic rural areas, passing through rolling green downs and golden grain fields to visit Cambooya, Nobby, Clifton, Allora, Warwick, Killarney and Leyburn.

6. Granite Belt Heritage Trail

The cool high country of the Granite Belt is like no other part of Queensland. From Dalveen, take the 'fruit run' through Amiens to Stanthorpe, then visit Ballandean, Girraween National Park and Wallangarra.

7. Sunshine Coast Hinterland Heritage Trail

Surf and sand give way to dairy farms and fields of sugarcane and pineapples. Travel past the Glass House Mountains to Landsborough, Maleny, Montville, Mapleton, Nambour, Palmwoods, Yandina, Eumundi, Noosa, Pomona, Kin Kin and Gympie.

8. Forest Ranges Heritage Trail

Head for the hills and discover rich dairying country, whispering pine forests and clear mountain streams. The trail links Dayboro, Mount Mee, Woodford, Kilcoy, Jimna, Kenilworth and Kandanga and connects with the Sunshine Coast Hinterland Trail at Gympie.

Heritage trails provide a wonderful way to enjoy Queensland's Great South East and sample all the region has to offer: enjoy the regional food, taste the local wines, go bushwalking, fishing or canoeing, pack a picnic hamper, or simply relax in the country. Visitors with a full day to spare can follow a trail from start to finish. Others may choose to pick up a trail, or leave it, at any convenient point.

Code of Conduct for Visitors

Places featured in this guide have been selected because of their interest and historical importance. National parks and heritage theme parks are also included. Many of the places described are privately owned and visitors should respect the rights of owners and occupants. Most privately owned heritage places featured in this guide can be viewed from public thoroughfares without entering private land. Most of the homes and homesteads are not open to the general public without appointment.

Intending visitors should obtain permission from landholders before entering private property. Visitors to state forests should remain on the main roads. Permits are available from regional forestry offices for authorised travel on other forestry roads.

Remember that the places included in this guide are of natural and cultural heritage value; visitors should treat them with care and consideration to ensure their conservation and sustainable use for the benefit of future generations.

REGIONAL KEY MAP

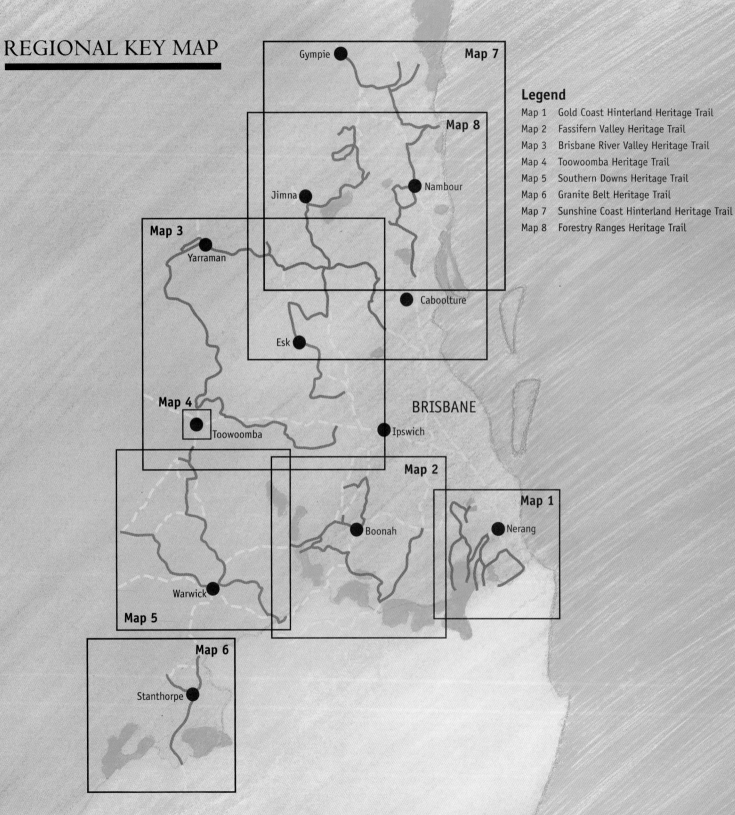

Gympie

Map 7

Map 8

Jimna

Nambour

Map 3

Yarraman

Caboolture

Esk

BRISBANE

Map 4

Toowoomba

Ipswich

Map 2

Map 1

Boonah

Nerang

Warwick

Map 5

Map 6

Stanthorpe

Legend

Map 1   Gold Coast Hinterland Heritage Trail
Map 2   Fassifern Valley Heritage Trail
Map 3   Brisbane River Valley Heritage Trail
Map 4   Toowoomba Heritage Trail
Map 5   Southern Downs Heritage Trail
Map 6   Granite Belt Heritage Trail
Map 7   Sunshine Coast Hinterland Heritage Trail
Map 8   Forestry Ranges Heritage Trail

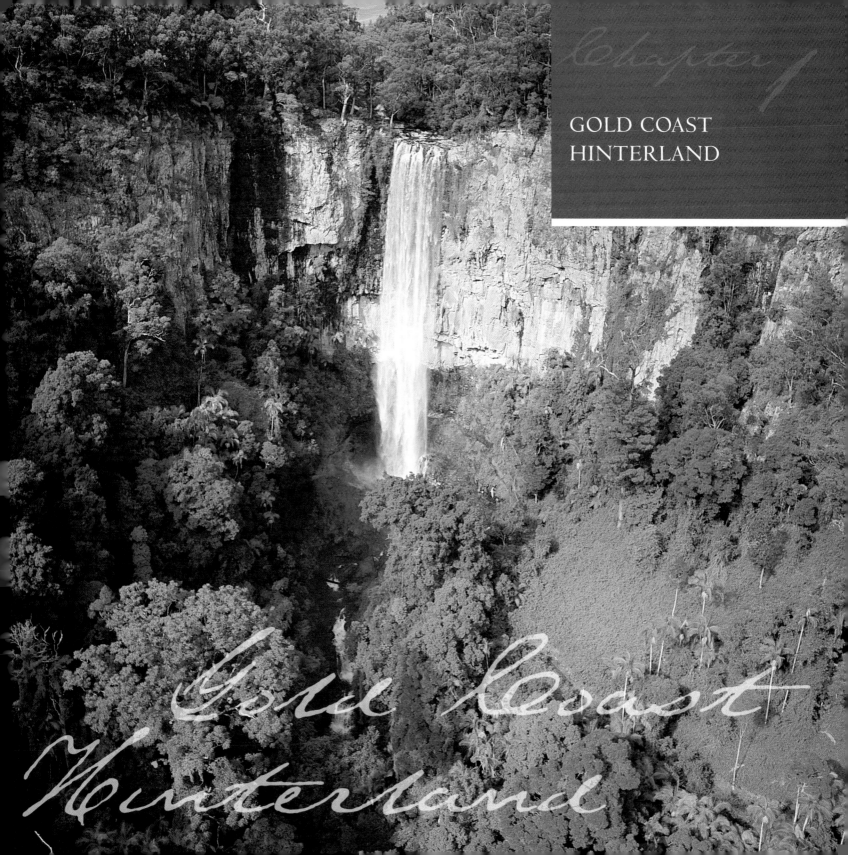

MAP I
Gold Coast Hinterland

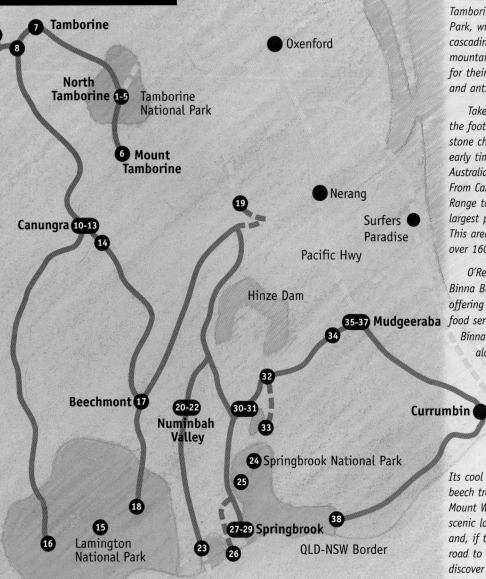

Tamborine 7 9 8

Oxenford

North Tamborine 1-5

Tamborine National Park

6 **Mount Tamborine**

19

Nerang

Surfers Paradise

Pacific Hwy

Canungra 10-13

14

Hinze Dam

35-37 **Mudgeeraba**

34

32

30-31

Beechmont 17

20-22 **Numinbah Valley**

33

Currumbin

24 Springbrook National Park

25

18

38

15

27-29 **Springbrook**

16 Lamington National Park

23 26

QLD-NSW Border

Inland from the Gold Coast, discover dramatic green ranges, rainforests and mountain streams. The trail starts on Tamborine Mountain. Tamborine National Park, with its abundant rainforest walks and cascading waterfalls, covers much of the mountain. The mountain's villages are known for their cafes, art and craft markets, galleries and antique shops.

Take the road to Tamborine township at the foot of the mountain to see the historic stone church at Mundoolun before visiting the early timber town of Canungra, near the Australian Army's jungle warfare training centre. From Canungra, the trail ascends the McPherson Range to Lamington National Park, Australia's largest preserved subtropical rainforest. This area boasts more than 500 waterfalls and over 160 kilometres of graded walking tracks.

O'Reilly's Green Mountains Guesthouse and Binna Burra Lodge are mountain resorts offering excellent accommodation and fine food served in licensed restaurants. From Binna Burra, return through Beechmont along the Nerang road to the Numinbah Valley and the beautiful Natural Bridge. From Numinbah Valley, take the road to Springbrook, visiting the spectacular Purling Brook Falls on the way. Springbrook is on the rim of an ancient volcanic crater. Its cool rainforests contain ancient Antarctic beech trees. Enjoy breathtaking views of Mount Warning and the Tweed Valley from the scenic lookouts. Return through Mudgeeraba and, if time permits, take the Currumbin Creek road to Mount Cougal National Park and discover cascading falls and mountain rock pools. Take a short walk through the forest to the remains of an old sawmill.

THE GOLD COAST HINTERLAND

The earliest exploration of the Logan River district was undertaken from the Moreton Bay penal settlement during the 1820s but not until 1842 did the first comprehensive exploration of the Gold Coast hinterland take place. In the early 1860s surveyors attempted to map the Queensland border across the thickly forested mountains and high plateaus. Timber-getters coming up from the Tweed River found the Numinbah Gap, which allowed the hinterland forests to be opened up for timber-cutting and land selection. A rough track used by coaches and bullock teams between Tweed Heads and Nerang was linked with the Brisbane road. Coastal communities became established for fishing and transporting timber from the upper valleys.

Nerang became the principal port for the south coast district and the transport centre for trading vessels, coaches and bullock teams. The completion of the railway from Brisbane to Nerang in 1889 and to Tweed Heads in 1903 provided a major boost to settlement. The railway allowed access to newly opened farming blocks. Dairying became the main pursuit, although agricultural crops were tried with mixed success. Evidence remains of a thriving arrowroot industry on the Coomera River. The difficulty of access from the coast meant that the Tamborine plateau developed slowly and was more orientated towards Beaudesert, which was linked to Brisbane by rail in 1888. The rail link provided transport for the timber industry and also for the local dairy farmers and contributed to the life of the settlements.

A major influence on the region's historical development was the national parks movement. The first national park in Queensland, Tamborine's Witches Falls, was gazetted in 1908. Over the next two decades, other parks were gazetted on Tamborine and on the Lamington and Springbrook plateaus. With the exception of Southport, towns rarely generated sufficient wealth to require the upgrading of buildings from a functional timber-and-tin style. An active religious and community life produced appropriate structures and facilities, however, many displaying beautiful locally cut and milled timbers and a high level of design and craftsmanship.

Dam building also had a great effect on the environment and changed the landscape. But the major influence on the character of the area has been the rapid development of the Gold Coast for tourism, and the associated development of new transport routes, housing and commercial centres. Tourism's effect has radiated beyond the coastal strip to the hinterland, resulting in a change from rural to semi-urban settlement patterns, but it has also increased population numbers and revived the economy of the small towns.

(Left) Crossing Canungra Creek, c1897 (John Oxley Library)

(Right) Curtis Falls, Mount Tamborine National Park

GOLD COAST HINTERLAND HERITAGE TRAIL

1. Tamborine Mountain

Tamborine Mountain was first settled in 1875, when John O'Callaghan selected a small parcel of land near the present North Tamborine Village. Most early settlers were involved in maize growing and dairying. They led a precarious existence, having to cart all produce for market down the mountain. In 1889 the Geissman family opened Capo di Monte, the first guesthouse at North Tamborine. Other guesthouses followed and Tamborine became widely known as a holiday and convalescent area. In 1916 O'Callaghan's land was subdivided into small farms, leaving the frontages for commercial development. This was the beginning of North Tamborine Village.

Access to the mountain improved when the tourist road was completed in 1924. The Village, with its school, post office and a range of shops, became the mountain's business and social centre. The North Tamborine Public Hall, completed in 1923, is still in use as the Zamia Theatre. Creation of national parks over the decades made Mount Tamborine a haven for birdwatchers, bushwalkers and naturalists. The poet Judith Wright lived at Mount Tamborine from 1949 to 1976. Many of her finest poems were inspired by the mountain and the rainforests, including 'The Cycads' (1949), 'Flame Tree in a Quarry' (1949), 'The Cicadas' (1953) and 'At Cedar Creek' (1976). The mountain is now the centre of a thriving tourist industry.

2. Tamborine National Park

After the first application for a lease on Mount Tamborine in 1875 settlement expanded and within 30 years much of the rainforest had been cleared for farming. The move for a national park at Mount Tamborine began as early as 1895, in association with the campaign for Lamington National Park. The concept of 'national parks' had taken hold in the United States in 1870, with the creation of Yellowstone National Park, and quickly spread to other parts of the world. By 1900 parks had been established in New South Wales and Victoria, but it was not until 1906 that a National Parks Act was introduced in Queensland. The State's first national park, Witches Falls, was declared in 1908. Palm Grove National Park was proclaimed in 1925 and over the next 40 years other areas on the mountain were protected.

3. Witches Falls,
Tamborine National Park

By the early 1900s, Mount Tamborine residents were becoming concerned about the need to preserve an area of the mountain's natural rainforest and wildlife. In 1907, Sydney Curtis and Joseph Delpratt, of the Tamborine Shire Council, persuaded the government that a section of the mountain should be set aside as a reserve. Witches Falls was the first park in Queensland, declared in 1908 under the new National Parks Act. Curtis's daughter explained the name arose when, as children, they used to bring the cows home after school. Some evenings they were very late returning and crossing the creek near the falls was eerie, so they called them the 'Witches Falls'.

❶ *Zamia Theatre, North Tamborine*
❷ *Rainforest: Tamborine National Park (EPA)*

4. Curtis Falls,
Tamborine National Park

In 1887 the Curtis family established a water-powered sawmill on Cedar Creek, upstream from Curtis Falls. The mill was equipped with a large water wheel. The creek was dammed at night above the falls and the water was released the next day to power the wheel. After turning the wheel, the water ran back into Cedar Creek through a channel in the rock that had been blasted to accommodate the wheel. The area around the falls was later declared a national park. Very few traces of the mill remain today, although the channel in the rock where the water wheel operated is still visible.

5. The Old Church,
Long Road, Eagle Heights

The venue for hundreds of weddings since its relocation from Nerang in 1993, the former St Andrew's Wesleyan Church is one of the earliest surviving churches of the Gold Coast hinterland. It was built about 1880.

6. St Bernard's Hotel,
Alpine Terrace,
Mount Tamborine

Tamborine pioneers John Pindar and his family opened St Bernard's as a guesthouse in 1889. Formerly the manager's house for Robert Muir's sugar plantation, it was re-erected on the mountain after the sale of Muir's estate. The Siganto family purchased St Bernard's in 1905. They extended it in 1910, obtained a liquor licence in 1915 and laid out the gardens on the eastern escarpment. Used as an Army convalescent home during World War II, St Bernard's has had several owners since its sale soon after the war. Despite extensive renovations and extensions, the structure of the original house is still evident. St Bernard's remains a landmark in Tamborine's history, as the last and possibly the best known survivor of Tamborine's early guesthouse era.

4   *Cedar Creek water wheel (John Oxley Library)*
5   *Old St Andrew's Church, Eagle Heights*
6   *St Bernard's Hotel, Mount Tamborine*

7. Tamborine

Although little remains of the small town settled in the early 1870s, Tamborine is important for its association with the first organised immigration of Irish settlers to Queensland. After Separation in 1859, Bishop Quinn formed the Irish Immigration Society to increase the number of Irish settlers. Many of the families who arrived in Brisbane in 1862 on the *Erin-go-brach*, the first ship financed by the Society, took up selections in the Tamborine district. Others arrived on the *Fiery Star* the following year. They were later among the first to select farming blocks at Tamborine. By the 1870s, the town served a small but rich agricultural district. The extension of the railway from Bethania to Beaudesert in 1888 bypassed the town, however, and by the early 1900s new settlement focused on Tamborine Mountain and the Canungra area.

8. Tamborine House

'Tambourine' grazing run was taken up in 1843 by the surveyor Robert Dixon. After 1844 it had a succession of owners, and in 1870 was purchased by Joseph Delpratt, who had arrived in Australia in 1860. For almost 100 years, the Delpratt family engaged in dairying and breeding draughthorses and shorthorn cattle. By 1967, when it was sold, Tamborine station had been dramatically reduced in size. The homestead, probably built in the late 1860s, was extended to its present size in 1914. Despite extensive renovations, the house's original core is still evident and its interiors retain many original features. Visits to Tamborine House are by appointment only.

9. St John's Anglican Church, *Mundoolun*

Services are still held regularly at this simple but imposing church, built in memory of John and Anne Collins, who settled at Mundoolun in 1844. Following their deaths in the late 1890s, John Buckeridge, the Brisbane Anglican Diocesan Architect, was commissioned to design the memorial chapel, which was consecrated in 1902. The square Norman-influenced tower was added in 1915. The church, built of stone quarried on the property, has interior fittings of red cedar. The walls hold plaques commemorating members of the original Collins family and the Delpratt family of the adjoining Tamborine run. The graveyard contains the graves of John and Anne Collins and other family members, as well as the grave of Bullum (John Allen), a lifelong associate of the family and a member of the local Wangerriburra people.

10. Canungra

Logging of the district's massive red cedar trees had begun when, in 1852, A.W. Compigne took up Sarabah, Canungra's first pastoral run. With other grazing runs, Sarabah was cut up for closer settlement in the late 1860s and the town of Canungra grew up around several farming selections first settled in 1873. Development increased after the opening of Lahey's sawmill in 1884 and the arrival of mill workers, timber-getters and bullock drivers. Canungra was well established by the 1890s, but was not surveyed until 1915, the year the rail link to the main Brisbane–Logan line was completed. This allowed easier access to markets. New settlers flocked in as more farming blocks became available, and dairying became as important as the timber industry.

During World War II a jungle warfare training centre was developed and the railway was used to transport troops and equipment.

By the late 1940s, much of the available timber had been logged and many sawmills had closed. The railway ceased operating in 1955 due to competition from road transport. Recession in the timber and dairying industries contributed to Canungra's decline. The military facility was revived during the 1960s and used extensively during the Vietnam War. In 1975, it began a broader training role as the Land Warfare Centre. Canungra is now the access point for visitors wishing to explore the natural beauty of the adjacent national parks.

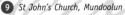

9 St John's Church, Mundoolun
10 Arrival of the mail at Canungra, c1911 (John Oxley Library)

11. Canungra Hotel,
Kidston Street

This site was originally occupied by a guesthouse, Bellissima, built by David Lahey in 1916 and named after the ship that had brought the Lahey family to Sydney from Ireland in 1861. The guesthouse accommodated many visiting dignitaries over the years. In 1927 it was sold to Bernie Conaghan, who renamed it the Canungra Hotel. It became Canungra's first licensed premises, as the Laheys had always refused to allow alcohol to be sold in the town. The hotel was destroyed by fire in 1937, and the present hotel was built soon afterwards. It was occupied by the students and teachers of Brisbane's Stuartholme School during World War II.

12. St Luke's Anglican Church,
Kidston Street

St Luke's Church dates from 1916. Its original site on the hill was sold in 1927, after the congregation complained about the difficulty of reaching the church. The building was then moved on log rollers down the hill to its present location.

13. St Margaret Mary's Catholic Church,
Kidston Street

Catholic residents of the Canungra district began their campaign for a church in 1919. Construction began in March 1934 and the church was dedicated three months later.

14. Canungra Tramway Tunnel,
Duncan Street

In 1884 David Lahey obtained timber leases over large tracts of rainforest and opened a sawmill in Canungra. The mill was destroyed by fire in 1897, but was rebuilt on a larger scale the following year. As logging increased, hauling the timber by bullock wagon proved too slow, so work began on a tramway in 1900. The timber tramway from Canungra across and up the Coomera Valley was surveyed in 1900. It was a major engineering feat: severe grades were used to reduce costs and specially geared locomotives were needed to handle the steep grades at low speed.

By 1904 half of the proposed 16-kilometre tramline had been laid and a tunnel 90 metres long had been completed. The line was complete and in full operation by 1905.

The mill burnt down again in 1906 and was rebuilt to almost double its original capacity. The Commonwealth War Service Homes Commission purchased the mill and tramway from the Laheys in 1920, but ceased operations after a few months. Lahey's timber firm reacquired the mill soon after. The mill was finally closed in the late 1930s and the tramway was dismantled after World War II.

11 *Canungra Hotel*
12 *St Luke's Church*
14 *Canungra Tramway locomotive, c1915 (above top) (John Oxley Library)*
14 *Canungra Tramway tunnel (above)*

Lamington National Park (EPA)

15. Lamington National Park

In 1895 Beaudesert pastoralist Robert Collins began the campaign for a national park to preserve the area's remaining forests. He made many journeys into the McPherson Ranges studying Aboriginal languages and customs. Collins died in 1913, before his dream for Lamington became a reality. Romeo Lahey, an engineer and son of the Canungra sawmill owner David Lahey, continued the campaign. Lahey's approach was far from passive. In 1912 he protested to the government against the dairying selections taken up by the O'Reilly family at Green Mountains. Early in 1915 he began a door-to-door campaign in the district, giving lectures at public meetings, and in June that year presented a petition signed by over 500 of the Lands Minister's electors. The long campaign was won and Lamington National Park was gazetted in 1915. The park was named in honour of the governor, Lord Lamington, although Lahey believed that parks should not be named after people and had favoured the name Woonoongoora.

In 1994 Lamington National Park was listed as part of the Central Eastern Rainforest Reserves World Heritage Area, which includes one of the world's most extensive areas of subtropical rainforest, most of the world's warm temperate rainforest and nearly all of the Antarctic beech cool temperate rainforest. Antarctic beech trees are evergreen and are confined to areas of highest elevation on mountain tops along the southern border ranges. The trees have been described as being thousands of years old, but it is only their roots that are so ancient. The trees send up suckers, which grow as the older trunks die. The trunks and branches may be only a few hundred years old. The roots of the oldest Antarctic beech in Lamington National Park are estimated to be over 5000 years old. The beech forests demonstrate the evolutionary course of Australia's natural history.

Lamington has inspired a great number of works of literature, art and music over a period of more than eighty years including paintings by important Queensland artists such as Vida Lahey and Lois Beumer. Artist camps were held in the 1930s to take advantage of the inspiration afforded by the rainforest. The landscape paintings of William Robinson (1980s-90s) further illustrate the aesthetic values of Lamington, as does an orchestral work by Raymond Curtis, 'Journey Among Mountains' (1989). Arthur Groom wrote *One Mountain After Another* (1949) about the development of Binna Burra Lodge and the Scenic Rim concept for a series of national parks along the Main Range. The acclaimed English poet Rodney Hall was inspired by bushwalking in the rainforests of Lamington National Park to write 'The Climber' (1962) and 'Australia' (1970).

16. O'Reilly's Guesthouse,
Green Mountains

In 1912 eight young men of the O'Reilly family each selected a block of farming land on Roberts Plateau in the McPherson Range. They named their selections Green Mountains, the subtropical equivalent of the Blue Mountains near their earlier farm in New South Wales. They cleared the dense rainforest and established a dairy farm on the land, working as timber-getters to gain income. Survival became so difficult the O'Reillys considered forfeiting the land. The selections were in the centre of Lamington National Park gazetted in 1915, and with the growing tourist interest in the area, the O'Reillys decided to open a guesthouse. Completed in 1926, O'Reilly's Green Mountains Guesthouse offered very basic accommodation. Guests came on horseback via the precipitous mountain track from Kerry until the first road was completed in the 1920s.

Still run by the O'Reilly family, the guesthouse has been extended and modernised. Recently renovated, the 1930s farmhouse with red cedar interiors is the oldest dwelling on the mountain.

16 *First section of O'Reilly's guesthouse, 1928 (John Oxley Library)*

16 *St Joseph's Church, Green Mountains*

A memorial in the grounds commemorates the bushcraft of the late Bernard O'Reilly, who found the wreckage of the Stinson aircraft that had crashed in mountainous country near the border in 1937 and played a major part in the rescue of the two surviving passengers. The story is now part of the district's folklore.

St Joseph's Catholic Church

Originally erected at Gleneagle near Beaudesert about 1875, St Joseph's Church was moved to the O'Reillys' Green Mountains property in 1955 and was opened by Archbishop Duhig and Monsignor Steele of Beaudesert. Monsignor Steele had celebrated the first mass at Green Mountains at O'Reilly's farmhouse in 1922.

17. Beechmont

On the edge of Lamington National Park, the Beechmont area was settled by timber-getters who harvested the giant red cedars from the mountain forests. A settlement at Beechmont developed between 1882 and 1892, Irish and Scottish emigrants being among the first to take up land. Until they cleared the land for small crops and dairying, many farmers survived on timber-cutting and cartage services. Fruit growing, begun in the 1890s, was successful until the industry was devastated by fruit fly in the early 1900s. Dairying then became the main industry, assisted by improvements in the road to Nerang and other local towns. Beechmont became a popular mountain holiday destination in the 1920s and guesthouses were built. The town developed as a retreat for artists, including the acclaimed painter William Robinson. The Canungra Land Warfare Centre and the Hinze Dam have changed Beechmont's rural character, while improved road access from the Gold Coast has resulted in an increase in tourism and residential development.

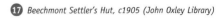

17 *Beechmont Settler's Hut, c1905 (John Oxley Library)*

18. Binna Burra Lodge

The engineer Romeo Lahey, who had played a significant role in establishing Lamington National Park, met the freelance journalist Arthur Groom at the formation of the National Parks Association of Australia in 1930. Lahey was voted in as president and Groom as secretary. In 1933 Lahey and Groom acquired land on Lamington Plateau to establish a guesthouse. A Canungra boarding house, built in 1902, was dismantled and taken up to Binna Burra by packhorse to become the dining and recreation room. The old building is still used as a reception room. By 1934 volunteer labourers had erected the first timber slab huts for guests.

Graded walking tracks designed by Lahey, were constructed under the State Government's unemployment relief works program. A track between Binna Burra and O'Reilly's was opened in 1938, but the access road up the mountain was not completed until 1947. Binna Burra is now a social and educational centre and an internationally known tourist attraction. Groom's former house, begun in 1935, was refitted as an environmental study centre in 1980 and is still used for meetings of the Lamington Natural History Association.

18

18

18 Arthur Groom's former house, Binna Burra (above)

18 Building the first cabin at Binna Burra, 1933 (below left) (John Oxley Library)

19. Rivermill Restaurant, *Mount Nathan*

Arrowroot, used primarily in the manufacture of starch for clothing, was grown in the Nerang area from the 1870s and several mills were operating by the end of the century. Built in 1910, this river mill was the largest arrowroot mill then operating in southern Queensland. It was erected by the Walker family, who began farming from their homestead, Sherwood, in 1870. The Walkers sold the mill in 1954, but it was still operating in the 1970s. Some of the factory machinery, including the water pump, is displayed in the grounds of the restaurant, which also houses an interesting display of early photographs.

20. Numinbah Valley

Cedar-cutters were active in the Numinbah Valley from as early as 1845, but Edward Harper and Robert Duncan were the first to take up land in the 1860s after they found a route through the range from the Tweed Valley. The area became known when surveyors mapped the Queensland border between 1859 and 1863. The border runs through the top of the valley and a border gate operated there until Federation. During the 1870s, land was selected under the government's closer settlement provisions.

The main industry was timber-getting and logs were hauled by bullock teams to Nerang for transport by paddle-wheel steamer to Brisbane.

The families of the timber-getters and bullock drivers formed a small settlement at Numinbah Valley during the 1880s. Living conditions were harsh, heavy rain and floods posing a constant challenge to the development of agriculture and dairying. The opening of the railway to the Tweed in 1902 and the gradual improvement of road access to coastal towns brought stability to the district. Dairying, pig raising, small crops and fruit growing joined timber as established industries. The history of the settlement after 1910 is associated with Yaun's sawmill, which operated until 1944. Today the settlement remains the centre for the Numinbah Valley's beef cattle and fodder-growing industry.

21. Numinbah Valley School of Arts, *Numinbah Valley*

Since its opening in 1925 the school of arts has been the social centre for the Numinbah Valley. Dances and sports days raised funds for its construction, and all the timber was donated and cut and dressed free of charge by workers at Yaun's sawmill. Similar community efforts went into improvements made over the years. The murals on the interior walls were painted by one of

21

21 School of Arts

a group of prisoners from the Numinbah Prison Farm who assisted with extensive alterations carried out in the early 1980s.

22. Chigigum House,
Numinbah Valley

David and James Yaun moved their Pine Mountain sawmill to the Numinbah Valley in 1909 to be closer to the hoop pine stands near Numinbah. Their family home, Chigigum, was built in 1910 with timber from the mill opposite. Yaun's sawmill was responsible for bringing new settlers and workers into the Numinbah Valley. The mill continued to operate until it was destroyed by fire in 1944. After the sawmill burnt down the Yauns turned to full-time dairying and guesthouse operations centred around Chigigum. The family continued to occupy the house until 1976.

23. Natural Bridge
National Park

A volcano centred over the present Mount Warning erupted about 23 million years ago, pouring out layers of hard volcanic rocks. The Numinbah Valley resulted from erosion caused by a north-flowing stream on the volcano's northern flank. Natural Bridge is the eroded lip of an old waterfall, which developed over a hard resistant basalt flow. The Natural Bridge is formed at the junction of the basalt layer and a softer volcanic layer beneath, called agglomerate. European timber-getters came to the Numinbah Valley around the 1870s. Magnificent trees felled in the area included a giant red cedar taken in 1893 from near Natural Bridge. A section of this tree was displayed at the Paris World Fair. By 1920 large areas of the Valley had been cleared and dairy farms were expanding. To preserve what remained, Natural Bridge was declared a recreation and scenic reserve in 1922 and was gazetted as a national park in 1959. It now forms part of Springbrook National Park.

24. Springbrook National Park

Springbrook National Park comprises a number of national parks previously known as Mount Cougal, Warrie, Wunburra, Gwongorella and Natural Bridge. These parks were amalgamated in 1990. Extensive clearing in the Springbrook area had, by the 1930s, led to public pressure to preserve the native plants and animals for future generations. Warrie National Park was gazetted in 1937, followed in 1938 by Mount Cougal and in 1940 by Gwongorella. The present park comprises three sections, Springbrook Plateau, Mount Cougal and Natural Bridge, and has over 30 kilometres of walking tracks. With its towering, 2000-year-old Antarctic beeches and protected rainforests, the park is the centre of the Central Eastern Rainforests Reserves World Heritage Area. The Springbrook parks have inspired many artists and photographers since the early 1900s. Prominent painters to depict this district have been Vida Lahey and Fred Williams; while the poems of Silvana Gardner such as 'Madonna of the Springbrook Rain' (1993), describe the aesthetic values.

22 *Chigigum House, Numinbah Valley*

23 *Natural Bridge, Springbrook National Park (EPA)*

24 *Springbrook axemen, 1906 (John Oxley Library)*

25. Purling Brook Falls

The escarpment was formed on two rhyolite flows creating high waterfalls such as Purling Brook Falls and lookouts offering spectacular views of the surrounding lower country.

26. Best of All Lookout

Overlooking the Tweed River are the spectacular remnants of the northern rim of an extinct volcano that was centred on the present-day Mount Warning, a dramatic volcanic plug. The most breathtaking vantage point on the escarpment is Best of All Lookout, offering sweeping views south from Point Danger across the Tweed Valley and Mount Warning. The Antarctic beech trees on the track to the lookout are remnants of vegetation that grew in a much wetter and cooler climate.

27. Canyon Guesthouse and Lookout

This house is a rare survivor of the guesthouse era at Springbrook. The home of the Dodd family, local dairy farmers, it was purchased in 1939 by Mrs Greenlees, who turned it into the very successful Highways Guesthouse.

At that time the Canyon was the tourist centre of the mountain, and half a dozen guesthouses were located nearby. After operating for some time as a tearoom, the house is again open as a guesthouse. The Canyon Lookout opposite commemorates the opening of Warrie National Park. The area was declared a timber reserve in 1911 and an inspection of the plateau by the Land Commissioner in 1915 resulted in the first recommendation for reservation of the Canyon. During the early 1930s relief workers built an access road to the Canyon. Proposals for logging the area resulted in calls for the Canyon to be preserved and Warrie National Park was declared in 1937.

28. Springbrook

Springbrook Village was settled after 1906 by the Springwood Group, settlers from northern New South Wales. The early settlers struggled to establish their farms despite poor roads and very high annual rainfalls. Timber-getting provided a basic living and as forest areas were cleared, dairying became the mainstay. Springbrook school opened in 1911 and Rudder's Hall was the centre for social events until the community hall was built in 1947. In the 1920s, the mountains became a popular holiday destination and over a dozen guesthouses were established on the plateau by the 1930s. By the 1950s the dairying and tourist industries had declined and the school closed in 1971. In recent years, Springbrook has again become popular as visitors to the Gold Coast discover the beauty of its national parks.

26 *Antarctic Beech Trees, Springbrook National Park*
27 *Canyon Guesthouse, Springbrook*

29. Springbrook State School

Springbrook's oldest building is the former state school, which opened in 1911 with an enrolment of 15 pupils. After its closure in 1971, the school fell into disrepair. The building was converted into the National Parks Information Centre in 1986 and now contains interpretive displays on the park's natural values. In front of the Centre is the stump of a gigantic New England blackbutt tree, estimated to have been close to 1000 years old when it was felled about 1911.

30. Mudgeeraba– Springbrook Road

Lack of access delayed settlement of the Springbrook Plateau prior to 1906. However, once land was advertised for selection the government was required to provide a road and two local selectors, Hardy and Trapp, blazed a track from Mudgeeraba by following Little Nerang Creek. By the 1920s it was decided to survey a new route onto the mountain and a Swiss engineer named Juries was employed to conduct the initial survey. Tenders were called and C.J. Hicks, a road contractor from northern New South Wales, started work on the new road in 1925. The section between Neranwood and Wunburra proved the most difficult, the six kilometres of backbreaking roadwork not being completed until 1928. When the road was opened, a toll was payable for each journey. The water trough on the Wunburra Range section is a reminder of the days when the road was used by horse and bullock teams.

31. Curved Bridges, *Mudgeeraba–Springbrook Road*

The curved wooden bridges on this section of the road were the work of bridge builder Charlie Kolb. After almost 70 years of service, they cope with the increased volume of traffic with the same degree of soundness that they have always had. The skills required to maintain and replace components of timber bridges like these are vanishing.

32. Neranwood Sawmill

Sawmilling had been long established in the district when the Nerang Hardwood Company was formed in 1923. The company, which largely represented grazing interests, was unusual because it built a locomotive-operated tramway to transport sawn timber to the State railway, rather than unsawn logs to a mill. Such tramways were common in Victoria but not in Queensland. The enterprise was substantial, having a two-foot gauge tramline from the railway yard at Mudgeeraba across the range to the upper Nerang River. The township of Neranwood sprang up around the sawmill, which was powered by a large boiler from the World War I cruiser *Sydney*.

The operation proved unprofitable and had only a short existence. In 1928 the assets were sold. The Depression delivered the final blow, and by the end of 1930 the tramway siding at Mudgeeraba was out of use. The heavy concrete foundations for the steam engine can now be seen within the grounds of Polly's Country Kitchen tearooms.

33. Little Nerang Dam

Prior to the opening of the Little Nerang Dam the water supply for the district was obtained from a pumping station on Mudgeeraba Creek. The project commenced in 1955 and the dam was completed in 1962. Most of the water for the Gold Coast and hinterland is now supplied by the vast Hinze Dam, the first stage of which was opened in 1977.

34. Rayner's Sawmill, *Mudgeeraba–Springbrook Road*

Before the advent of cardboard and other materials, hundreds of case mills provided timber for fruit cases. One of the last operating sawmills in the Gold Coast hinterland began life around 1943 as a case mill on a property at Little Nerang and was subsequently moved to its present site, where it has been operated for half a century by the Rayner family. Now electrically powered, the mill has changed little from the type of mill operating a century earlier. A tractor is used to handle logs and sawn timber, and a chainsaw supplements the fixed equipment and increases productivity. When the fruit-case market collapsed, many of the mills turned to producing rough sawn timber for building.

29 *Blackbutt stump at Springbrook school*
30 *Roadside water trough, Wunburra Range*
31 *A curved bridge on the Springbrook road*
32 *Neranwood sawmill engine foundations*

35. Mudgeeraba

A short-lived attempt by the Manchester Cotton Company to grow cotton under the government cotton bounty scheme opened up the area in 1863. Sugar was also tried briefly during the 1860s. German migrants were among the first settlers when the original pastoral leases became available for selection. Located on the track from the hinterland mountains to Nerang, the town of Mudgeeraba began to develop in the late 1880s after the railway to Nerang opened. When the line was extended to Tweed Heads in 1903, Mudgeeraba became the transport centre for the district's timber and dairying industries. The Depression years of the 1930s had a severe effect. The town was assisted by unemployment relief projects but its principal industries were in decline. By the 1950s, after the railway closed, Mudgeeraba had lost its commercial importance as development was centred on the Gold Coast. With the Gold Coast's tourist expansion, the town is once again a gateway to the Springbrook Plateau.

36. Nerang Council Chambers,
Railway Street

Although local government was established in the Nerang–Mudgeeraba district as early as 1880, this timber building constructed in 1927 was Nerang's first purpose-built Council Chambers. Its modest size and design reflected the Council's lack of financial resources, despite Mudgeeraba being the centre of a thriving farming community. In 1950 Nerang Shire was absorbed into the newly formed Albert Shire, with headquarters at Southport. The Council Chambers were converted for use as the Mudgeeraba Post Office, operated by the Cuddihy family from 1950 until Australia Post took over the service in 1981. The building remained an official post office until its closure in 1994.

37. Wallaby Hotel,
Robert Street

Local publican W.H. Laver built a new hotel opposite the Mudgeeraba Railway Station in 1914. Named the Exchange, it superseded Laver's original Mudgeeraba Hotel, which had started trading about 1885. The Exchange remained in the Laver family until 1958, when it was purchased by a syndicate and renamed the Wallaby Hotel, probably after Wallaby Creek near the township. The building, which now overlooks the busy Pacific Highway, has had a number of owners and has undergone many extensions and renovations.

38. Mount Cougal Sawmill,
Springbrook National Park

This sawmill, in the Mount Cougal section of Springbrook National Park, is a reminder that few wilderness areas, even in national parks, have not been logged by Europeans. The mill cut softwood timber for banana cases.

35 *Mudgeeraba Railway Station and the Exchange Hotel, c1917 (John Oxley Library)*

John Tracey established the sawmill at the head of the Currumbin Creek valley in 1942 and felled timber from scrub land owned by the Dolan family that now forms part of the national park. In 1948 Tracey sold the mill to Albert Bunney, who replaced the original kerosene engine with a V8 engine and installed a larger breaking-down saw and bench for cutting hardwood. Tony Stephens, who had worked with Tracey, bought the mill in 1951. The mill closed in early 1954, after six months' heavy rain. Bunney repurchased it but was killed in an accident on the mountain in 1959. His son John acquired the mill in the 1970s and removed much of the machinery.

38 *Mount Cougal sawmill, Springbrook National Park*

Fassifern Valley

MAP 2
Fassifern Valley

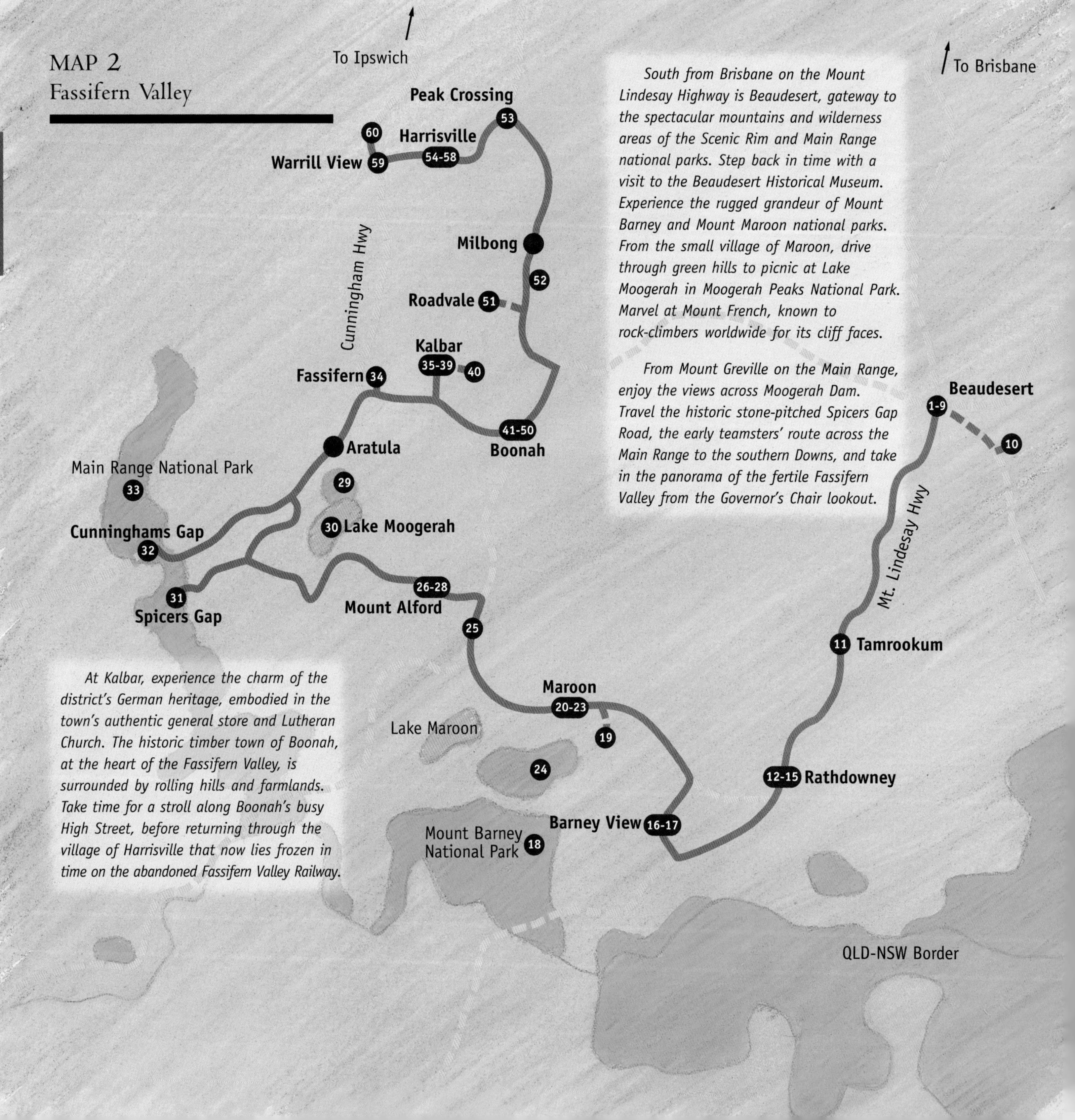

To Ipswich

To Brisbane

Peak Crossing **53**

60 Harrisville **54-58**

Warrill View **59**

Cunningham Hwy

Milbong **52**

Roadvale **51**

Kalbar
35-39 **40**

Fassifern **34**

41-50

Aratula **29** Boonah

Main Range National Park

33

30 Lake Moogerah

Cunninghams Gap **32**

31 **26-28**

Spicers Gap Mount Alford

25

Maroon
20-23

Lake Maroon **19**

24

12-15 Rathdowney

Mount Barney National Park **18**

Barney View **16-17**

Mt. Lindesay Hwy

Beaudesert **1-9**

10

11 Tamrookum

QLD-NSW Border

South from Brisbane on the Mount Lindesay Highway is Beaudesert, gateway to the spectacular mountains and wilderness areas of the Scenic Rim and Main Range national parks. Step back in time with a visit to the Beaudesert Historical Museum. Experience the rugged grandeur of Mount Barney and Mount Maroon national parks. From the small village of Maroon, drive through green hills to picnic at Lake Moogerah in Moogerah Peaks National Park. Marvel at Mount French, known to rock-climbers worldwide for its cliff faces.

From Mount Greville on the Main Range, enjoy the views across Moogerah Dam. Travel the historic stone-pitched Spicers Gap Road, the early teamsters' route across the Main Range to the southern Downs, and take in the panorama of the fertile Fassifern Valley from the Governor's Chair lookout.

At Kalbar, experience the charm of the district's German heritage, embodied in the town's authentic general store and Lutheran Church. The historic timber town of Boonah, at the heart of the Fassifern Valley, is surrounded by rolling hills and farmlands. Take time for a stroll along Boonah's busy High Street, before returning through the village of Harrisville that now lies frozen in time on the abandoned Fassifern Valley Railway.

THE FASSIFERN VALLEY

Pastoral occupation of the Fassifern Valley began in the early 1840s. Grazing runs taken up included Fassifern, Maroon, Dugandan, Normanby and Coochin Coochin. At this time, the small local population consisted of station workers and teamsters. In the early 1860s, after Queensland had become a separate colony, land tenure was more secure and self-contained villages grew around the homesteads. The location of towns such as Boonah, Coulson and Harrisville on pastoral runs emphasises the importance of the continuing economic and social links between station and town.

From the early 1870s, predominantly German families took up the small farming blocks as the large runs were subdivided for closer settlement. Agricultural settlement took on a more permanent character from the late 1880s, largely due to the completion in 1888 of the railway from Ipswich to Boonah. The line assisted settlers struggling to establish dairy farms and encouraged the development of commerce at rail sidings, prompting the establishment of new towns. More German settlers came to the Fassifern from the 1890s and Boonah became the district's business centre.

In the Beaudesert area the completion of the railway line from Brisbane in 1888 opened up more land for selection, largely by Irish settlers, and provided access to the markets on which the timber and dairying industries depended. As the railway terminus, Beaudesert became the principal town of the upper Logan and Albert Rivers district. It was formed on the Beaudesert pastoral run taken up in 1842. The Lahey brothers began sawmilling operations in 1888 and laid the foundation for the continuing importance of the timber industry to the district. The unprecedented demand for timber after World War II increased the number of sawmills in operation but depleted timber supplies. This led to the subsequent decline of the industry as a mainstay of the local economy.

Construction of the Moogerah and Maroon dams provided water for irrigation, and enabled farmers to diversify into small crops after dairying declined in the 1960s. Renewed growth has taken place in recent years as the value of the district for pastoral and agricultural production is more widely appreciated. The attractions of the Scenic Rim national parks and the development of the Moogerah and Maroon lakes as recreational centres have contributed to an increase in tourism. Removed for many years from the principal development areas of south-east Queensland, the Fassifern Valley has retained many examples of its early buildings.

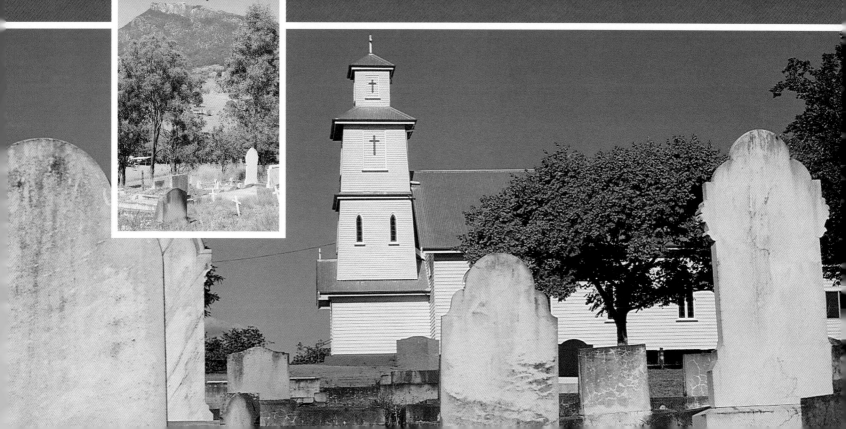

Mount Maroon Cemetery

FASSIFERN VALLEY HERITAGE TRAIL

1. Beaudesert

With completion of the railway in 1888, Beaudesert became the principal town of the upper Logan and Albert district. Its history dates from 1842, when Beaudesert run was taken up by Edward Hawkins. He named the property after his birthplace, Beau Desert Park, in Staffordshire, England. His partner, J.P. Robinson, formed a partnership with William White, who later took over the property. A private town was surveyed on Beaudesert run in the 1870s. Growth was slow until the mid-1880s, when closer settlement encouraged some interest in local development, mostly associated with the local timber and dairying industries.

Of several sawmills operating in the area from the late 1880s, Lahey's remained in operation the longest and made a lasting contribution to the town's economy. The Logan and Albert Co-operative Butter Factory opened in 1904 but it was undermined in 1931 by the transporting of whole milk direct to Brisbane by rail. Beaudesert received a boost from the construction in 1930 of the Brisbane–Sydney railway line through to Kyogle and additional primary industry facilities such as feedlots and abattoirs were established. Descendants of the district's early settlers still play a part in the town's community life.

2. Enright's Sawmill, *Brisbane Street*

When the railway reached Beaudesert in 1888 Lahey brothers' sawmill was located alongside the line with its own siding. A steam traction engine, known as 'Lahey's Folly', hauled logs to the mill and sawn timber was railed to Brisbane.

Construction of the Beaudesert Tramway in 1904 enabled the mill to tap most of the country south to the New South Wales border. The mill was substantially enlarged in 1906, the Lahey brothers and Nicklin then being the proprietors. When it burnt down in 1919 a new mill was built. Lahey's Beaudesert mill was sold to Patterson's of Toowong in 1948. Six years later the property was acquired by Enright's, the current owners, who continue to operate a large modern sawmill and timber yard at the site.

3. Beaudesert Railway Station, *Brisbane Street*

The station office dates from 1888, when the line from Loganlea to Beaudesert was completed. A daily train service linked Beaudesert to South Brisbane and from the 1890s a special siding was used to load timber from Lahey and Nicklin's sawmill.

In 1904 the station became the terminus for the Beaudesert Tramway, built by noted railway engineer George Phillips and operated by the Beaudesert Shire Council. A very profitable venture serving the district's timber and dairying industries, the tramway was extended to Rathdowney and Hillview in 1911. The line operated until 1944, when it was closed due to competition from road transport. For some years, the Shire Council chambers were located in the station office, which is now used by the Beaudesert Historical Society.

4. Beaudesert Hotel, *Brisbane Street*

The original Beaudesert Hotel was a two-storey timber building opened in 1885 when the town's commercial centre was developing. The present brick hotel, built in 1940 for Queensland Breweries to a design by Addison and McDonald, reflects the influence of modern architecture pioneered by Le Corbusier and the Bauhaus school of design.

5. Beaudesert War Memorial, *Brisbane Street*

An impressive example of the work of Brisbane stonemason W.E. Parsons, the memorial was constructed under the supervision of Brisbane architect A.H. Conrad and unveiled by the Queensland Governor, Sir Maurice Nathan, in 1921. A major landmark in the town, it was originally located at the centre of the intersection but was moved in the 1980s.

6. Logan and Albert Hotel, *Brisbane Street*

A hotel of the same name has been trading on this site since the late 1880s. The present hotel, designed by architects Hall and Phillips, was built in 1934.

7. Beaudesert Times Office, *William Street*

This building, completed in 1905, was formerly the Beaudesert School of Arts. Vacant from the early 1960s, it was taken over by Frank Hodgson of the *Beaudesert Times* newspaper, before the launching of the weekly *Logan and Albert Times* in 1967. The paper was renamed the *Beaudesert Times* in 1985. Hodgson originally purchased the paper in 1930 and his family still retain an interest in the company.

5 Unveiling Beaudesert War Memorial, 1921 (John Oxley Library)
6 Logan and Albert Hotel
9 St Mary's Church, Beaudesert

8. Beaudesert Showground Grandstand, *Albert Street*

This timber and iron grandstand is typical of those built by agricultural societies and race clubs in many centres throughout Queensland from the 1880s. Local pastoralist Ernest White donated land to the Logan and Albert Agricultural and Pastoral Association when it was formed in 1889 and the first annual Beaudesert show was held that year. Within a few years the show ring had taken shape, but the grandstand was not built until 1906. In the same year the ring was improved and yards were erected for the monthly cattle sales. The showground and grandstand have been in continuous use for local events.

9. St Mary's Catholic Church, *Boonah Road*

The first Catholic church on this site was a timber building of beech and cypress pine erected in 1889, next to a presbytery built in 1885. It was soon too small for Beaudesert's rapidly expanding population and a larger, more elaborate timber church, designed by G.M.H. Addison, was completed in 1907. Two sets of memorial stained-glass windows, one depicting St Patrick and St James and the other St Anne, were crafted by M. Moroney of Brisbane and installed in 1915. In 1901 a two-storey timber convent for the Sisters of Mercy was built adjacent to the church; additions designed by Hall and Dods were made in 1914. The convent was destroyed by fire in 1929, but within 12 months a new convent funded by public subscription had been built. The two-storey brick building, designed by leading Catholic church architect J.P. Donoghue, featured spacious verandahs, a chapel and accommodation for boarders.

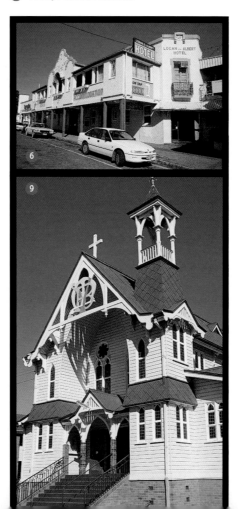

10. Nindooinbah Homestead

Built by A.W. Compigne about 1860, the timber homestead is a fine example of the rural architecture associated with Queensland's early squattocracy. The woolshed, one of the oldest and most intact in Queensland, dates from 1857. It was one of many buildings comprising the homestead village. Compigne held the property until 1867 when Robert Towns, who held the mortgage, foreclosed on Compigne and soon after sold the property to William Duckett White.

By 1901, when William Collins took up residence, the homestead was in a dilapidated state. After purchasing the property from White in 1906, Collins engaged noted Brisbane architect Robin Dods to extend the house. Dods' work, including the entrance gate, altered little of the original design. His wife, a plasterer, created the dining room's curved plaster ceiling. The house contains Collins family furnishings, ornaments and memorabilia gathered over three generations. Often described as having the ideal design for rural Queensland life, the homestead has had many distinguished visitors. The ballroom was built for the Prince of Wales's visit in 1920, but the Prince failed to attend the ball given in his honour. Nindooinbah homestead is not open to the public.

10 *Nindooinbah Homestead*

11. All Saints Anglican Church, *Tamrookum*

The Collins family completed this church in 1915 as a memorial to Robert Collins, pioneer pastoralist and a Member of the Queensland Parliament. Collins had lived at Tamrookum homestead since 1879 and had marked out the church site before his death in 1913. Described as unique in Australian church architecture, the church is built of hardwood and cedar cut on the property and demonstrates the distinctive style of its architect, Robin Dods. Tamrookum run was first settled by John Campbell in 1842. It was purchased by John Collins in 1878 and subdivided in 1931. The Collins family retained the homestead block with the church and cemetery where Robert Collins and other family members are buried. Also in the cemetery are the graves of Constable Doyle and Albert Dahlke, manager of Carnarvon, a Collins property in the Carnarvon Ranges. They were killed by the outlaw Kenniff brothers at Carnarvon in 1902.

11 *All Saints Church, Tamrookum (above)*

11 *All Saints Church under construction (below) (John Oxley Library)*

12. Rathdowney

Rathdowney has a comparatively young history. The town's development dates from the early 1900s, when the Collins brothers' grazing property Rathdowney was subdivided and sold under the government's closer settlement scheme. The already established timber industry was supported by Campbell's sawmill, and as the forests were cleared dairying and pig raising became important local industries. Transport of produce remained a problem until the Beaudesert Tramway was extended to Rathdowney in 1911. The town developed as the terminus for the tramway. By the 1920s, Rathdowney's growth reflected its status as a farming centre, commercial activity increasing during the construction of the Kyogle railway line in 1930. Improved access to the area after the railway line and the highway opened in the 1930s fostered a small tourist industry. Rathdowney declined with the downturn of the dairy and timber industries in the 1950s, but remains important as the focus of the district's community activities.

13. Rathdowney Tramway Station, *Mount Lindesay Highway*

The building was constructed in 1911 as the terminus for the Beaudesert Tramway. Recently relocated to the Rathdowney Historical Museum, it remains largely unchanged and is now used by community groups.

14. St David's Anglican Church, *Prior Street*

Before the construction of the Anglican and Catholic churches in 1929, services were held in the local hall and in family homes. An unusual feature of fundraising for the Rathdowney churches was that the local Catholic and Anglican communities held joint fundraising functions.

14 *St David's Church, Rathdowney*
17 *Site of Mount Barney school*

15. St Joseph's Catholic Church, *Mount Lindesay Highway*

The church was built in 1929 with funds raised by the local Catholic and Anglican communities. Need for the church arose with the arrival of construction workers on the Kyogle railway line.

16. Barney View Uniting Church

Built in 1908 by local Baptist, Presbyterian, Anglican and Methodist parishioners, this became the Methodist Church until it was renamed the Uniting Church in 1977. The Salvation Army also held services here for many years. Headstones in the cemetery date from the church's early period.

17. Mount Barney School

The plaque commemorates the site of a provisional school established in 1901 for the children of selectors and farm workers in the Mount Barney district. The school closed in 1962 after local population numbers declined, a reflection of the general decline in the district in that period.

18. Mount Barney National Park

In 1828, Captain Logan, Commandant of the Moreton Bay Penal Settlement, and botanists Allan Cunningham and Charles Fraser were the first Europeans to climb Mount Barney, Queensland's third highest mountain. The mountain is the centre of the national park, which in 1994 was included in the Central Eastern Rainforests Reserves World Heritage Area. The park covers a range of rainforest types and is home to rock wallabies, platypuses and the endangered Coxen's fig parrot.

One of the most distinctive peaks of the Scenic Rim, Mount Barney is composed of granophyre, a granite-like rock formed below the earth's surface as a dome-shaped intrusive mass. This intrusion and the overlaying sandstone were pushed up and then stripped by erosion, leaving the mountain's distinctive twin peaks. The locality is extremely rugged and of natural heritage significance, having many protected plant species, particularly on the higher peaks. Creeks flowing down the mountain, with cascades and rock pools, are fringed with she-oaks and patches of rainforest. The prominent colonial artist Conrad Martens depicted the mountain in a painting in 1851.

19. Cotswold Cottage

Frederick Cook built this cottage at the foot of Mount Maroon in 1891. Cook was a native of the Cotswolds in England, and his home was known as Cotswold Cottage. The walls were of local sandstone rubble, held by a cow manure mortar mixture. The roof was sheeted in handmade timber shingles and many of the windows were made of lantern slide plates. The only cement used in the building was in the northern wall of the sitting room, which still stands. The home comprised two bedrooms, dining room, kitchen, sitting room and workshop. Active in the local community, Cook was also an artist, whose paintings won prizes at the Royal National Show in Brisbane in the 1930s. On Cook's death in 1940 the house fell into disrepair.

20. Maroon

In 1843 Bettington and Haley took up the earliest grazing run in this district, naming it Melcombe. The name was later changed to Maroon. As settlers moved into the area, a school, post office and store were built. However, the area did not begin to develop until 1914, when the original stations were subdivided and opened up for closer settlement. In that year part of Maroon station was sold and broken up to establish about 30 dairy farms.

19 *Ruins of Cotswold Cottage*
20 *Maroon community hall and store*
22 *Maroon school war memorial*

21. St Andrew's Anglican Church

The first Anglican service in Maroon was held in the school of arts in 1906. The following year the Church of St Andrew was dedicated and incorporated into the Boonah Parish. The timber and shingle-roofed church was built by Fred Cook on donated land. The altar was carved from cedar from Mount Maroon station. St Andrew's was renovated in 1957 and six pencil pines were planted in the grounds two years later to celebrate Queensland's Centenary and the diocesan Jubilee.

22. Maroon State School War Memorial

The war memorial in the school grounds commemorates the 41 men (16 of whom lost their lives) from the Maroon district who served in World War I, and 35 who served in World War II. The figures represented a high proportion of the district's male population. Trees have been planted around the memorial, which is maintained by the school, and a commemorative ceremony is held at the site each year on Anzac Day.

23. Maroon Cemetery

On a grassy hillock on what was part of the original Maroon homestead paddock, lies a small cemetery with graves and headstones dating back to 1856. The graves, revealing high infant mortality, bear testimony to the hardships endured by early settlers in rural districts.

24. Mount Maroon National Park

Mount Maroon, one of seven national parks in the Fassifern district, was gazetted in 1938. The summit offers views of the Great Dividing Range, from Cunninghams Gap to Wilsons Peak and the Lamington Plateau. Rosa Campbell Praed mentioned the mountain in *My Australian Girlhood* (1902), and the colonial artist George Hart Taylor depicted it in 1894, as did Godfrey Rivers in his painting 'A Study near Maroon' (1906).

25. Coochin Coochin Homestead

Coochin Coochin run was first taken up by David Hunter in 1842, followed by John Kent in 1844. Kent adopted the name Coochin Coochin, said to be an Aboriginal word. Typical of 1840s houses, the original homestead had internal cedar joinery and low verandahs to keep the walls cool. The home was built on the valley floor but was moved to higher ground in 1871. The property changed hands frequently until 1882, when it was purchased by James Bell, a member of a family long associated with pastoralism in Australia.

As Bell's family expanded, so did the homestead. Pavilion rooms were built, and spaces between the additional rooms were planted with tropical plants and fig trees. Famous for its large parties, the house was visited by the Prince of Wales and other dignitaries. Trees planted by well-known visitors adorn the landscaped garden. Coochin Coochin was a base for the colonial artist Conrad Martens in 1851 and Godfrey Rivers undertook a series of paintings of the station and the nearby Main Range in 1905. The homestead is not open to the public.

26. Mount Alford

Originally known as Reckumpilla, the town was renamed after Thomas Alford, manager of Coochin Coochin station from 1868 and later a part-owner. The large pastoral runs in the district were broken up in the 1870s and in the 1880s the township that became Mount Alford developed as selectors moved to the district.

27. Mount Alford State School War Memorial

Erected under the supervision of the Mount Alford School Committee in 1918 in recognition of local students who had served in World War I and in memory of those killed. The memorial also contains a student honour roll for World War II.

28. Mount Alford General Store

Around 1887 August Anders opened a general store, reputedly the first building in the township. In 1910 the store was sold to J.R. Brown, who rebuilt it in 1913. The store has traded continuously for over a century and has had many owners.

29. Moogerah Peaks National Park

Mount French, Mount Greville, Mount Moon and Mount Edwards are peaks in the four separate parks that make up Moogerah Peaks National Park. Of volcanic origin from about 23 million years ago, these residual peaks now cradle the Moogerah Dam. The vegetation is predominantly open eucalypt forest with montane heath on the exposed rock faces and rainforest in some sheltered areas. Much of the fertile Fassifern Valley was covered by dry rainforest before it was cleared for agriculture in the 1880s.

Only a small remnant of this vegetation type is protected within Mount French National Park, an increasingly popular recreation destination. The relative inaccessibility of the peaks ensures that much of the district's natural values remain intact.

30. Moogerah Dam

Plans to build a dam across the Mount Edwards Gorge to supply water to Brisbane were first mooted in the early 1900s. Land was resumed for the purpose in 1916 and 1917 and by 1917 local advocates were promoting the dam, but construction did not begin until 1959. The main wall was completed in 12 months. The dam was named Moogerah, after the nearby settlement. Local farmer-irrigators use the dam water for vegetable growing, but the main user is the Swanbank Power Station near Ipswich.

25 *Coochin Coochin Homestead*
28 *Mount Alford general store*
30 *Moogerah Dam*

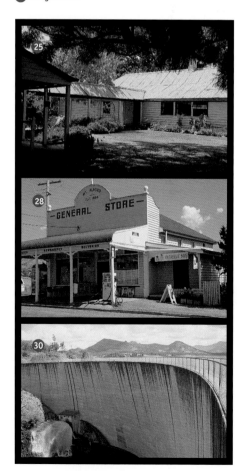

View from Governor's Chair Lookout

31. Spicers Gap Road

Squatters on the southern Darling Downs continued to search for a more convenient pass through the Great Dividing Range and in 1847 Henry Alphen, a stockman from Canning Downs run, rediscovered the gap identified by Cunningham in 1827. Although the *Moreton Bay Courier* launched an appeal for construction of a road through Spicer's Gap, little public support was forthcoming and squatters Patrick Leslie and Fred Bracker put up most of the money to clear the road and lay a 'corduroy' or pine log surface. By early August 1847 two drays had travelled to Ipswich using the new road, saving three days on the trip. From the 1850s until the 1870s, Spicer's Peak Road (as it was then known) was the major transport route from the southern Downs to Ipswich, enabling travellers to avoid a lengthy journey by way of Gorman's Gap near Drayton. Two hotels opened on the new road, Balbi's Inn at Clumber and the Main Range Hotel near the pioneer cemetery.

Between 1860 and 1865 a properly designed and constructed road, surfaced with stone pitching and corduroy logs, was built under the direction of Robert Austin, a surveyor and later Engineer of Roads. Sections of this surface can still be seen through Spicers Gap. Austin's improvements allowed the use of horse teams as well as bullock teams, but the popularity of the road was short-lived. Spicer's Peak Road was virtually abandoned in 1871, when the railway from Ipswich to Warwick via Toowoomba was opened. Cunninghams Gap was declared as a national park in 1909. Interest in the track was revived in the 1920s with the development of the motor car and recreational driving. In 1935 the Main Roads Commission decided to build a highway through Cunninghams Gap and the Spicers Gap Road was no longer maintained. In 1998 action was taken to conserve the road and the surviving historical section is now a walking track within the Spicers Gap Road Conservation Park, part of the Main Range National Park.

32. Cunninghams Gap

Cunninghams Gap is named after British botanist and explorer Allan Cunningham, who undertook the earliest European exploration of the Darling Downs. In 1827 Cunningham led a party from the Hunter River district to explore the land beyond the Dividing Range. He made the first recorded European discovery of the Darling Downs and identified a possible dray route (later known as Spicer's Gap) through the range to the coast. Cunningham returned to Sydney, where he reported to Governor Darling on the quality of the country and the potential for an access route to Moreton Bay.

In 1828 Cunningham returned to Moreton Bay to search for the pass through the Dividing Range. Instead, he discovered a new gap, now Cunninghams Gap. In his report to Governor Darling, Cunningham noted the economic significance of this gap, which connected the coast lands with the extensive pastoral country to the west. In commemoration of Cunningham's achievements the composer Colin Brumby wrote 'The Vision and the Gap' (1984), a cantata for chorus and orchestra with libretto by the poet Thomas Shapcott.

Stone-pitched road formation

Site of the pioneer cemetery

Balbi's Inn Site

Early in the 1850s Alexander Balbi, a native of Malta, built a public house on Spicers Gap Road at Clumber, at the foot of the Main Range. Known as Balbi's Inn, the establishment was still operating in 1866. The site is now marked by clumps of introduced trees and bamboo.

Main Range Hotel Site and Pioneer Graves

A low stone wall is all that remains of the public house on Spicers Gap Road, run by Casper Burdorff, who petitioned for a licence in 1863 but had left by 1866, defeated by the competition from Balbi's Inn. The remains of about twelve people who lost their lives on Spicers Gap Road are interred in a small pioneer cemetery nearby. The original wooden grave markers have decayed and the site is marked by a more recent stone cairn.

Moss's Well

The well beside Spicers Gap Road commemorates Edward Moss, who was contracted to corduroy sections of the original road in the late 1840s.

Governor's Chair Lookout

This large rock, perched on the edge of the cliff face, was reportedly a popular resting spot for early governors of Queensland when their journeys took them through Spicer's Gap. Lord Kerr and Lord Scott visited it as early as 1851. Sir Charles Fitzroy and Queensland's first governor, Sir George Bowen, are said to have sat on the rock in 1854. The panoramic view takes in Mount Greville and Moogerah Dam.

32 *Memorial at Cunninghams Gap*

33. Main Range National Park

The national park is the western part of the Scenic Rim. Its four sections contain impressive peaks, escarpments and ridges that are part of the Great Dividing Range. From the New South Wales border northward, the sections are Queen Mary Falls, Mount Roberts, Cunninghams Gap including Spicers Gap, and Mount Mistake. The term 'Scenic Rim' was first coined by the author Arthur Groom to describe the curved line of prominent ranges to the south and west of Brisbane. The ranges include more than 40 peaks over 1000 metres high; the highest is Mount Superbus (1375 metres). The Scenic Rim contains some of the largest areas of natural vegetation remaining in south-east Queensland and the largest area of rainforest. Vegetation types include subtropical and temperate rainforests, open forests and woodlands. In 1994 the World Heritage Committee declared the Central Eastern Australian Rainforest Reserves World Heritage Area over the Scenic Rim, including the Main Range parks.

34. Fassifern Pioneer Cemetery

Fassifern run was taken up by John Cameron in 1842. The town of Fassifern was surveyed as early as 1855, and the first land sales were held in 1862. The township cemetery reserve contains three memorials, including the grave of Sarah Mercer, buried in 1855 at the age of four. She was the daughter of the local innkeeper.

35. Kalbar

About 1876 August Engels began trading from his home on the site of the present township of Kalbar. The following year he subdivided his land, keeping a portion for his store. By 1890 a small settlement had been established around the store, with a hotel and a butcher, essentials for a pioneering settlement. These businesses were soon joined by others, including the Engelsburg Dairy Company. Previously known as the Fassifern Scrub, the town in 1879 was named Engelsburg, after the first storekeeper. The rise in anti-German feeling during World War I prompted a change of name, and Engelsburg was formally renamed Kalbar in 1916 when the Fassifern Branch Railway reached the town.

34 *Fassifern pioneer cemetery*

36 *Wiss Brothers' original store (below) (John Oxley Library)*

36 *Pressed metal facade on Wiss Brothers' store (right)*

36. Wiss Brothers' Store, *George Street*

The Wiss brothers were among the earliest storekeepers in Kalbar, establishing their business in 1890. As the business grew Lionel Wiss acquired more land in George Street and in 1905 he commissioned an Ipswich architect, M.W. Haenke, to design the building for the brothers. In 1909 they erected a larger and more attractive store next to their original building. This store, reflecting the growth not only of the Wiss business but also of Kalbar, featured an elaborate decorative facade of Wunderlich pressed metal designed to imitate bricks.

37. Kalbar School of Arts, *Edward Street*

The Kalbar School of Arts committee was formed to raise funds for a building in 1904. The new hall was opened in 1906 and soon housed a library of 2000 books. Disaster struck in 1920, when the hall and half the businesses in Kalbar were destroyed by fire. Only the honour board and piano were saved. Fundraising began for a new hall on a new site and the Mercer brothers built the present hall in 1923. The honour board was reinstated and the building was named the Kalbar School of Arts and Memorial Hall. A verandah and various stage improvements have been made to the building, now used annually for commemoration of Anzac Day.

38. Blake's Cottage, *Ann Street*

Blake's Cottage has been connected with people and events of importance in the early growth of the Kalbar area. The small timber and corrugated iron farmhouse was built elsewhere in the district in the 1890s and was moved to this site by a local German farmer, Heinrich Scholz, upon the residential subdivision of Engelsburg in 1912. At that time the town comprised little more than a few businesses around the main intersection. The Pennell family bought the cottage in 1928 and in 1947 the title was transferred to Charles Blake's family. The cottage eventually passed to their son, also named Charles Blake, who died in 1994.

39. Wiss House, *Ann Street*

This large timber home was built in 1912 for Lionel Wiss and his family. By then, Wiss Brothers' store was successful and Wiss had become one of the most important businessmen in the town. The house was owned by the Wiss family until 1975. Still privately owned, it is not open to visitors.

40. St John's Lutheran Church, *Edward Street*

The present church, dedicated in 1930, was the third St John's Church to be built for Kalbar's Lutheran congregation. The first, of hand-sawn timber with a shingle roof, was dedicated by Pastor Heiner in 1882. In 1901 a larger church was built to serve the congregation, reunited after a period of division, and a school was built at the same time. When the manse at Milbong burnt down in 1922, the congregation wanted the new manse to be built at Kalbar. Its building assisted by donations of materials and services from Kalbar businessmen and church members, the manse was dedicated in the following year. The cemetery remained open for burials until 1945; in it is the grave of Julius Domjahn, who arrived in 1875 and was the district's first Lutheran minister.

38 *Blake's Cottage at Kalbar*
40 *Cemetery at St John's Church, Kalbar*
41 *High Street Boonah, 1936 (John Oxley Library)*

41. Boonah

This land was taken up as part of the Dugandan run from 1844. The first farming settler in the area, James Johnson, arrived in 1870. As more land was opened for closer settlement during the 1870s, new settlers, many of German origin, moved into the area. After Max Blumberg opened the first store in the early 1880s, on what is now the site of the Commercial Hotel, the settlement was known as Blumbergville. When the railway arrived in 1887, the rail siding was named Boonah and the terminus retained the name Dugandan. Floods in that year caused the commercial centre to shift towards Boonah and the name was officially recognised in 1895.

In 1888 the town was selected as the headquarters of the Goolman Divisional Board. The Board became a Shire in 1904 and was renamed Boonah Shire in 1937. Boonah became the centre for the district's dairying industry. The first butter factory opened in 1901 and dairying, together with pig raising and fodder crops, expanded steadily over subsequent years. The completion of Moogerah Dam and the upgrading of the Cunningham Highway have contributed to Boonah's continuing importance as the district's principal town.

42. Fassifern Butter Factory, *Railway Street*

Since the early 1900s dairying has been the dominant industry in the area. The district's first creamery was established at Coulson in 1892 and by 1900 Boonah had three creameries. Most farmers had their own separators until the Fassifern Butter Factory was established in 1901. In 1916 a new factory was built on the present site, which was then beside the railway. Extensive additions were completed in 1933 and butter production at Boonah surpassed that of all other factories in the Fassifern and Lockyer Valley districts. In addition to producing butter and dairy products, the Boonah factory generated electricity for the township and supplied water to the hospital. Declining production led to the factory's closure in 1974. The building was subsequently converted to a drive-in fruit and vegetable store.

43. Boonah War Memorial, *Yeates Street*

Erected by public subscription, the Boonah War Memorial records the names of the 374 local residents who served in World War I. The foundation stone of the memorial entablature was unveiled in 1920 by General Sir W. Birdwood; the completed monument was unveiled several months later by Mrs G.A. Bell of Coochin Coochin station on the occasion of the visit of the Prince of Wales.

42 Former Fassifern Butter Factory, Boonah
43 Boonah War Memorial
45 Post Office and the Commercial Hotel
46 Showground pavilion and grandstand

44. Boonah Post Office, *High Street*

Boonah's post office was opened by the Postmaster-General, W.H. Wilson, in 1899, not long before the transfer of all post offices to the Federal Government. The simple timber building was of a standard design prepared for small townships by the Government Architect's Office.

45. Commercial Hotel, *High Street*

The Commercial Hotel, originally the Royal Exchange, was built in the 1890s. In 1903 it was acquired by Charles Meredith and was renovated. The exterior of the hotel, always a popular gathering place on market days, is little changed. Its timber cross bracing and ornate verandah balustrade are typical of substantial regional hotels of the period.

46. Boonah Showground Pavilion, *Oliver Street*

The first Fassifern and Dugandan Agricultural Exhibition was held in Boonah in 1898, when a militia drill shed was used as the show pavilion. The Boonah showgrounds were established on the present site in 1911.

47. Bruckner's Sawmill, *Rathdowney Road*

Bruckner and Hertzberg constructed a sawmill in Boonah in 1883. Bruckner acquired sole ownership in 1889 and remained in control until his death in 1934. His family continued to manage the business until the mill was sold in 1971. The Bruckner and Cossart mills played an important part in the daily lives of the town's residents, who set their clocks by the steam whistles until electricity replaced steam in the 1960s.

48. Cossart's Sawmill, *Mount French Road*

In 1887 James Cossart entered into partnership with the Ipswich sawmiller John Hancock to rebuild Hancock's Boonah mill, which had been destroyed by floods. Cossart became sole owner of the mill a few months later. The mill was destroyed by fire in 1897 and was rebuilt on its present site, which was then beside the railway line. Cossart's business continued to expand and in 1899 he opened a hardware store in Boonah's High Street. The number of employees continued to grow, particularly after the establishment of a case mill, reaching a peak of 240 people in 1939 when the mill was the largest producer of butter boxes in Australia. The sawmill, with its own siding, accounted for much of the traffic on the Fassifern Branch Railway until the railway closed in 1964. Cossart died in 1922 but the business remained a family concern until 1981, when it was sold. Part of the sawmill is currently used by a timber recycling company.

49. Dugandan Hotel, *Rathdowney Road*

A hotel was operating at Dugandan by 1885. As the new settlement of Boonah developed nearby, the present hotel was opened about 1909. The building remains relatively unchanged and the extensive original cross bracing used in the walls is still visible.

50. Trinity Lutheran Church, *Rathdowney Road*

The first Trinity Lutheran Church was erected at Dugandan in 1883. The present church was completed in 1907 to a design by a well-known architect, Henry Wyman, and the old church was moved to Kalbar. Although some improvements were carried out in 1937, this remains a typical rural Lutheran church of the period.

48 *Saw-dust kiln at Cossart's mill, Boonah*
51 *Roadvale general store*
52 *Lutheran cemetery, Milbong*

51. Roadvale

The railway reached Roadvale in 1887. Although the settlement was not intended to become a major station, this part of the Fassifern Valley became densely populated and a sizeable township had developed by the early 1900s. Disaster struck in 1915, when most of the town was destroyed by fire. Humphries and Tow's store, established in 1914, was one of the few buildings to survive. Although many of the businesses were rebuilt, the town never regained its former status.

52. Milbong

Known as the One Eye Waterhole in the early 1860s, the Milbong area was one of the first to be opened for settlement in the Fassifern Valley. English settlers were followed in the late 1870s by a large number of German immigrants, who stayed when other settlers moved on. After early failed attempts to grow cotton and sugarcane, farmers turned to dairying. More land was opened up in the 1880s and Milbong developed as the town for the district. A store, the Farmers Arms Hotel, a Lutheran church and a school were among the buildings constructed. The Milbong Co-operative Dairy opened in 1898 and until the 1930s the town remained the centre for a small dairying and mixed farming district. Milbong was one of a number of towns in the Fassifern Valley that declined in importance as development became concentrated in Boonah. The cemetery is one of the few surviving reminders of the large Lutheran congregation that worshipped at Milbong until the 1920s.

53. Peak Crossing

Peak Mountain station was taken up by William Wilson in 1868. The township of Peak Crossing was formed at the crossing of Purga Creek at the junction of the Old Warwick Road and the Harrisville and Fassifern Valley roads.

54. Harrisville

The town was named to honour George and John Harris, who in the 1870s opened a store and a cotton gin on what is thought to have been a portion of the original Normanby run. When the railway line was extended to Boonah in 1888 the township of Harrisville developed around the railway station.

55. Harrisville School of Arts,
Queen Street

The first section of this building was constructed about 1889 to the designs of architect Henry Wyman. In 1891 the trustees of the school of arts purchased the hall from Robert Dunn and began building extensions. The school of arts became the district's concert hall and entertainment centre. About 1909 a reading room and library were added to the complex to encourage further education. The building is still used regularly for community activities.

56. Commercial Hotel,
Queen Street

The original Commercial Hotel was built in 1901 for Miss Ellen Butler. It was sited close to the railway line to attract the custom of the railway gangs. It burned to the ground in 1939 and was replaced by the present hotel in the same year.

57. Former National Bank of Australasia,
Queen Street

Opened as the Royal Bank of Queensland, this building operated as the Bank of Queensland from 1917 to 1922 and then as the National Bank of Australasia. It has been used as a residence and antique shop since its closure as a bank. The Federation-style building has a hipped roof and a central gable with a decorative fretted bargeboard and overhanging eaves. Its timber decoration is typical of the period of its construction. The elaborate timber entry on the left-hand side of the building was the original entrance to the banking chamber.

57 *Former National Bank at Harrisville*
58 *Royal Hotel*
60 *Normanby Homestead*

58. Royal Hotel,
Dunns Avenue

The first hotel on this site was the Harrisville Inn, opened in 1875. A new licensee, Margaret Wholley, renamed it the Royal James Hotel in 1878. That building is thought to have burned down in the 1920s and to have been replaced with the present hotel.

59. Warrill View Showground Hall

The planned village of Warrill View was overshadowed by nearby Harrisville and did not expand until the 1930s. This two-storey warehouse was moved here from Roma Street in Brisbane in 1934 to become the settlement's new showground hall.

60. Normanby Homestead

The house was constructed in 1866-67 for George Thorn, to a design by the Ipswich architect and surveyor Charles Balding. Normanby run was originally known as Rosebrook and is thought to have been settled about 1843 by Donald McIntyre. George Thorn, a prominent Ipswich citizen, took over the property in 1845, renaming it after the Marquis of Normanby. Subdivision of the run began in 1860 when the village of Normanby, now Warrill View, was established. In 1886 the property comprised 20,000 acres and carried 25,000 wethers for fattening for markets. Declining fortunes led to its subdivision in 1899 and the homestead was sold with just 32 acres (about 13 hectares) of land. Members of the Macarthur family, of merino sheep fame, bought Normanby in 1961 and the house has since been restored. The homestead is not open to the public.

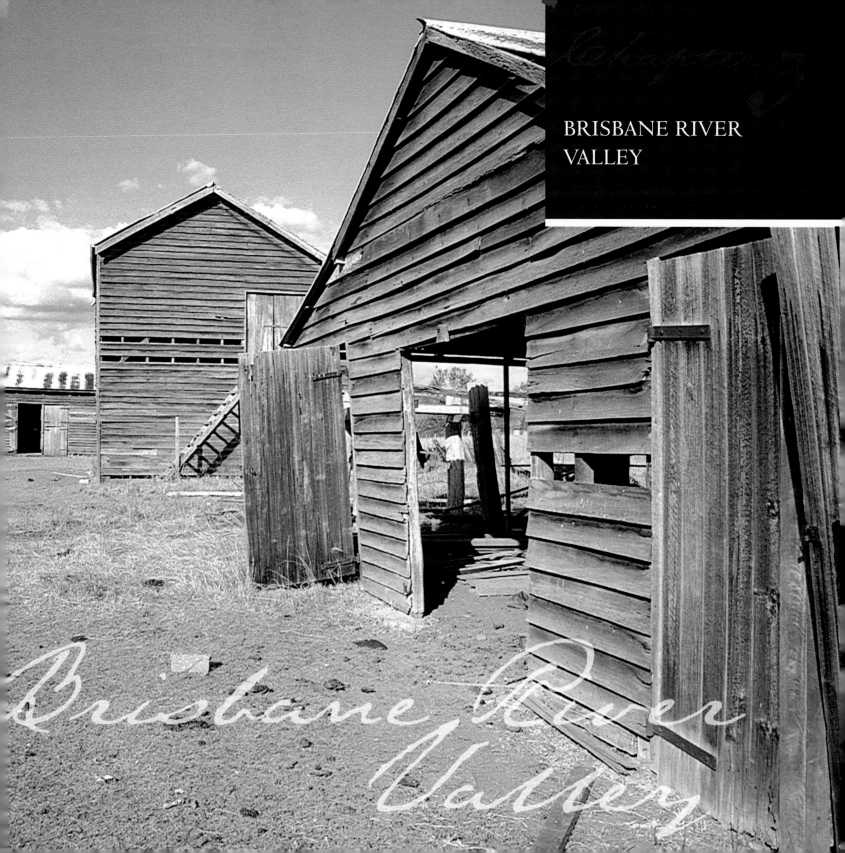

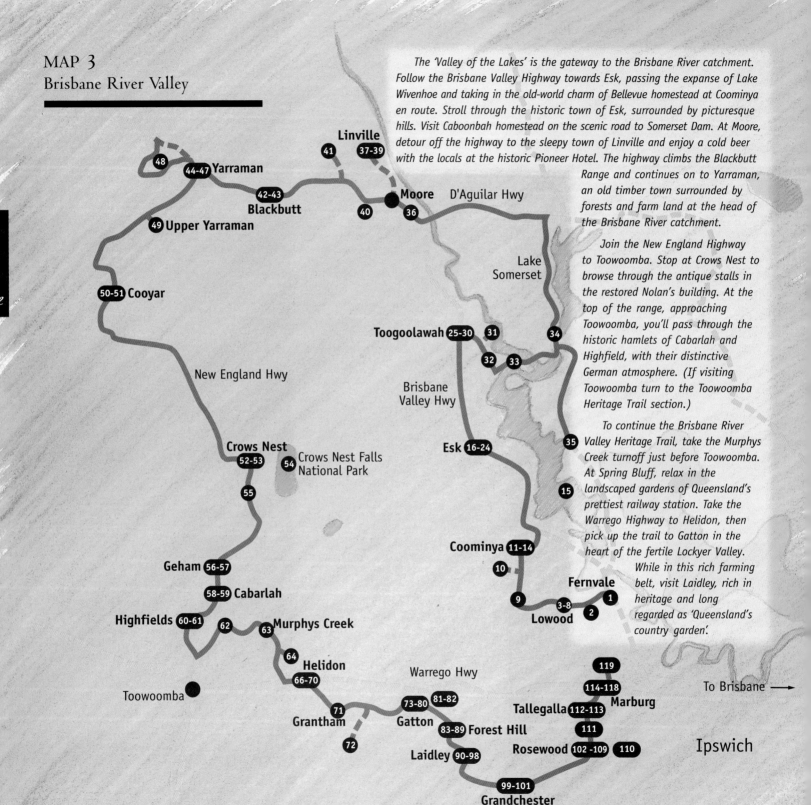

MAP 3
Brisbane River Valley

The 'Valley of the Lakes' is the gateway to the Brisbane River catchment. Follow the Brisbane Valley Highway towards Esk, passing the expanse of Lake Wivenhoe and taking in the old-world charm of Bellevue homestead at Coominya en route. Stroll through the historic town of Esk, surrounded by picturesque hills. Visit Caboonbah homestead on the scenic road to Somerset Dam. At Moore, detour off the highway to the sleepy town of Linville and enjoy a cold beer with the locals at the historic Pioneer Hotel. The highway climbs the Blackbutt Range and continues on to Yarraman, an old timber town surrounded by forests and farm land at the head of the Brisbane River catchment.

Join the New England Highway to Toowoomba. Stop at Crows Nest to browse through the antique stalls in the restored Nolan's building. At the top of the range, approaching Toowoomba, you'll pass through the historic hamlets of Cabarlah and Highfield, with their distinctive German atmosphere. (If visiting Toowoomba turn to the Toowoomba Heritage Trail section.)

To continue the Brisbane River Valley Heritage Trail, take the Murphys Creek turnoff just before Toowoomba. At Spring Bluff, relax in the landscaped gardens of Queensland's prettiest railway station. Take the Warrego Highway to Helidon, then pick up the trail to Gatton in the heart of the fertile Lockyer Valley. While in this rich farming belt, visit Laidley, rich in heritage and long regarded as 'Queensland's country garden'.

Linville
41 37-39

48 44-47 Yarraman
42-43 Moore D'Aguilar Hwy
Blackbutt
40 36

49 Upper Yarraman

Lake
Somerset

50-51 Cooyar

Toogoolawah 25-30 31 34
32 33

New England Hwy

Brisbane
Valley
Hwy

Esk 16-24 35

Crows Nest
52-53 54 Crows Nest Falls
National Park

55 15

Coominya 11-14
10
Fernvale
9 3-8 1
Geham 56-57 2
58-59 Cabarlah Lowood
Highfields 60-61
62 63 Murphys Creek
64
Toowoomba Helidon
66-70

119
114-118

Warrego Hwy Marburg
71 73-80 81-82 Tallegalla 112-113
Grantham Gatton 111
72 83-89 Forest Hill
Rosewood 102-109 110
Laidley 90-98

To Brisbane →

99-101
Grandchester Ipswich

THE BRISBANE RIVER VALLEY

The New South Wales Surveyor-General, John Oxley, and the botanist Allan Cunningham explored the Brisbane River Valley to the vicinity of the present Ipswich in 1824. Pastoral settlement on the Darling Downs spilled into the valley from 1841, when the McConnel family occupied Cressbrook run, near Toogoolawah. While land was sought for sheep grazing, the dense forests with their rich resources also attracted timber-getters. The logging of native forests and, more recently, the establishment of pine plantations have been dominant influences on the history and heritage of the Brisbane River Valley. Queensland's first railway line opened from Ipswich to Grandchester in 1865 and was extended to Toowoomba on the Main Range by 1867.

Clearing the dense scrub in areas such as Rosewood was a necessary step to the establishment of dairying. Along with pig raising, dairying provided the principal economic support for the majority of the Valley's farming population until the 1950s. The economic depression and the introduction of the cream separator in the 1890s fostered the establishment of farmers' associations and the building of co-operative dairy factories.

The high level of military enlistment throughout the district during World War I meant that by the early 1920s most towns had an active returned servicemen's association and a war memorial surmounted by a statue of a 'digger'. The period saw an increase in the number of churches, convents and schools built.

Community school of arts halls were extended or rebuilt to accommodate an increasingly active social life, and many sporting associations were formed to take advantage of showgrounds developed by agricultural associations. Weekend picture shows also became popular. The travelling picture show man who used local halls took up permanent residence in major towns, where halls were converted for film projection when talking pictures arrived in the 1930s. Although the heritage character of towns and a range of rural industrial sites has been altered by fires and the consequences of economic decline, the relative absence of change or pressure for redevelopment has resulted in the retention of many significant heritage buildings.

During the difficult Depression years, the most important influence on the life and character of the Brisbane River Valley was the construction of the Somerset Dam, designed to control the floods that had devastated the Valley since the 1870s. Completed in 1953, the dam provided employment for hundreds of workers. While the dam caused the loss of a vast area of arable land, it also secured town water supplies and made possible the irrigation systems that assisted the fruit and vegetables industry. The construction of the Wivenhoe Dam, opened in 1985, had similar effects. The extensive lakes formed by both dams have been developed for recreational activities and are used by increasing numbers of visitors each year.

Holmes railway camp, Main Range, c1867 (John Oxley Library)

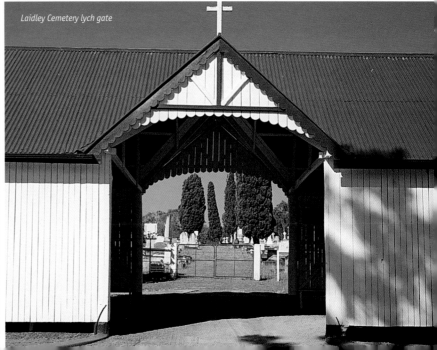

Laidley Cemetery lych gate

BRISBANE RIVER VALLEY HERITAGE TRAIL

1.   Fernvale

In 1842, when Moreton Bay was first opened up to free settlers, Fernvale was a stopping place on the early teamsters' route from Ipswich to the South Burnett Region. The Brisbane Valley Branch Railway was extended through Fernvale to Lowood in 1866 and the town was the centre of a brief cotton boom. Many German immigrants had settled on newly opened agricultural blocks by the early 1870s and the town began to develop. Church communities were established and the school opened in 1874. Dairying had become the most important industry by the early 1900s. The construction of the Wivenhoe dam from 1977 to 1985 brought a large temporary workforce to the area. The population has continued to increase as a result of rural subdivision development.

2.   Vernor Baptist Cemetery

The cemetery, on the old Fernvale–Lowood road, is the only reminder of the strong religious life of the early German settlers in this area. In 1886, members of the German Baptist congregation at Fernvale built their own church at Vernor Railway Siding. This church fell into disrepair after the congregation moved back to Fernvale, where a new church was built in 1925. In 1949, the Vernor church was relocated to South Lowood and then to Tarampa, where it remained in use as a Baptist church until recently.

3.   Lowood

Previously known as 'The Scrub' or 'Cairnhill', Lowood developed as a railhead town after it became the terminus for the first section of the Brisbane Valley Railway in 1884. German immigrants, the first to farm the district, had been joined by a substantial number of English settlers by 1890. Timber and dairying were the principal industries. As the railhead for the district's produce and supplies, Lowood developed steadily throughout the 1890s and, despite the setbacks of drought and flood, was well-established by the 1920s. Much of the main streets' pioneer character disappeared in disastrous fires during the 1920s and 1930s. Dairying and rail freight were the basis for the town's prosperity until the 1960s.

4.   Lowood Railway Station

This early Brisbane Valley Branch Line reached Lowood in 1884 and the station office was constructed about this time. By 1926 the station had been expanded to include a refreshment room, and the complex was further expanded in 1946. By then it included a goods shed, pig shed, freight shed and station-master's quarters, evidence of the growth in traffic and freight on the line that continued until the 1960s, when road transport took over.

5.   Former National Bank of Australasia, *Railway Street*

The Royal Bank of Queensland opened a branch at Lowood in 1901. For about 20 years it was the only banking establishment in the town. When the Royal Bank and the Bank of North Queensland merged in 1917 to form the Bank of Queensland the Lowood branch was relocated to its present site. In 1922 the Bank of Queensland merged with the National Bank of Australasia and the building remained a branch of the National Bank until 1986. It is currently used as a dental surgery.

6.   Jubilee Theatre, *Walters Street*

Built in the 1930s by a local retailer Jack Walters, the theatre with its canvas chairs and Raycophone film projector, has remained intact and unused since its closure in 1966.

2   *German settlers' graves at Vernor Cemetery*
5   *National Bank Lowood, c1922 (John Oxley Library)*
6   *Lowood's Jubilee Theatre*

7. Former Cairn Hill Cream Factory, *Park Street*

The Cairn Hill Farmers Co-operative Dairy Company was formed in the 1890s as a small, local factory. By the turn of the century it had become a successful venture with twenty-five local farmers supplying milk to the factory. The present building erected by the co-operative in 1905 now serves as a private residence and an antiques shop.

8. St James Anglican Church, *Prospect Street*

When the church was built in 1894, it was dedicated to commemorate St Mark's Church at Wivenhoe, destroyed in the 1893 Brisbane River floods. The Lowood church was rededicated as St James's when the new Wivenhoe church was built. Designed by the Anglican Diocesan Architect J.H. Buckeridge, the church was constructed by a Lowood contractor, Joseph Irwin. Extensions were added in 1928 and other changes to the structure and interior finishes have been made over the years. The building remains typical of Buckeridge's church designs.

7 *Former Cairn Hill cream factory*
9 *Airfield bunker ruins on Mount Tarampa*
10 *Banff Brothers' Winery (top)*
10 *Fermentation room at Banff's Winery (bottom)*
(John Oxley Library)

9. Lowood World War II Airfield, *Mount Tarampa*

With Japanese forces moving south, an operational airfield was quickly established at Mount Tarampa near Lowood, as part of the defence of the Brisbane area during World War II. American forces took over the airfield in mid-1942, at the height of the emergency. A semi-underground operations bunker and bomb storage pads were installed on the slopes of Mount Tarampa. After the emergency passed, Lowood remained a grass field until 1944, when a gravel strip was completed and later sealed. The field was used for the training and re-equipping of Royal Australian Air Force squadrons until the end of the war. In the 1950s the Queensland Motor Sports Club used the single runway and taxiway circuit as a car-racing venue. The ruins of the operations bunker can still be seen from the road at the base of the mountain.

10. Banff Brothers' Clinton Winery, *near Coominya*

Vineyards were first established around Fernvale and Coominya in the 1870s on the arrival of German settlers in the area. Jacob Banff and his wife arrived as immigrants in 1863 and moved from Fernvale to take up the Clinton property in 1880. Banff's Clinton wines became extremely popular in the early 1900s and the cellars were expanded. In 1914 new cellars capable of holding 158,000 litres of wine were built. The Banffs also operated a brandy distillery and by 1917 the vineyard was the second largest wine and brandy producer in Queensland. By the 1950s the Banffs were no longer making wine, the sale of fresh grapes being more profitable. The historic winery building is still in use as a fruit packing shed. The early timber homestead stands nearby. Though grapes are still grown, the original vines have been replaced with an orchard.

11. Coominya

A town, originally named Bellevue, was slowly established around the railway siding built to serve Bellevue pastoral station. Only the hotel had been built by 1905 when J.R. Atkinson surveyed town allotments for sale around the station. The town was renamed Coominya soon afterwards. For many years, the town continued to be linked to Bellevue station, although by the end of the 19th century it had become well known for the wine industry based on Gutteridge's Norman and Banff brothers' Clifton vineyards. In the early 1920s soldier settlers were established alongside the township on blocks of 160 acres (71.5 hectares). The blocks were too small for survival and the settlement lasted little more than five years. During the 1920s and 1930s, Coominya thrived as a typical small railway town. In 1975, when Bellevue station was resumed for construction of the Wivenhoe Dam, the National Trust relocated the homestead at Coominya. The town has become a popular tourist centre and its population has increased as a result of rural subdivisions.

12. Coominya Railway Station

The branch line between Lowood and Esk was opened in 1886 and the station office was built in the same year. The goods shed had been built by 1891, when the platform and station building were relocated on the other side of the line.

13. St Francis Saviour Catholic Church

Until 1920, services for all religious denominations in Coominya were held in the hall behind the hotel. In 1921, Archbishop Duhig opened St Francis Saviour Catholic Church, built by Jack Madden of Ipswich.

A feature of the church is its decorative timberwork over the front porch. Many parishioners donated to the church: John Newman donated the land and the pine board for the lining, Arthur O'Connor donated the hardwood and Roger Hanrahan donated the altar, while Mick Newman made no charge for carting all the timber.

14. Bellevue Homestead

Bellevue was originally part of the Wivenhoe run that was transferred to Fairney Lawn station in 1858. The station was resumed for closer settlement in 1869. The oldest parts of the present homestead were probably constructed after Bellevue was transferred to Campbell and Hay in 1872. The leasehold was converted to freehold in 1879, and in 1884 was acquired by James Taylor, whose son George and his family occupied the homestead. George Taylor died in 1899 but his widow remained at Bellevue and married the pastoralist Charles Lumley Hill in 1901. Bellevue was the social centre of the district in the early decades of the 20th century. The property remained in the Taylor family until the early 1950s. In 1975 Bellevue was resumed as part of the Wivenhoe Dam project, and the buildings were acquired by the National Trust and moved to nearby Coominya township. Bellevue homestead is today located close to the original entrance to the property.

13 *St Francis Saviour Church, Coominya*
14 *Bellevue Homestead*

15. Wivenhoe Dam

Ferriter and Uhr took up Wivenhoe run in the early 1840s. The grazing run was resumed and thrown open for farm selection in 1869. Wivenhoe was investigated in the 1890s and again in 1933 as a dam site for the Brisbane River catchment area, for water supply and flood mitigation purposes. The dam project was authorised in 1971 and construction began in 1977. The dam, requiring the resumption of more than 30,000 hectares of agricultural and dairying land, had an enormous influence on the Brisbane River Valley. In 1979, the Wivenhoe dam township was completed to house 750 dam workers and their families. The dam filled in 1983, and was completed in 1985. The entire Wivenhoe project including the Split-Yard Creek dam and hydro-electricity facilities cost $450 million. The 400-kilometre long foreshores of Lake Wivenhoe have been landscaped and the area developed for recreational activities. A rowing course on the Sheep Station Creek reach of the lake is the venue for the annual 'Head of the River' school's regatta.

16. Esk

From the late 1860s, selectors began farming in this district on resumed sections of the original pastoral runs taken up in the 1840s. The township of Esk was established in 1873 to serve the Eskdale and Cressbrook Creek copper mines. The first mining boom was short-lived, but operations continued on a small scale. Several sawmills were established, including one owned by Lars Andersen, the contractor for many buildings in the district. Esk became the headquarters for local government in 1880 when the Durundur Divisional Board was constituted. Renamed the Esk Divisional Board, it later became the Esk Shire Council. Further growth took place after the railway line was extended from Lowood in 1886.

15 *Grammar eight on Lake Wivenhoe (Photo Active)*

Dairying had become important by the early 1900s and the butter factory, opened in 1904, was a mainstay for the town and district until it closed in 1973. The timber industry declined in the 1920s, and fires and depressed economic conditions brought further changes in the 1930s. In the postwar period, Esk profited from the upgrading of local roads as motor transport took over from the railways, but the roads eventually took business to the larger towns in the district. The downturn in the dairying industry from the 1960s marked the beginning of Esk's decline as a major rural centre. Today it is largely supported by cattle and hobby farmers and visitors enjoying Lake Wivenhoe's recreational facilities.

17. St Agnes Church and Rectory, *Brisbane Street*

Plans for the church were prepared in late 1888 by the architect John Buckeridge. The building was erected in 1889 by the Esk sawmill proprietor Lars Andersen. Buckeridge also designed the rectory, built in 1902. Since 1928, when the Esk and Toogoolawah parishes combined to form the Brisbane Valley parish, the rector has lived at Toogoolawah and St Agnes rectory has been rented. Currently it is leased to a local arts and craft society. The gateway pillars, erected in honour of former parishioner and Brisbane Valley pioneer Francis Bigge, were designed and built by stonemason Andrew Petrie of Toowong in 1920.

18. Esk War Memorial, *Ipswich Street*

The memorial was commissioned by the Esk Patriotic Committee. Subscriptions commenced in 1916, and the Ipswich architect George Gill called for tenders in 1919. The Ipswich firm of Frank Williams carried out the masonry work and Wunderlich Limited of Sydney supplied the art metalwork. The memorial was unveiled in 1921. A stone memorial erected in the park in 1984 commemorates Captain Patrick Logan, commandant of the Moreton Bay penal settlement, who was killed while exploring the Brisbane Valley in 1830.

19. Lyceum Hall, *Highland Street*

Sawmill owner Lars Andersen erected Esk's first school of arts in 1891. The building was moved to a site near the railway station in 1904 and a committee was formed to raise funds for a new school of arts. Opened in 1909, the building became known as the Lyceum Hall. While the school of arts continued to operate a library and meeting rooms, the hall became an increasingly popular venue for local dances and arts and crafts exhibitions. From 1914, silent movies were shown regularly and 'talkies' were introduced in 1931. The Shire Council purchased the hall in 1972 and in 1976 carried out major extensions to complement the several extensions carried out previously. The building is a landmark and a link with Esk's social history.

20. Staging Post Inn, *Brisbane Street*

This was formerly the well-known Metropole Hotel. The original hotel, built in 1907, was one of the largest hotels outside Brisbane. It burnt down in the fire that destroyed much of Esk's business centre in 1932. The present two-storey hotel was built on the same site in the following year. The hotel reopened under its present name during the 1970s, after renovations carried out to modernise it. The 1930s decor has been retained and since 1981 the building has operated as a guesthouse and restaurant.

18 *Esk War Memorial*
19 *Lyceum Hall*
20 *Metropole Hotel, c1914 (John Oxley Library)*

21. Club Hotel,
Brisbane Street

Opened as the Central Hotel at Sandy Creek in 1890, the hotel was renamed the Club Hotel after it was moved to its present location in 1906. The roof and the spacious ground- and first-floor verandahs with their decorative balustrades were taken off for the move. During World War II, the hotel was taken over to provide accommodation for children from the Wooloowin orphanage in Brisbane.

22. Esk Co-operative Dairy Factory,
Factory Lane

The factory was one of the most successful dairy farmers' co-operative ventures in the Brisbane Valley. The first factory was erected in 1904 by the Queensland Meat Export Company to encourage farmers to move into dairying. Objections to the company's low prices led to the formation in 1906 of the Esk Co-operative Dairy Association. The Association soon took over the factory, and within a few years the rapidly increased number of suppliers and higher level of butter production ensured its success. After the building burnt down in 1926, the refrigeration engineering firm of Waugh and Josephson erected the present factory, which opened in 1927. The problems faced in export markets and the gradual decline in milk suppliers through the 1960s led to the factory's closure in 1973. The Esk Pottery began production here in 1990, and has built up a thriving business on export orders.

21 Club Hotel
23 Esk Railway Station
25 McConnel family of Cressbrook, c1887 (John Oxley Library)

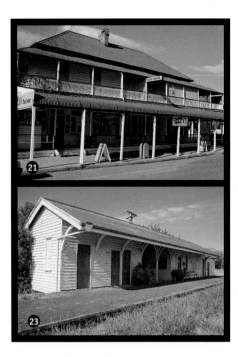

23. Esk Railway Station

Esk became the terminus for the Brisbane Valley Branch Line when the extension from Lowood opened in 1886. The principal township in the valley, Esk became a major livestock trucking centre until the Toogoolawah extension was opened in 1904. In addition to cattle and pigs, freight included condensed milk from Toogoolawah and timber from the Blackbutt forests. Refreshment rooms provided in 1912 were finally closed and demolished in 1978. Services on the Brisbane Valley Branch Line were discontinued in 1993.

24. Esk Hospital,
Highland Street

The Esk Nursing Home was opened on this site in 1907. In 1925 the government agreed to build a new maternity hospital on the site, to be known as the Stanley Memorial Hospital, and to move the old nursing home building to another location.

The maternity block, opened in 1926, is now the earliest portion of the present hospital. By the 1930s, with a large construction camp established at Somerset Dam, the district's population had increased significantly. The entire hospital was remodelled in 1936 and a new main block and general ward were added. The new building, which remains the entrance to the hospital, was opened in 1938.

25. Toogoolawah

The first European settler in the Brisbane Valley was David McConnel, who took up the Cressbrook run in 1841. In the late 1890s his son James established a condensed milk factory on Cressbrook Creek, and subdivided a large part of the run into dairy farms and the township of Cressbrook Creek (later Toogoolawah). The McConnel family was deeply involved in Toogoolawah's economic and social development, encouraging cultural, religious, sporting and economic activity. They employed a contractor to build homes for their farmers, donated land for church purposes and promoted a variety of district clubs, organisations and societies. Expansion of the town coincided with the rail connection to Ipswich in 1904 and the purchase of the factory by the Nestlé and Anglo-Swiss Condensed Milk Company in 1907.

26. St Andrew's Anglican Church, *Mangerton Street*

This timber church is a fine example of the ecclesiastical work of Brisbane architect Robin Dods. St Andrew's was constructed in 1912 for the Anglican congregation in Toogoolawah, on land donated by the McConnels of Cressbrook station. Dods was well known to the McConnels, having designed the chapel at Cressbrook. St Andrew's was erected by a local contractor, A.D. Menzies, who constructed most of the buildings in Toogoolawah until the mid-1920s. The rectory was built in 1925. The Anglican parishes of Esk and Toogoolawah were amalgamated in 1928, and since then the rector has lived at Toogoolawah. Some time after 1930 the walls of the church were buttressed, following storm damage. The original split cedar shingles were replaced in 1966 with sawn shingles of local ironbark.

27. Toogoolawah War Memorial, *Cressbrook Street*

This public park was established about 1906 on land donated by Cressbrook station. The World War I memorial was commissioned by the citizens of Toogoolawah in 1916. It was crafted by Ipswich monumental mason Frank Williams. The predominantly sandstone memorial honours the 197 local men who served in World War I, including 38 killed in action. Unveiled in 1917, it was the second World War I memorial erected in Queensland. A brass band was formed in Toogoolawah in 1919 and about this time a small bandstand was erected in the memorial park.

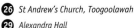 St Andrew's Church, Toogoolawah
Alexandra Hall

28. Toogoolawah Railway Station

Extension of the branch line from Esk to Toogoolawah opened in 1904. The new township of Toogoolawah was the location of the successful Cressbrook condensed milk factory and the station shows the role of railways in the development of rural industries.

29. Alexandra Hall, *Cressbrook Street*

Named after Queen Alexandra, the original hall opened in 1913 as the headquarters of the Toogoolawah Amateur Gardening and Progress Association. It survived a fire in 1926 but was burnt down in 1930, largely due to a lack of water and firefighting equipment. A much larger hall incorporating a stage was built from timber cut locally and opened in 1931. A licence to show movies was granted the same year to a Mr Trattles and the hall has been used as a movie theatre since then.

30. Nestle's Condensed Milk Factory, *Factory Road*

The factory operated during the most productive years of the dairying industry and made a substantial contribution to the prosperity of both town and district. Its construction in 1898 was financed by the McConnels of Cressbrook. By 1900 the factory posed a serious challenge to the Nestlé and Anglo-Swiss Condensed Milk Company, which dominated the condensed milk market. Further expansion followed and in 1907 the Nestlé Company purchased the factory, also purchasing dairy farms in the district. A house, named Inverness, was erected for the factory manager in 1917. The house is now privately owned.

The farmers and the factory management began to disagree over prices and conditions. Nestle's merged with the Standard Dairy, resulting in the closure of the condensed milk factories at Lowood and Colinton. The Toogoolawah factory was closed in 1929, when Nestle's began producing its entire output from Victoria.

32. Caboonbah Undenominational Church

As the name suggests, the church was built to serve all religious denominations in the district when lack of funds precluded the building of separate churches. Constructed in 1905, it demonstrates the importance of religion and community endeavour among the early settlers. The land was donated by the Somerset family of Caboonbah station and social and sports events were organised to raise funds. Local sawmiller Lars Andersen built the church, using timber cut on the site. In 1975 the church was moved to its present location above the flood levels of the Wivenhoe dam.

33. Caboonbah Homestead

The homestead was built for grazier Henry Plantagenet Somerset, who had arrived in Moreton Bay in 1871 intending to stay only until he could obtain an English army commission. Instead, he took up stock and station management. In 1879 Somerset married Katherine McConnel of Cressbrook station and in 1888 he secured land in the Mount Stanley area of the Brisbane River Valley as a grazing property that he named Caboonbah. The Somersets occupied their new homestead in 1890, and remained there until Katherine's death in 1935. Somerset died the following year. Following Katherine Somerset's death, the house was sold to the Grieve family, who operated Caboonbah as a guesthouse until 1962. The property was resumed in 1973 as part of the Wivenhoe Dam project and was transferred to the Brisbane Water Board. Caboonbah is now the headquarters of the Brisbane Valley Historical Society and is open to the public.

31. Toogoolawah World War II Airfield, *Watts Bridge*

This grassy field was selected as a base for the transport and spotting squadrons of the Australian Army, relocated here from Toowoomba in 1942. Grass runways were graded and gravelled by the end of 1943. Because Toogoolawah was planned as a temporary airfield, it had no permanent buildings and accommodation was in tents. The airfield was de-licensed in 1947, but later reopened as Watts Bridge Airfield, named after a nearby bridge over the Brisbane River that was destroyed in the 1974 floods. It is now used for gliding and recreational flying by the Queensland Vintage Aeroplane Group and other organisations.

The closure had a devastating effect on the town, almost half the population being forced to move in search of employment. The factory was dismantled in 1938 and the remaining buildings, apart from the packing shed, burnt down in 1951.

30 Nestle's condensed milk factory (top) (John Oxley Library)

30 Packing shed of the Nestle's factory, Toogoolawah (above)

31 Grass runway at Watts Bridge

32 Caboonbah Church

Somerset Dam under construction, 1937 (John Oxley Library).

52

Construction worker's huts at Somerset, c1937 (John Oxley Library)

CORONATION HALL

Coronation Hall

34. Somerset Dam

Henry Somerset of Caboonbah station was the first to suggest the site of the present Somerset Dam. Following the 1893 floods and their devastating effects on the Brisbane River Valley, various flood mitigation schemes were proposed, but not adopted. In 1906 Somerset invited the Water Board to inspect the Stanley Gorge, suggesting that a dam across the gorge would provide flood mitigation in the Brisbane River Valley and increased storage for Brisbane's water supply. A 1928 commission of enquiry recommended a reservoir on the Stanley River, but no action was taken until 1933 when the Forgan-Smith Labor Government adopted the Brisbane River flood mitigation and water supply scheme as a major employment-generating project during the Depression.

By 1935 work on the Stanley Dam had commenced. Hundreds of men were engaged in diverting the Stanley River and accommodation was erected for almost 1000 construction workers and their families. In that year district residents requested that the dam's name be changed to Somerset, in honour of the man who had first proposed the site. The town established for the dam workers was also named after Somerset. The dam was almost finished in 1942, when the workforce was diverted to the war effort. The dam was opened in 1953 and in 1958 it was officially named after Henry Somerset.

Construction Workers Cottages

When construction work on the dam began in 1935, it became difficult to retain Depression relief workers in an isolated location away from their families. To overcome the problem, the government built workers' cottages, together with single men's barracks, shops, a school, churches and recreational facilities, establishing the town of Somerset Dam. The concept was modelled on the towns constructed for the Hume, Nepean and Woronora dams in New South Wales. After World War II a Commonwealth Government plan to buy the cottages for relocation as public housing came to nothing. The cottages were reoccupied during the final stage of the dam's construction. Although some were subsequently sold for removal, many retain their original structure and character and are used as holiday accommodation.

Coronation Hall

The hall was designed by a consulting engineer, H.H. Dare, who had previously advised on the planning of townships associated with the construction of major dams in New South Wales. Built to accommodate over 200 people, it was first named the Jubilee Hall, but was renamed Coronation Hall to mark the coronation of King Edward VIII. Opened in 1936, the hall was the venue for major social events and movies were shown there most weekends.

St Joseph's Catholic Church

To foster community life in the new town of Somerset Dam, the Stanley River Works Board assisted in the building of the Anglican and Catholic churches. Both were opened on 30 August 1936 in a special ceremony that brought hundreds of people to the town. St Joseph's was blessed by Archbishop Duhig, who had travelled from Brisbane for the occasion.

35. Castleholme Homestead, *Bryden*

Castleholme was established following Hugh Conroy's selection of the small grazing property in 1875. Conroy and his wife were Catholics and for 22 years mass was celebrated in their home until St Anne's Church was built nearby in 1901 on land donated by the Conroys. By 1916 the small cedar dwelling at Castleholme had become a rambling, fourteen-roomed house. The principal activity was dairying. Castleholme remained in the Conroy family until it was acquired in 1978 as part of the Wivenhoe Dam project. The homestead survives as an example of an early farm selection. The church was recently removed but the early cemetery remains.

36. Colinton War Memorial

Queensland's first World War I war memorial was an honour board erected at the Colinton School of Arts building in 1916. This stone memorial was erected in 1917, the year the Toogoolawah war memorial was unveiled. It is one of the earliest World War I memorials in Queensland.

35 *Castleholme farm buildings*
36 *Colinton War Memorial*

37. Linville

Linville became the settlement for farmers who took up selections from the resumed Mount Stanley and Colinton pastoral runs from the early 1880s. It was known as the Nine Mile Receiving Office until 1901. After 1910, when the railway was finally extended from Toogoolawah, Linville developed as the railhead for the local timber industry. A sawmill was opened in 1912 and the timber industry remained important in the town until the 1950s. The town also served as the centre for local dairy farmers and for the short-lived soldier settlement farms allocated in 1920. By the 1950s, dairying had given way to cattle raising. The town declined when road transport reduced the need for cattle loading yards and the railway service was subsequently discontinued.

36

38. Linville Railway Station,
George Street

The Brisbane Valley Branch Line reached Linville in 1910 and was extended to Benarkin in 1911. The station office was probably built about that time. A small war memorial at the entrance to the station was erected in 1921; it features a German machine gun, captured on the Western Front in 1918. The Brisbane Valley Line was closed in 1993.

39. Pioneer Hotel,
George Street

The hotel, built in 1892, was cut into two sections and moved three times by bullock wagon ahead of the construction of the railway. It was re-erected on the present site in 1910, when William Warlow was the licensee. It was known for some years as the Linville Hotel. Apart from some internal modernisation, the timber hotel remains much as it was at the end of the 19th century. Bullock team yokes and tools used by early timberworkers decorate the internal walls.

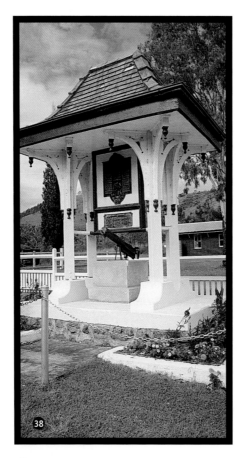
38

39

38 *Linville Railway Station and war memorial*
39 *Pioneer Hotel*
40 *The Stone House (right)*
40 *William's Homestead, 1926 (below) (John Oxley Library)*

40. The Stone House,
Moore

Located at the foot of the Blackbutt Range, the Stone House was on the main road from Esk to the Seven Mile gold diggings near Nanango and was a regular coach stop and horse change. It was built about 1869 by Robert Williams, one of a family of brothers who had come from England to the colony. The Stone House is part of a group of stone and timber huts that formed the homestead on Williams' selection. The buildings are constructed of stone quarried nearby and laid with a lime mortar. Some of the walls are partly constructed with timber slabs. The house served as an inn during its early years. Adjoining buildings once formed a kitchen, store and living quarters. The homestead is mentioned in the popular drovers' ballad 'Brisbane Ladies' — *'we pulled up at the stone house on Williams' Paddock, and early next morning we crossed the Blackbutt'.*

40

40

41. Taromeo Sawmill

Established in 1910 as a pine sawmill by A.J. Raymond and Company, Taromeo mill was acquired as a State enterprise in 1915. In 1920 the property was transferred to the Forestry Service, along with all other State-owned sawmills. After a change in government policy in 1933, Taromeo sawmill and the Newstead timber yards in Brisbane were sold to Yarraman Pine Pty Ltd. In recent decades the sawmill has been converted to electricity and new plant has been installed. The early office building at the entrance to the mill is reported to have served as an agency for Cobb and Co. coaches and a bank. An early well and hand pump are still located nearby on the old road to the Seven Mile gold diggings. Taromeo and Yarraman are surviving examples of the former State sawmill system initiated by the Ryan Labor Government. The remaining sawmill workers' cottages are probably a legacy of the State enterprise period of the 1920s.

42. Blackbutt

The town is located on Taromeo pastoral run, first taken up by Walter Scott in the 1840s and resumed for agricultural settlement after 1888. Local settlers built the school in 1896 and the town reserve was proclaimed in 1900. The name Blackbutt, that of a local eucalypt species, was first used in the town survey carried out in 1908. The difficulties of transporting a large amount of logged timber to the mills led to the opening of the railway over the Blackbutt Range to the town in 1911. Already well established around the two sawmills, the town saw further development associated with railhead services to the timber, dairying and agricultural industries. Timber remains the most important industry and Blackbutt is widely referred to as 'Timber Town'.

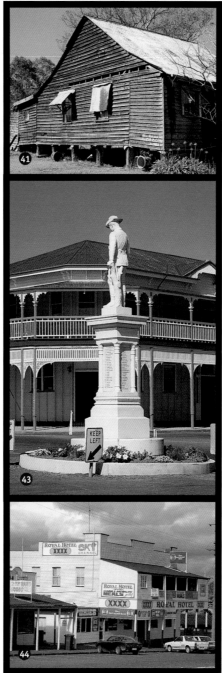

43. Hotel Radnor and Blackbutt War Memorial, *Hart Street*

Originally the Grand Hotel, built around the time the railway was completed in 1911, this is the only survivor of five hotels erected for the railway trade. The spacious, two-storey building still displays the original exposed stud construction work. The war memorial in the centre of the main intersection is inscribed with the names of nearly 100 men from the district who served in World War I. The monument was carved by a Brisbane sculptor and transported to Blackbutt to be unveiled on Anzac Day in 1920.

44. Yarraman

The town was established when the Queensland Pine Company's sawmill opened there in 1912. With the arrival of the railway the following year, the company opened a pulp mill, with a siding connecting the mill to the railway station. A company hotel and mill workers homes were also built during this period. The mill was sold to the Forestry Board in 1926. Coalmining is also a key industry in the area. The first recorded coal find was in 1913 and today coal is mined at the nearby Meandu Mine for use at Tarong Power Station. Livestock handling facilities were built at the railway station in the 1920s and 1930s when farming was at its peak, but timber has long been Yarraman's most important industry. The town remains the centre for forestry reserve and plantation timber operations.

41 Sawmill worker's cottage, Taromeo

43 Hotel Radnor and Blackbutt War Memorial

44 Yarraman's main street

45. Sisters of Mercy Convent, *Miller Street*

Completed in 1945 for the Sisters of Mercy, this building served as a boarding convent for boys from 1946 until its closure in 1966. Following some changes, the former convent continued to be used by the Catholic Church for seminars and retreats. In 1988 it was handed over to the church administration at Cherbourg for use as Aboriginal hostel. After being empty for some time the property was acquired in 1997 by the Yarraman and District Historical Society as a centre for a historical museum. The convent is now known as Heritage House. Our Lady of Dolours church, which stands nearby, continues as a place of worship.

46. Yarraman Railway Station and Fuel Tanks

The Brisbane Valley Branch Line terminated at Yarraman in 1913. An authorised extension to Nanango never proceeded. The station served the Queensland Pine Company at Yarraman until the sawmill closed in 1972. The trucking yards were closed in 1991 and the line itself was closed in 1993. During World War II, with the North Coast Railway vulnerable to attack, an alternative inland defence road was built and the Brisbane Valley Railway was used to convey fuel. Large underground storage tanks were built on the hillside adjacent to the railway station. They continued to be used as a railway fuel depot for the South Burnett region until the 1980s.

47. Yarraman Sawmill, *Mill Street*

The Queensland Pine Company was floated to acquire the assets of Millar's Karri and Jarrah at Yarraman Creek. In 1912 it established a pulp mill at Yarraman.

The mill was meant to use pine tops, commonly treated as waste. In 1926 the mill was purchased as a State enterprise, and a tramway was constructed from the pine mill to a forestry camp known as 'The Stables'. The pulp mill was destroyed by fire in 1929. It was rebuilt on a smaller scale and sold to the Yarraman Pine Company in 1933, along with the Taromeo sawmill and Newstead timber yards. The Yarraman pulp mill was the first commercial wood-pulping operation in Australia using the then relatively new kraft pulping process: it used chips made from the waste timber from the sawmill, a conservation measure not widespread in Australia until the 1970s. The sawmill, which is now owned and operated by Yarraman Pine Pty Ltd, is not open to visitors.

48. Yarraman Forest Drive
Yarraman Tramway

By 1924 the Yarraman sawmill was having difficulty obtaining enough logs as a result of industry arrangements favouring Brisbane sawmillers. The State Labor Government decided to solve the problem by purchasing the mill as a State enterprise in 1926 and providing it with a guaranteed supply of timber. A tramway more than four kilometres long was constructed, with steel and wooden rails and a single switchback beyond which the locomotive could not work. A tramline continued, terminating at a loading bank near The Stables forestry camp. Part of the route has now been made into a walking track.

The Stables Camp Site

Before the introduction of more comfortable quarters, this site was a camp for more than 50 forestry workers. The camp was known as The Stables because it was a stabling area for the horse teams that hauled hoop and bunya pine logs to the timber tramway used to carry logs to the sawmill in Yarraman. Gravity propelled the loaded wagons to a switchback, and from there they were hauled into the township by a locomotive.

 Yarraman Sawmill
 The Stables site, Yarraman Forest Drive

49. Upper Yarraman Farmers' Hall

Before its removal to the present site, the hall was one of two public halls built at Blackbutt around 1912. Owned by a Mr W. Crumpton, it was known as Crumpton's or the Phoenix hall.

50. Cooyar

Cooyar was an outstation of Rosalie Plains run, which was taken up by Robert Ramsay in 1848. By 1889 it was the settlement for timber-getters working the Cooyar Range and for farmers who had selected the land resumed from Cooyar station. Following the construction of a tunnel through the Cooyar Range, the railway reached the settlement in 1913. The town developed throughout the 1920s and 1930s to serve the timber and dairying industries. When they declined in the early 1960s, the railway closed and many businesses moved to larger towns. A major flood in 1988 destroyed the memorial hall and the bridge built in 1924 to give dairy farmers access to the railway station. Cooyar now provides community facilities for local properties.

51. Cooyar Hotel and War Memorial

The only survivor of the three hotels built after the railway was extended to Cooyar to serve the timber trade, the building was extensively damaged by floods in 1988. The Cooyar war memorial, unveiled in 1923, was constructed with funds raised locally by public subscription. The pedestal was produced by monumental masons R.C. Ziegler and Son of Toowoomba, but the 'digger' statue was imported from Italy. Originally two German machine guns were mounted near the monument, but these have since been removed.

52. Crows Nest

Large sections of the Crows Nest sheep run first taken up in 1849 were opened for selection in 1875. The declaration of two forest reserves, together with land clearing, supported a timber industry, while German, English and Irish settlers successfully established dairy farming. There was also a brief tin mining boom in 1873 and 1874. The town was declared in 1876 and the rapid development of its community life owed much to the efforts of early residents including sawmiller E. Pechey and storekeeper J.T. Littleton. The branch railway from Toowoomba, completed in 1886, followed a steep circuitous route designed to serve several sawmills and a large dairying district.

As the railhead for this prosperous district, Crows Nest was a substantial town by the early 1900s. A large block of shops built for James Nolan in 1916 is now occupied by Salt's Antiques. The town enjoyed steady growth during the 1920s and timber remained a viable industry, supporting the town until after World War II. In 1949 it became the administrative centre for an enlarged Crows Nest Shire.

The population contracted through the 1950s and 1960s as rural industries declined. Fires in 1949 and 1967 destroyed many of the buildings in the main streets. Crows Nest is now the commercial and administrative centre for one of the fastest growing shires in south-east Queensland.

53. Crows Nest Shire Office

This original section of the former shire council chambers was completed in 1940. The building now serves as the council library.

49 Upper Yarraman Farmers' Hall
52 Salt's Antiques recycle Nolans' Block
53 Crows Nest Shire office

55 *Pechey forestry arboretum*

54. Crows Nest Falls National Park

The rugged landscape of the national park contrasts with the low rolling hills adjacent to Crows Nest township. The geology is dominated by granites with characteristic domed outcrops containing large amounts of the mineral felspar, which sparkles in the sunlight, hence the name the Valley of Diamonds for the principal gorge. The park's vegetation is predominantly open-eucalypt forest, although the distinctive grouping of weeping bottlebrush, river she-oak and swamp mahogany occurs along the creek banks. Hoop pines can be seen in the gorge below the Valley of Diamonds Lookout. The park has small patches of heathland, and spring wildflowers provide colourful displays. The original area of the national park, near Crows Nest, was declared in 1967. The Perseverance Dam area was declared in 1978. The two areas were amalgamated in 1980 to form the present park.

55. Pechey Forest Arboretum

Arboreta are plots of land where different varieties of trees and plants are planted by researchers to study their suitability under particular climate, soil type and topography conditions. By 1910, because of the rate of felling of old-growth pine timbers, it was apparent that the needs of the Queensland timber industry would have to be met by importing pine wood from overseas or establishing plantations of exotic varieties on land incapable of producing local species for milling. Pechey Forest Arboretum was established for scientific research into suitable varieties of exotic plantings for local introduction. The Forestry Department purchased the initial areas of the Pechey State Forest from the estate of E.W. Pechey in 1926. A nursery was established on the site in 1927 and the arboretum was established in 1928.

56. Geham

A small settlement grew up around Alexander and Duncan Munro's Argyle sawmill built on Geham Creek in 1874. Apart from the resident mill workers, there were German, English and Irish settlers who established dairy farms in the district. Geham declined as the timber and dairying industries declined and in recent years much of the land has been subdivided for housing development. About 1919, returned World War I soldiers were offered parcels of second-rate farming land at Geham, that first needed to be cleared to make a living. Most soldier settler families failed in their attempts to survive on their blocks.

57. Argyle Homestead, *Geham*

This picturesque chamferboard residence, set in a garden amongst a variety of mature trees, was built in the 1870s for Duncan Munro, a timber merchant and prominent Toowoomba businessman. Munro, with his brother Archibald, had established the Argyle Sawmills at Geham. It is likely that Argyle Farm was named after his birthplace, Argyllshire in Scotland. Munro moved to Toowoomba early in the 1900s, and remained there until his death in 1926. From 1903, Argyle was leased to a number of people until Munro sold the property to Johann Kahler in 1920. The Kahler family had been among the early European settlers in the Geham district. In 1942, the property was transferred to David Kahler, who died in 1983, bequeathing Argyle homestead to the National Trust. The Trust subsequently sold the property at public auction.

58. Farmers Arms Hotel, *Cabarlah*

William Wilkes was the first licensee of the original hotel in 1876 when it was a Cobb and Co. staging post on the road to Crows Nest station. The original hotel closed in 1902.

59. Cabarlah Cemetery

The cemetery is a reminder of the early German settlers who took up land in the area from the 1860s.

60. Highfields

First known as 'Koojarewon' or 'Top of the Range', Highfields developed as a timber town and the site of the Highfields sawmilling company. Sawmills operated in the town from the 1860s until the 1920s and were responsible for much of the town's importance during that period. The completion of the Main Line up the Main Range to Spring Bluff in 1867 assisted the timber industry and made land in the district accessible for dairy farming. The Highfields Divisional Board was constituted in 1879. Separate shires of Crows Nest and Highfields were proclaimed in 1913, but Highfields became part of the new Shire of Crows Nest in 1949. Specialised plant nurseries and fruit and vegetable growing are recent industries. The town retains its rural character although it is now part of the suburban development that stretches from Toowoomba.

61. Christ Church Lutheran Church, *Highfields*

This is the third church built on this site, the first having been dedicated in 1876. In 1907 the new Christ Church was erected, the bell tower being added later. The English language replaced German for church services and Sunday school in 1915. Christ Church was renovated and rededicated in 1925. Descendants of the Lutheran pioneers still make up a large proportion of the congregation.

62. Spring Bluff Railway Station

Opened in 1867, this was the principal station on the Main Range climb between Murphys Creek and Toowoomba and was used as a watering point for steam engines. Originally known as Highfields, or the Main Range Station, it was named Spring Bluff in 1890 because of the abundance of natural spring water. Construction of the Ipswich to Toowoomba Main Line started in 1864. The Main Range was regarded as the most difficult section because the steepness of the climb necessitated the construction of nine tunnels.

In 1914 the Railways Department launched a garden competition to encourage staff to beautify the stations and grow vegetables. Station-master Ralph Kersop and his wife Lillian planted the gardens at the station from the 1920s, extending and terracing them during the 1930s and 1940s. Their efforts were rewarded with first prizes for many years. When the station was threatened with closure in 1991, local residents fought successfully to preserve the buildings and the gardens. Today many people visit Spring Bluff each year, and the grounds and the picnic area nearby are always popular.

63. Murphys Creek

The creek was named after Murphy, a shepherd who had a hut nearby during the 1864 railway survey of the area. The township grew around the railway station, located on the former Helidon run, which was occupied in the early 1840s. The line between Ipswich and Toowoomba was completed in 1867. Bricks were fired in the area from the early 1860s and were used in the construction of the Victoria tunnel through the Main Range. Quarries were being worked by the mid-1860s and the stone was used in several of Toowoomba's public buildings. Railway operations and mixed farming supported the small population.

64. Murphys Creek Railway Station

Tenders were called for the construction of the railway station buildings in 1867, only months before the line opened for traffic. In 1877 further buildings were needed and a booking office and platform were constructed. The steel water tank and tower bear testimony to the era of steam locomotives in Queensland between the 1860s and 1960s. The tank was used to replenish steam engines operating over the Main Range. Murphys Creek Station was closed in 1992.

65. Lockyer Creek Railway Bridge, *Guinn Park*

This bridge, located at the end of Thomas Street, was among the first three reinforced-concrete arch rail bridges built in Australia; all were in Queensland. Designed in 1909 under William Pagan, the chief engineer of the Railways Department, it has one of the largest spans of its type in Queensland.

66. Helidon

'Hellidon' run was taken up in 1841 by Henry McDermott of Sydney. Sheep to stock the new run were brought down the Toowoomba Range by Peter Murphy and James Pearce. Murphy was engaged to build slab huts and settle in before the shearing season. William Turner took over the run in 1849. He built a large homestead and remained until his death in 1878. By 1866, about 18 families lived in the area, which had four hotels, a number of stores and a church and school under construction. Helidon is perhaps best known for its spa water and sandstone quarries.

The springs were first noted by Allan Cunningham in the late 1820s. In the 1880s Gilbert Primrose purchased the Helidon spa and established the Helidon Spa Water Company.

The spa water achieved international fame, winning medals at the Colonial and Indian Exhibition in London in 1886 and later exhibitions. This company was later taken over and traded under the name Kirks, becoming a well-known soft drink maker. Helidon sandstone, with its distinctive pink toning, was first quarried in the district in 1889. The best known quarry is Wright's Quarry, provider of stone used in many public buildings in Brisbane including the City Hall, The University of Queensland, St Stephen's Cathedral and St John's Cathedral, and more recently at Bond University on the Gold Coast.

63 *Murphys Creek store and tank stand*
65 *Lockyer Creek railway bridge, Guinn Park*
66 *Helidon Spa Water Company, c1890s*
   (John Oxley Library)

67.   Criterion Hotel,
Railway Street

The Criterion Hotel was first licensed in 1895 as a single-storey timber building. The present two-storey brick hotel was built about 1918 after fire destroyed the original building.

68.   Former Bank of New South Wales,
Railway Street

A branch of the newly formed Australian Bank of Commerce opened in Helidon in 1910 and shifted to permanent premises in 1921. Following a merger in 1931 it became a branch of the Bank of New South Wales. This building's character and appeal arise from the unusual arrangement of the banking chamber and the residence. The bank closed in 1970 and the building is now a private residence.

69.   St Joseph's Catholic Church

The Catholic parish of Helidon was formed in 1880 when worshippers regularly walked from Flagstone to attend mass. The first St Joseph's Church, built in 1880, was demolished by a cyclone in 1914. The parishioners' fundraising efforts resulted in the construction of the present church in 1915.

70.   Sisters of Mercy Convent

The first convent school in Helidon was built in 1874 for the Sisters of St Joseph. The order left Queensland in 1879, to be replaced by the Sisters of Mercy. This two-storey convent was erected for the Sisters of Mercy in 1916, and for some years was used as a boarding school. The Sisters of Mercy left Helidon in 1963 and the former convent became a Christian Brothers novitiate. The building is currently the headquarters of a religious movement.

67 *Helidon's Criterion Hotel*
68 *Former bank and residence, Helidon*
72 *St Stephen's Church, Ma Ma Creek*

71.   Grantham

Grantham run was occupied in 1841 for George Mocatta, the first in a long line of lessees. In 1866 a railway siding was established on the Toowoomba Main Line to serve Grantham head station and a settlement grew up around the railway.

By 1872 the Sandy Creek Hotel was operating here on the main Gatton–Toowoomba road, but the railway station was not established until the mid-1870s. During the 1880s the station was developed to handle the transshipment of sheep and cattle and by 1900 large quantities of agricultural produce were being consigned from Grantham. A provisional school was opened in 1905. The township prospered following the opening in 1907 of the Queensland Farmers' Co-operative Company Butter Factory. The original timber dairy factory was replaced in 1926 by the present brick building, which operated until 1971.

72.   St Stephen's Anglican Church,
Ma Ma Creek

The first church at Ma Ma Creek, a small wooden building with a shingle roof, was erected in 1888. In 1892 the congregation initiated plans for a new church but it was not until 1911 that the foundation stone was laid by the Archbishop of Toowoomba. The new church, designed by architect W.D. Voller, was consecrated by the Archbishop of Brisbane in 1912. One of the most picturesque churches in the diocese, St Stephen's is built of concrete blocks, with a square tower that adds dignity to the church and the surrounding graveyard.

The war memorial was commissioned by Fleurine Andrews, a widow who was mourning the loss of three sons killed in action in World War I. Erected about 1920, the monument was made by the masonry firm of Andrew Petrie of Toowong and features a life-sized statue of an Australian soldier wearing a cap instead of the usual slouch hat. Although it was a private monument marking a personal tragedy, erected directly behind the family plot in the cemetery, the memorial has become the site for the public commemoration of Anzac Day at Ma Ma Creek.

73. Gatton

Gatton is at the heart of the Lockyer Valley, one of the most productive agricultural districts in Queensland. After the railway extension from Grandchester was completed in 1866, the centre of the town moved from the hill location surveyed in 1859 to the present site near the railway. Land was opened for selection soon afterwards, attracting many German settlers under the immigration scheme organised by Lutheran Pastor Heussler. A small village developed from the mid-1870s and further expansion took place during the 1880s. Local government was established in 1880 with the Tarampa Divisional Board, which became Gatton Shire in 1938.

Timber was an early established industry and by the end of the 19th century agriculture, particularly the growing of maize and fodder crops, dairying and pig raising were the mainstay of the district's economy. The expansion of the 1920s was followed by the Depression years. Recovery was slow but irrigation, farm mechanisation and the success of cotton, wheat and vegetable growing re-established Gatton's importance as the centre for the Lockyer Valley from the late 1960s. The town has also continued to benefit from its association with the Gatton Agricultural College, now a campus of The University of Queensland.

74. Imperial Hotel,
Railway Street

Gatton's oldest hotel was built in 1886 and named the Brian Boru after a legendary Irish king. It was renamed the Imperial in the early 1900s. For many years the hotel was well known as the social centre for the weekly stock sales. In 1993, new owners began a program to restore the hotel's original character. Its high ceilings and wide verandahs are again visible and its interiors retain many original features.

75. Royal Hotel,
Railway Street

The Plough Inn, built in 1866 by William Cook, was the first hotel on this site. It was moved from its original location in the old town, probably in 1885, by James Tuckett, the second licensee. He renamed it the Royal. The first hotel was destroyed in a fire and the present two-storey brick hotel was built in 1914.

76. Commercial Hotel,
Crescent Street

The two hotels that have traded on this site provide an interesting example of the long-standing practice of name-changing by new owners or licensees. The original hotel was the Universal, built in 1883. In 1885 it became the Willmott and H.J. Atkinson renamed it the Scariff around 1912. After a fire in 1926 the hotel was rebuilt and was named the Commercial.

73 Ballantine's store, Gatton. c1900 (John Oxley Library)
75 The Royal and the Commercial, Gatton

77. Gatton Railway Station and Boer War Memorial, *Crescent Street*

The Main Line from Ipswich to Toowoomba was opened through Gatton as far as Helidon in 1866. The present station office was erected about 1900. A waiting shed on the Brisbane platform and the distinctive timber footbridge were built about 1914. The second of two memorials built in Queensland to commemorate the Boer War (1899–1902) was erected in honour of four local soldiers who died in the conflict. Designs were called for in 1907 and that of a leading Toowoomba architect, William Hodgen, was selected. Walter Bruce, a monumental mason from Toowoomba, made the pedestal and the marble statue was imported from Italy. The memorial, unveiled at its original location on the corner of Railway and Crescent Streets in 1908, was relocated to the railway station in the late 1970s. In the 1980s the original Italian marble statue was replaced with a sandstone figure of an Australian light-horseman.

78. Lockyer Creek Railway Bridge

The crossing of Lockyer Creek at Gatton presented problems for the bridge designer, due to the width and depth of the valley at this point. The present steel truss bridge of three spans was constructed in 1903 to replace the original low-level timber bridge.

79. Weeping Mothers' War Memorial, *Hickey Street*

Few of Australia's World War I memorials are as emotive as the Gatton memorial, funded by residents as 'an expression of sympathy with the mothers of fallen soldiers'. Its foundation stone was laid in 1922. The work of leading Ipswich stonemason Frank Williams, the figure holds a scroll with the inscription 'Their name liveth forever more'. Inside the mausoleum are the names of those who died in the two World Wars and the Vietnam War.

78 *Lockyer Creek railway bridge, Gatton*
79 *Weeping Mothers War Memorial*
80 *Sisters of Mercy Convent, Gatton*

80. Walsh Centre and Sisters of Mercy Convent, *Maitland Street*

The Gatton parish was established after the arrival of Irish settlers in the district in the late 1880s. The efforts of parish priest Father Daniel Walsh to keep a parish school open failed and, after 1892, Catholic children attended the state school. A new campaign Father Walsh began in 1905 was successful. The convent was built for the Sisters of Mercy, who had accepted Archbishop Duhig's invitation to staff a Catholic school in Gatton. Both convent and school were opened in 1917. The original convent school was restored by St Mary's Parish Catholic Centenary Committee in 1986. It was named the Walsh Centre in memory of Father Walsh, who died in 1939. The convent was vacated by the Sisters of Mercy in the late 1980s and is now used for student accommodation.

81. Gatton Agricultural College

Establishment of an agricultural college was foreshadowed in 1891 when money was set aside by the government, but its construction was delayed until a suitable site was available. In 1895 the government selected land on the recently repurchased Rosewood station near Lockyer Creek. Additional land was acquired in 1896, providing a range of blacksoil creek flats, swampy timber country and a sandstone ridge for agricultural experimentation and training. The first buildings were constructed in 1896 and included the administration block (now the Foundation Building). The new Queensland Agricultural College was officially opened in 1897. In 1922 the college passed from the control of the Department of Agriculture to the Education Department. During World War II the United States Army took over the college for use as a general hospital. The college became a tertiary institution in 1962 and in 1990 came under the control of The University of Queensland.

82. Foundation Building and the Homestead

Both the Foundation Building and the Homestead are original college buildings constructed in 1896-97. Until 1977 the Foundation Building was home to the college administration. The building was restored as part of the college centenary celebrations. The Homestead was used as the Director's residence until 1973 and remains a staff residence.

83. Forest Hill

Forest Hill is on land that once formed part of Rosewood run, settled by Donald Coutts in the 1840s. Part of this land was reclaimed between 1863 and 1865 by Thomas Prior, the Post Master General. The second section of the Toowoomba Main Line was opened between Grandchester and Gatton in 1866.

Major A. Boyd, who purchased a small parcel of land near the railway in 1880, named his property Forest Hill, the title Cunningham had given to the district on his map. Boyd was granted a licence for a railway siding from which he could load timber and Boyd's Siding gradually became Forest Hill. Land was divided into the first town lots in 1886. Shops were soon established and a hotel was built in 1889. Custom came largely from the railway workers employed to upgrade the line and build a level crossing in the town. Local farmers began to bring their produce to Forest Hill instead of Laidley, however, and the town became established.

84. Former National Bank of Australasia, *Victoria Street*

The first bank in Forest Hill was the Queensland National Bank, which opened in 1901. In 1910, faced with competition from a new branch of the Commercial Bank, the Queensland National Bank put up a new building closer to the railway station. It comprised a banking chamber, a manager's office and living quarters at the rear. As a wartime precaution, the bank was closed in 1943, reopening in 1947. The bank merged to become the National Bank of Australasia the following year. The National Bank closed the Forest Hill branch in 1976 and the building is currently used as a second-hand store.

85. Lockyer Hotel, *Victoria Street*

Built by Alex McAllister in 1906, the Lockyer was the last hotel built in Forest Hill. In 1907 Janet Meredith, a hotelier of long standing in the town, acquired the licence and the hotel gained a reputation as a first-class establishment. Meredith purchased the Lockyer Hotel in 1911; on her death in 1956 the property passed to her daughters, who retained the building until 1969.

86. Forest Hill Hotel, *Victoria Street*

Originally the Station Hotel, the Forest Hill Hotel opened in 1898 under licensee James Campbell. The first hotel built in the town, it was originally only one storey in height. Faced with competition from three newer two-storey hotels in the town, the subsequent owner, O.E. Noffke, added a second storey and made other alterations in 1907.

81 *The Foundation Building, Gatton College*
83 *Forest Hill Hotel and shops*
85 *Lockyer Hotel, Forest Hill*

87. Forest Hill Railway Station

Forest Hill was designated as a station in 1881 when a gatehouse and platform were built about a kilometre from the present station site. A small station building served as a residence, booking office, goods office and waiting room and was the first house at Forest Hill. The present railway building was constructed in 1886 and a level crossing was built in 1888, west of the present crossing, which dates from 1927. The town's business revolved around the railway. By the 1960s, rail was superseded by trucks as the roads improved and the railway declined, Forest Hill Station closing in 1993.

88. Forest Hill War Memorial, *Gordon Street*

At a public meeting in 1920 the citizens of Forest Hill agreed to build a monument to honour soldiers from the district who had served in World War I. Council provided some funds and the remainder was raised through social functions, dances and special race meetings. Lowther and Sons were commissioned to build the monument, which was unveiled by the mothers and widows of the deceased soldiers in 1921; a banquet for 120 persons was held that day to commemorate the event.

89. Forest Hill School of Arts, *Railway Street*

Built in 1911 with money raised by the Progress Association and a loan from the National Bank, the original school of arts building consisted of a hall with a stage and dressing room at the back. A supper room, stage wings and a ticket office were added over the years. From 1944 until 1956 the school of arts was the venue for the regular Friday and Saturday night picture shows.

89 *School of Arts porch*
90 *Patrick Street Laidley, c1900 (top) (John Oxley Library)*
90 *Patrick Street shops (bottom)*

90. Laidley

The name Laidley's Plains was bestowed on the district by the explorer Allan Cunningham in 1829 in honour of James Laidley, the New South Wales Deputy Commissary-General. Laidley Plains pastoral run was first taken up in 1843 by John Robinson. The lease passed to Thomas Mort in 1849 and in 1852 the run was transferred to his brother, Henry Mort of Franklin Vale, and James Laidley Jr. By the 1850s much of the plains had been cleared for sheep. The district's population expanded as new settlers moved to the area to work on the railway. The first German migrants began arriving in 1861, and by 1890 more than 2000 Germans lived in the West Moreton area.

The settlement of Laidley developed during the 1850s as a teamsters' stop on the main wagon road from Ipswich to Toowoomba, after the difficult haul over the Liverpool Range. In the mid-1860s the Main Line section of the Southern and Western Railway was constructed about 1.5 kilometres to the north of the village, but there was little activity around the railway station until the mid-1870s, when the town gradually became the focus of the area. By the end of the 19th century, the Lockyer Valley was one of the most prosperous agricultural districts in Queensland. This prosperity was reflected in the flurry of building activity in Laidley, which saw the town nearly double in size as many of the early timber structures were replaced with substantial brick buildings.

91. St Patrick's Catholic Church, *Edward Street*

Laidley was originally part of the Ipswich Parish. In 1866 St Patrick's Chapel was built on Chapel Hill, Laidley. This church was a small timber Gothic building and almost half its congregation comprised Catholics from Germany, Prussia and Poland who had settled in the district. It was replaced in 1889 by a new church, which burnt to the ground in 1918. A decision was made to build a new church closer to the Catholic School and in 1918 Archbishop Duhig laid the foundations for the new St Patrick's Church on the present site. Designed by the Toowoomba architect Harry Marks, the church was consecrated in 1919. Its central stained-glass window, designed by the firm of M. Moroney at Petrie Bight, Brisbane, was made using English antique glass in strong colours to withstand the Australian sunlight.

92. Laidley Uniting Church, *Patrick Street*

Dedicated in 1933, this building served as the Laidley Methodist Church until the Uniting Church was formed in 1977. The church hall was built in 1956 and was extended in 1982.

93. Old Bakery Gallery, *Patrick Street*

Charles Whitehouse came to Laidley by a circuitous route from his birthplace in London. For 18 years he worked with the Railways Department as an engine driver. In 1885, Whitehouse established a successful bakery and confectionery business that he ran until 1904, when his son Benjamin took over the management.

The present two-storey brick establishment was built on the site of the original bakery before Whitehouse retired. Charles Whitehouse died in 1920. The property remained in the Whitehouse family until it was sold in 1950. The building has undergone several changes of ownership since this period. It is now open to the public as an arts and craft gallery operated by the Laidley Shire Council.

94. Das Neumann Haus Museum, *William Street*

This building was constructed in 1893 by the Neumann family and was used as a furniture shop and residence for many years. During World War II, crowds gathered to hear bands playing on the first-floor balcony. In 1980, after they closed the shop, the Neumanns gifted the building to the Laidley Shire Council. A vigorous community protest against the Council's plans for its demolition was successful. Under a restoration program, the furniture section was removed, a small park was established and the main building was converted for use as a tourist information centre and historical museum. It was officially opened in 1983.

95. Exchange Hotel, *Patrick Street*

Constructed in 1902, the Exchange reflects, in both style and materials, the confidence and optimism of one of Queensland's most prosperous country towns of the early 1900s. The hotel was built for Julius and Hansine Jocumsen, and replaced an earlier hotel of the same name on the site. When the new hotel was completed, the Royal Bank of Queensland occupied premises on the ground floor. Between 1904 and 1924 the hotel was owned by the Giesemann family. In 1924, the property was transferred to James King, who bought the Exchange following the destruction by fire of his own hotel. The Exchange remained the property of the King family until 1950.

92 *Laidley Uniting Church*
95 *Exchange Hotel*

96. Wyman's Store, *Patrick Street*

George Wyman learned the grocery business at Ipswich, before establishing himself at Laidley in 1883. In the following year he and his wife acquired land in Patrick Street, adjacent to the Exchange Hotel. Here they carried on their grocery business for many years. In 1902 George Wyman was elected Mayor of the first Laidley Town Council. He arranged for the construction of a new store on his land in 1906 and by 1907 he also had a store in nearby Forest Hill. Wyman died in 1911, his property passing to his widow. The store remained in trust, passing in turn to other members of the family until 1971, when it became Wyman's Pty Ltd. The economic decline of the township, brought about by better transport and the growth of regional centres, has led to a reduction in the services now offered by the store. It no longer has 22 staff, including trained drapers and milliners, as it had in its heyday in the early 1900s.

97 *St Saviour's Church, Laidley*

97. St Saviour's Anglican Church, *Orton Street*

St Saviour's was consecrated in 1909. Designed in neo-Gothic style, it is said to be the first reinforced-concrete church built in Australia. It was constructed on a steel frame, which was later filled in with cement. Fibrous cement tiles were used for the hip roof with its octagonal dome tower. The noted Brisbane firm of R.S. Exton was commissioned to make the stained-glass windows.

98. Laidley Hospital, *William Street*

A public meeting was held in Laidley in 1913 to discuss the establishment of a local hospital, as the nearest hospital was then at Ipswich. The site chosen was five kilometres out of town. Architects Coutts and Sons designed a nine-bed general hospital, to be called the Lockyer General Hospital. Built by George Neumann, it opened in 1915. The inconvenience of the location soon became apparent, however: it deterred patients and the hospital suffered financially. Neumann was employed to move the hospital to its present site in William Street. The main hospital building still features its original cupola and decorative front gable.

99. Grandchester

Originally known as Bigge's Camp, Grandchester developed as a settlement during construction of the Ipswich to Toowoomba Main Line railway in 1865. A town survey was undertaken and half-acre blocks were advertised for sale in 1866. Grandchester became the town centre for the surrounding rural community. It gained importance after 1893, when Charles Mort of Franklin Vale station opened a creamery and butter factory.

100. Grandchester Railway Station

The first railway in Queensland was the Southern and Western Line from Ipswich to the Darling Downs, linking Toowoomba, Dalby and Warwick. Construction was undertaken in sections, the first terminating at Bigge's Camp in 1865, when the present station building was half-completed. The railway station at Bigge's Camp was renamed Grandchester. Today the station is the town's most prominent feature, a classic railway station building that incorporates residential accommodation for the station-master. It was the first Queensland railway building built to a standard plan. The waiting room features a carved timber honour roll commemorating those who served in World War I. The complex still contains tanks for watering steam locomotives and a concrete dam.

100 *Grandchester Railway Station, c1900 (top) (John Oxley Library)*

100 *Station-master's house, Grandchester (above)*

101. Grandchester Sawmill

Started by the Gillam brothers in 1940, this is one of the few steam-powered sawmills remaining in Queensland. It is still in commercial use. The plant includes the boiler of a 1950s C17 railway locomotive built by Walker Brothers of Maryborough, fired by waste timber and sawdust from the circular saw. It was installed in 1971 to replace an earlier boiler. The steam engine was constructed by Marshall and Sons of Gainsborough, England, possibly as early as 1908. It was first used at Nestle's factory at Toogoolawah, then at the Lowood butter factory and subsequently at Hood's sawmill, Gatton.

102. Rosewood

The area was first settled in 1844 by Donald Coutts, who by 1846 had named his run Rosewood station. In 1866 the location became a stopping place on the Toowoomba Main Line and was known as Rosewood Gate. A railway station was constructed and the township developed as hotels, churches and a school were built. The first town blocks were sold in 1907. However, in 1914 at least nine buildings were destroyed in a fire so large that the glow could be seen in Ipswich. Despite this setback, many of the buildings were quickly rebuilt, creating the early streetscape that survives today. Rosewood's coal seams had been prospected since the 1860s, but were not developed until the early 1900s. Coalmining declined after World War II, a consequence of depleted reserves and disappearing markets.

101 *The steam engine, Grandchester Sawmill*
102 *Settlers in the Rosewood Scrubs, 1880 (above)*
   (John Oxley Library)
102 *Rosewood Hotel and shops (right)*

103. Glendalough House, *John Street*

One of the grandest homes in Rosewood, Glendalough was once owned by Thomas Bulcock, whose father was a prominent parliamentarian and a store owner in Brisbane. In 1908 Bulcock moved to Rosewood and bought a hardware business and a cottage in John Street. His business thrived and in the early 1910s the simple cottage was transformed into this twelve-roomed house. Its features include wide verandahs, high pressed-metal ceilings, a ballroom-sized living room for gracious entertaining and an extensive landscaped garden, which was used for many large social functions.

104. Rosewood Uniting Church, *John Street*

This church, one of seven churches in Rosewood, was built in 1875 as a Congregational Church. The nearby manse was opened in 1898. A significant feature of the church complex is the free-standing timber bell tower.

104 *Uniting Church and bell tower (below)*
107 *Carting cane to Rosewood, c1912 (right) (John Oxley Library)*
107 *Rosewood Railway Station (below right)*

105. Rosewood Post Office, *John Street*

This building was constructed about 1910 in Marburg and was relocated to Rosewood in 1941. Typical of post-Federation post offices in Queensland, it conforms to a standard government design.

106. Rosewood Hotel, *John Street*

The first hotel on this site was destroyed in the fire of 1914 and was replaced by this two-storey timber-framed building. Many of the hotel's original features survive, along with a detached kitchen wing. The Rosewood Hotel remains a distinctive element of the town's main street.

107. Rosewood Railway Station

A railway gatekeeper was appointed in 1866 when the settlement was known as Rosewood Gate. In 1875 a waiting room and a station-master's house were built. A new station office built in 1880 was replaced with the current station building in 1918. The new station was erected using concrete units, a construction method popular with the Queensland Railways Department at the time.

108. Rising Sun Hotel, *John Street*

One of the earliest hotels in Rosewood was the Rising Sun, built on this site during the 1860s after the arrival of the railway. The hotel was destroyed by fire in 1878, but was immediately rebuilt. In 1908 it was replaced by the present Rising Sun Hotel, a flamboyant example of Art Nouveau architecture. The building was designed by the Ipswich architect William Haenke whose stylistic approach is evident in the bell roof of the upper balcony, the corner roof turret, the decorative valances of the street awning and the large window of the public bar. Much of the original room configuration of the first floor survives, as does the original internal staircase.

109. St Brigid's Catholic Church and School, *Matthew Street*

Built in 1909, St Brigid's is among the largest timber churches in Queensland. Before its official opening by Bishop Duhig in 1910, mass was celebrated in the nearby Rising Sun Hotel until 1885, when a simple timber church, also named St Brigid's, was constructed. Rosewood continued to grow as a result of the sugar, timber and dairying industry as well as a burgeoning coalmining industry. This new church, intended to accommodate 1000 parishioners, was designed by the local priest, Father Andrew Horan, who also built churches elsewhere within the Ipswich Parish. The interior features a capacious gallery at the west end and a timber altar rail and pillars painted to resemble marble. The sanctuary end contains two painted frescoes that show the German influence. The ceiling is of Wunderlich pressed metal. Above the altar are three stained-glass windows depicting St Brigid in the centre, flanked by St Agnes and St Philomena. Two stained-glass windows added in 1935 were based on murals by the prominent Queensland artist William Bustard.

110. Normanton Colliery, *near Rosewood*

This coal-loading gantry is one of the few intact relics of the mining industry to survive on the West Moreton Coalfield. The Normanton tunnel was opened by two local families in 1922. Initially the owners could not afford mechanical power or access to the railway. The gantry was built in 1929, further down the paddock, and it was moved to this site and enlarged about 1946. A crusher and picking belt were later added to the site. The Normanton colliery had considerable reserves of coal and operated until the 1960s, its coal being sold to hospitals, a paper mill and power stations.

111. Rosewood Railway Museum, *Freeman Road, Kunkala*

The Australian Railway Historical Society operates a heritage railway service on a section of the former line from Rosewood to Marburg. This journey recreates a typical Queensland branch line service of the 1950s using a steam locomotive and a diesel rail motor known as 'Red Fred'.

109 *St Brigid's Church, Rosewood*
110 *Normanton Colliery loading gantry*
113 *Tallegalla Cemetery*

112. Tallegalla

Tallegalla was part of the densely covered area known as the Rosewood Scrub. It was almost impenetrable, forcing explorer Allan Cunningham to detour around it when searching for the headwaters of the Brisbane River in 1829. The name 'Tallegalla', meaning 'scrub turkeys', was adopted in 1876 when John Dart, the first selector in the area, applied to open a postal receiving office at his farm. Other selectors, many of German origin, gradually took up land resumed from Rosewood pastoral run and grew a range of cereal crops, fruit and sugarcane. A school was built in 1879, and a strong religious and community life developed throughout the 1880s. After 1911, the Rosewood–Marburg Branch Railway assisted farm production and local coalmining. The branch railway closed in sections from 1964 and, with the decline in rural industries, Tallegalla also declined in importance.

113. Tallegalla Cemetery

In 1876 the early selector Charles Freeman donated land on this ridge for the establishment of a Methodist Church and cemetery. Known as the Walloon Cemetery, by 1886 it had become the Rosewood Cemetery and by the 1920s, the Tallegalla Cemetery. With its commanding views, the cemetery is one of the region's most scenic burial places.

114. Marburg

This was a locality of many names, known to early settlers as First Plain, while the Minden area was named Second Plain. At one time it was also known as Back Plains. Later the township adopted the name Frederick, after one of the early settlers in the district. The adoption of the name Marburg, that of a town in the Prussian province of Hesse-Nassau, reflected the ethnicity of the district's population, four-fifths of whom were German. Nearby townships then adopted other German names. Anti-German feeling during World War I led to German names being replaced: Marburg became Townshend (after a British General), Minden became Frenchton, and Kirchheim became Haigslea. There was strong local opposition to these changes and in 1920 the names Marburg and Minden were reinstated, despite the objections of the RSL.

115. Marburg Hotel,
Edmond Street

The Marburg Hotel was originally a single-storey building erected about 1881 for a district farmer and publican, Weigand Raabe. One of the first buildings in the town, it provided accommodation for travellers, meals for local farmers and a venue for public meetings and clubs. Raabe died in 1883 and in the following year Otto Sakrzewski, a Marburg shopkeeper and carpenter, married his widow and renewed the hotel licence. It is thought that it was Sakrzewski who added the second storey in 1890. The Marburg Hotel has operated continuously since 1881, gaining increased patronage between 1923 and 1969 when the Brisbane–Toowoomba highway passed through the town. The hotel is the main focus of an annual Oktoberfest celebrating the town's German origins.

116. Former Queensland National Bank,
Queen Street

The first National Bank in Marburg was established in the school of arts in 1887. A new bank building was erected in 1888, but this was forced to close in 1893 following the nationwide banking crisis that year. The bank reopened in 1906 in a building formerly owned by the Weise brothers. In 1911 the Queensland National Bank purchased the site and erected a new bank designed by the Ipswich architect George Brockwell Gill. In 1970 the economic recession forced the closure of the bank but it continued to operate as an agency until it closed entirely in 1975. The building was sold to the Marburg and District Residents' Association and in 1976 was reopened as the Marburg Community Centre. The World War I memorial in front of the building was erected in 1920.

117. General Store,
Queen Street

The first building on this site was Frederich's store, which burned down on Christmas night in 1914. W. Dance erected a new store in its place in 1918. When Dance's store was destroyed in a fire in 1927 the Bielefields brothers, who were local storekeepers, purchased the site and erected the present store in 1931. They remained in business until 1975. The building is currently a second-hand collectables shop.

71

114 *Marburg Hotel and store*
116 *Marburg community centre, a former bank*
117 *Former general store, Marburg*

118. Shire Meeting Hall,
Edmond Street

The Walloon Divisional Board was proclaimed in 1879 and its first meeting was held at Plains Paddock. In 1903 the Divisional Board became the Walloon Shire Council. The existing council building was in need of repair and in 1913 a local builder, A. Jendrachowski, was contracted to erect a new hall for the council. Walloon Shire Council ceased to exist in 1917 when the shire was divided between the Ipswich and Rosewood councils and the hall became a branch office for Rosewood Council. From the 1930s until the 1970s the building was used by the Country Women's Association. The hall is currently used by the Rosewood Scrub Historical Society.

119. Woodlands House,
near Marburg

Once the centrepiece of a large sugar plantation, Woodlands was built in the years 1889–91 for Thomas Lorrimer Smith, who pioneered the sugar and timber industries in the district. Smith was a man of big dreams, and his house exemplified those dreams. Designed by Ipswich architect George Brockwell Gill, the mansion was lavishly decorated with iron lace and timber fretwork and featured bay windows, decorative plaster work and cedar panelling. Smith began to grow sugar in 1881; by 1886 he owned a rum distillery and in the following year he produced 270 tons of cane and 1300 gallons (5900 litres) of rum, using Kanaka or Melanesian labourers.

In 1906 the Marburg Sugar Company purchased the mill but Smith retained the home until his death in 1931.

After World War II the property was used by the Society of the Divine Word as a rest and recuperation centre for missionaries and for training novice priests. Since 1986 the building has been owned by Ipswich Grammar School and is used for school camps and as a corporate conference centre. Woodlands House is not open for public inspection.

 Woodlands House

Toowoomba

MAP 4
Toowoomba City

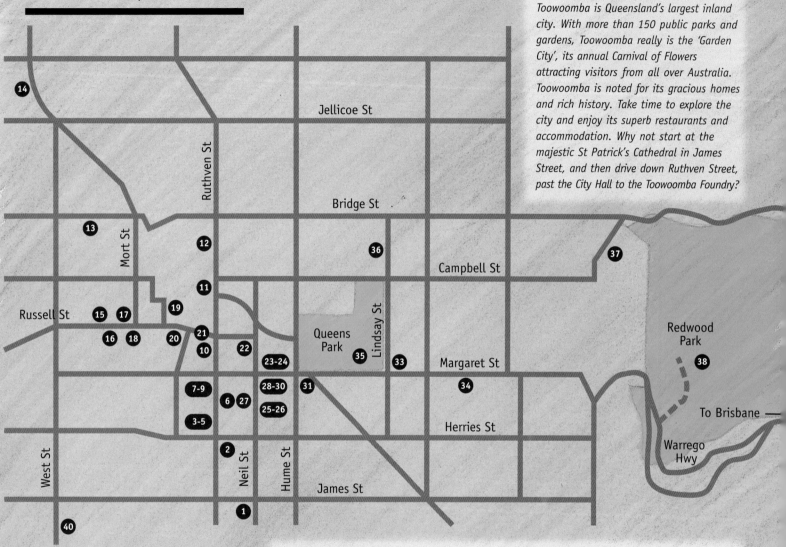

Perched on the edge of the Main Range and renowned for its magnificent views, Toowoomba is Queensland's largest inland city. With more than 150 public parks and gardens, Toowoomba really is the 'Garden City', its annual Carnival of Flowers attracting visitors from all over Australia. Toowoomba is noted for its gracious homes and rich history. Take time to explore the city and enjoy its superb restaurants and accommodation. Why not start at the majestic St Patrick's Cathedral in James Street, and then drive down Ruthven Street, past the City Hall to the Toowoomba Foundry?

Jellicoe St

Ruthven St

Bridge St

Mort St

Campbell St

Lindsay St

Queens Park

Russell St

Margaret St

Redwood Park

Herries St

West St

Neil St

Hume St

James St

To Brisbane

Warrego Hwy

74

Stroll down historic Russell Street whose winding route follows the original 1850s teamsters' track. Start at Vacy Hall, a restored colonial mansion that provides a retreat for discerning travellers; further along, inspect the authentic Victorian design and decor of Toowoomba Railway Station. Visit the early Russell Street shopping precinct where almost every building is a heritage gem.

Walk down Neil Street past the recently restored Empire Theatre with its magnificent Art Deco facade, to Margaret Street. Take in the imposing Court House, Post Office and Technical School, then picnic in Queens Park beneath hundred-year-old trees. Before leaving Toowoomba, visit the Cobb and Co. Museum, which houses Australia's finest collection of horse-drawn vehicles.

TOOWOOMBA CITY

Toowoomba was shaped by the early pastoral settlement of the Darling Downs. While the squatters made their fortunes from vast sheep runs on the eastern Downs, their wealth depended on reliable transport to overseas markets and they had to overcome the difficulty of moving wool and supplies over the Main Range. The discovery of an easier route to Ipswich resulted in settlement gradually moving from Drayton to Toowoomba, near the top of the range, where an adequate water supply was also available. The squatter James Taylor is regarded as the founder of Toowoomba. He bought town land in the 1860s and despite ridicule at the time over 'the Swamp', as the locality was then known, persevered with its development.

So fast did Toowoomba grow that in 1861 it was declared a town. Business development increased when the Ipswich–Toowoomba Main Line railway was completed in 1867. Squatters established town residences in Toowoomba and set about replicating the club, sporting and social life of Britain. However, drought in 1870 undermined the squatters' wealth. After that, town businessmen were sufficiently established to challenge the pastoralists' supremacy. They constituted an influential and expanding middle class.

Industry arrived with Griffiths' Toowoomba Foundry in the early 1870s. Other early industries included Perkins Brewery and several flour mills. Toowoomba was always popular as a mountain retreat in the fashion of colonial hill stations and its private, English-style gardens and landscaped public reserves added to its appeal. For Toowoomba, like many other Queensland towns, the 1880s were a golden era. The wealth of the land was reflected in the town's imposing public buildings. By the early 1900s, pastoralism had largely been replaced by agriculture and dairying as the government's closer settlement policy brought large numbers of small farmers to the Downs. By the late 1920s, the town had settled into a slower, more conservative life.

The economic Depression of the 1930s had less impact on Toowoomba than on many other centres. Its main influence was in the public works projects, such as the landscaping of Queens Park carried out by relief workers. Camps along the range accommodated up to 2000 unemployed men. During World War II, Toowoomba's transport facilities were important to the war effort. It was the service centre for nearby military installations and provided temporary accommodation for families evacuated from the coast. Over recent years, Toowoomba has retained a sound economic and community base. It is supported by solid growth in the service industries, the popularity of the university, and its role as the regional centre for government and business services. The recent revival of interest in Toowoomba's heritage has resulted in a series of projects to restore much of the city's historical environment in a way that is relevant to contemporary requirements yet contributes to the city's cultural life.

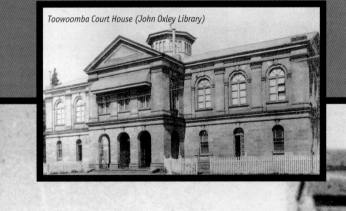

Toowoomba Court House (John Oxley Library)

Perkins Brewery, Toowoomba. 1871 (John Oxley Library)

TOOWOOMBA HERITAGE TRAIL

1. St Patrick's Catholic Cathedral,
James Street

Built as a parish church in the 1880s and consecrated in 1889, St Patrick's was constructed of bluestone from the council quarry, and was faced with freestone from a quarry near Murphys Creek. The building was conceived by a parish priest, Dr Dunne, but was built under the supervision of his successor, Father Thomas O'Connell. The architect was Harry Marks and the builder was Richard Godsall. The Toowoomba Diocese was created in 1929, with the Reverend James Byrne the first Bishop. His ambition was to improve St Patrick's to make it worthy of its new status as a cathedral. The building was completed and blessed by Archbishop Duhig in 1935. The bell outside the cathedral was donated by the St Patrick's branch of the Hibernian Catholic Benefit Society. Made in Dublin, the bell is affectionately known as Patrick in recognition of its benefactor, its maker and the cathedral.

2. St Luke's Anglican Church and Hall,
Ruthven Street

The first St Luke's to be erected on this site was one of the three Anglican churches established on the Darling Downs by 1859, and one of the four Downs churches named after the gospels. It was built by Charles Cocks, a Toowoomba sawmiller and building contractor. The present Gothic-style church was dedicated in 1897. Designed by the noted architect J.H. Buckeridge, it was built by James Renwick using bluestone with Murphys Creek freestone dressings. St Luke's Church Hall was designed by Toowoomba architect Harry Marks. This elaborate building, with its decorative ridge ventilators, was constructed in 1910 as a Sunday school and primary school.

3. Soldier's Memorial Hall,
Ruthven Street

When World War I was declared, the men of the Darling Downs, like many Australians, rushed to join up. The Darling Downs Regiment was formed in 1913 and the Downs horsemen were prominent in the Light Horse Brigade, which included the Desert Mounted Corps, commanded by Lieutenant-General Harry Chauvel, one of Australia's most famous military men. This hall was erected by the people of Toowoomba in 'memory of the fallen and in appreciation of the living'. The foundation stone was laid on Anzac Day in 1923 and the hall was officially opened in 1924 by the Governor of Queensland, Sir Matthew Nathan.

4. Toowoomba City Hall,
Ruthven Street

Toowoomba was declared a municipality in 1860 and the first elections were held the following year. In 1861 tenders were called for the construction of the town hall and the building was completed in 1862. It was the first purpose-built town hall in Queensland. As Toowoomba developed, a larger town hall was needed. A new building was constructed in 1880, to be replaced in 1900 by the current building. It was designed by the architect J. Willoughby Powell, who had successfully submitted a design for the Warwick Town Hall in 1885. The building became the city hall when Toowoomba was proclaimed a city in 1904. Toowoomba City Hall is now home to the regional art gallery and a theatre.

1 St Patrick's Cathedral
2 St Luke's Church hall
4 Toowoomba City Hall

5. Electric Light and Power Company Office, *Ruthven Street*

Formed in 1905, the company generated the first electric power for Toowoomba the following year using a steam-powered generating unit. In 1914, power supply was extended to the suburbs. Other towns on the Darling Downs and associated dairy and pig-processing factories were connected during the 1930s. By the early 1950s, the company was coordinating electricity supply for most of the region. Under an arrangement with the South East Queensland Electricity Commission, the company continued in this role until the industry reorganisation in the 1980s. During these years an office and a showroom for electric appliances was located in this building. It is now the Gallery Shop for Toowoomba Art Gallery.

6. White Horse Hotel, *Ruthven Street*

The White Horse Hotel has stood on this site since 1866. In 1906 the architects James Marks and Sons called for tenders for improvements to the hotel. Major renovations were undertaken about 1912 to the design of Reginald Marks, a son of James. The building was given an ornately detailed facade and a covered verandah that ran the length of the Ruthven Street frontage. Other substantial alterations appear to have been undertaken contemporaneously with the new facade. In 1914, the hotel was leased to William Hart, who advertised it as 'the most central and comfortable hotel in the Queen City of Queensland with hot and cold baths and first class cuisine'. By 1978, the verandah overlooking Ruthven Street had been removed and an awning was in place. The hotel was closed in 1986 and extensive work was undertaken by the new owners to turn it into office and retail facilities.

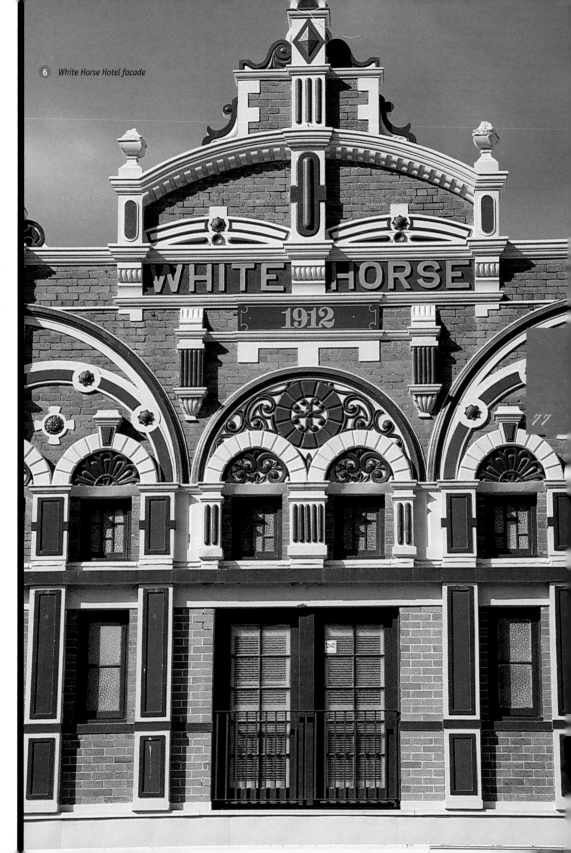

6   *White Horse Hotel facade*

7. Alexandra Building, *Ruthven Street*

Named for Queen Alexandra, the wife of King Edward VII, this architecturally distinctive building dates from 1902. Erected by James Renwick for caterer T.K. Lamb in 1902, it housed two shops and a supper hall at street level, and a large hall for dancing on the first floor. With the opening of the Cafe Alexandra, the building was a popular social venue for many years.

8. Harrison Printing Company, *Ruthven Street*

The long-established Toowoomba printers, Harrison, have occupied this building first as tenants and then as owners since 1909, when it was built for the Krimmer brothers.

9. Westpac Bank, *Ruthven Street*

The Bank of New South Wales had a long association with Toowoomba, having opened an agency here in 1860. This is the third bank building to occupy the site. The classical sandstone, granite and concrete building was erected in 1940.

7   *Alexandra Building facade*
9   *Westpac Bank building*
10   *Pigott's destroyed by fire, 1909 (John Oxley Library)*

10. Pigott and Company's Store, *Ruthven Street*

The growth of this store, constructed in a number of stages from 1910 to the 1960s, reflected the development of Toowoomba as a major commercial centre. Michael Pigott established the first Pigott's store at South Brisbane in 1886. In 1896, he opened a branch in Russell Street, Toowoomba, which became his principal store. In 1902, Pigott and Company moved to rented premises on the present Ruthven Street site. After a fire in 1909 destroyed the two-storey building, Pigott's was rebuilt with double the floor space. Pigott and Company purchased the site in 1914 and extensive additions were made. By the 1950s the family business had become Toowoomba's largest retail store. Further expansion took place in 1956 and during the 1960s. The store was later leased to McDonnell and East until 1990, when Pigott and Company sold the building.

11. Defiance Flour Mill, *Ruthven Street*

Patrick and Ellen O'Brien were Irish migrants who, since the 1880s, had operated a successful produce and grocery store in Russell Street. In 1898 the O'Briens entered into a partnership with George Crisp and established the Defiance Flour Mill. Crisp became the manager and miller at the new mill, which was designed by the architects James Marks and Sons and was described as being 'fitted with the latest machinery from England and America'.

Following Patrick O'Brien's death in 1906, his wife Ellen subsequently acquired the business from Crisp. In 1911 a new milling building designed by the architect W. Hodgen was erected on the Ruthven Street site. Substantially damaged by fire two years later, it was rebuilt, forming the core of the present structure. The business remained family-owned until 1955. Many changes took place in flour production and marketing during the 1960s, when the first of the silos that now dominate the site were built. The mill underwent further remodelling in 1976. The main building continues to function as a flour mill. The remainder of the complex comprises a pre-mix cake and bread plant, a retail flour plant and the office.

12. Toowoomba Foundry, *Ruthven Street*

A small foundry and machine shop was established in 1871 by George Griffiths, who had recently arrived in Toowoomba from Bristol, England. In 1876 Griffiths began development of a larger foundry and engineering machine shop on the present site, building Simplex windmills and steam engines. The business expanded after 1881 as a railway stock manufacturer. Production was supplemented by the mass construction of Southern Cross windmills, which found a ready market on the Downs. Toowoomba Foundry became a public company in 1884, but was still controlled by the Griffiths family. During World War II the foundry employed more than 1000 people, producing shell primers and engines for the war effort. The postwar boom in manufacturing saw the firm move into component casting and machining for the automotive and farming industries. By adapting to its changing market, the business has survived for over 100 years, outliving all its competitors.

13. Holy Name Catholic School, *Bridge Street*

The Holy Name School was established in Toowoomba early this century by the Sisters of Mercy. The school was destroyed by fire in 1919. Construction of the present building began and the school was opened in 1921 by Archbishop Duhig. The building is still in use as a school, though some alterations have been made over time to accommodate new teaching needs. A new primary school building was added in 1956 and a preschool was established in 1963.

13 *Entrance to the Holy Name School*
14 *Early kiln at The Maltings*

14. The Maltings, *Mort Street*

In the 1900s Toowoomba continued developing as an industrial town. One of the earliest industries was the brewing of beer.

The town's first brewery was opened in 1869 by the Perkins brothers, who established the Downs Brewery. They later moved to Brisbane, becoming famous as the makers of XXXX Beer. Toowoomba Maltings comprise a complex of buildings erected in several stages, in 1899 and 1906. The first malt house was erected on the site in 1897 for the Darling Downs Malting Company. It was operated by a well-known malting family, the Redwoods.

The maltings that survive today were built for the English maltsters William Jones and Sons who, in 1906, were able to expand their premises and lay claim to being the leading maltsters in the State. This plant was modelled on their business at Shrewsbury in England. In 1923 the property was acquired by the State Wheat Board. It was subsequently leased to several brewing companies and underwent major modernisation in the late 1960s before transfer to Carlton United Brewers in 1973. Toowoomba Maltings plant is now operated by the Barret Burston Malting Company.

15. Vacy Hall,
Russell Street

This single-storey brick residence was built in 1899 for Gilbert Cory and his wife Ann, the daughter of James Taylor. It is one of a number of substantial residences along Russell Street. Designed by the notable Toowoomba architect James Marks and erected by Alexander Mayes, a prominent Toowoomba builder, it was the second residence on this site. The first is believed to have been built in the mid-1870s, possibly as a present from Taylor to his daughter on her marriage to Cory in 1873. It was damaged by fire late in 1898 and the new house was built in 1899. After Ann's death, the property passed to Gilbert Cory, who remained at Vacy Hall until his death in 1924. Vacy Hall then had a succession of owners. It remained a private home until the 1950s, when it was converted to a boarding house. The present owners acquired Vacy Hall in 1986, refurbishing the building to provide guest accommodation.

16. Clifford House,
Russell Street

This house was built in 1860 as a squatters' residential club. In 1869 it became the private residence of James Taylor, who named the property Clifford House, after his father's village in Yorkshire. Taylor was a Cecil Plains squatter who rose to a position of wealth and influence, serving as a Member of Parliament from 1860 until his death in 1895. His wife Sarah remained at Clifford House until her death in 1908. The property passed to her son James, who lived there for a number of years; during this time much of the grounds was subdivided and sold. Clifford House was converted to a restaurant and reception centre during the 1970s. In 1993 the ground floor area was refurbished and leased to the Queensland Government.

17. St James Anglican Church,
Mort Street

Built about 1868, this is the oldest church in Toowoomba. It was constructed on land donated by James Taylor, who is credited with taking a leading role in Toowoomba's early development. The church was designed by the renowned architect Richard Suter, who also designed St Mark's Anglican Church in Warwick in the same year.

15 *Vacy Hall*
16 *Clifford House, c1908 (John Oxley Library)*
18 *St James Parish Hall*

18. St James Parish Hall,
Russell Street

Built in 1912 on land given to St James Anglican Church some 45 years earlier by James Taylor, St James Parish Hall is a picturesque example of an Arts and Crafts-inspired church hall. Designed by local architect Harry Marks, the building features unusual construction methods and details including hollow-wall construction. At the opening ceremony, the hall was described as 'a model of architecture' with ample facilities for the uses it was to be put to; it included reading rooms, library and lounge, and served as a venue for Sunday school and meetings.

19. Toowoomba Railway Station, *Railway Street*

In preparation for the opening of the Toowoomba Railway Station in 1867, an imposing two-storey building was to be sent to Toowoomba ready for erection. However, the need to conserve funds after the 1866 banks failure forced the abandonment of this structure and the construction of makeshift buildings. They were soon inadequate and in 1873 the Colonial Architect, F.D.G. Stanley, designed a new Italianate station building.

It was opened in 1874 and a new goods shed was erected in 1896. The railway refreshment room was built in 1902 and a tearoom was added in 1915. Further extensions were made to the refreshment room in the 1920s. After World War I a magnificent timber honour board was unveiled at the northern end of the station. Crafted at the Ipswich Railway Workshops, it pays tribute to the Toowoomba railway workers. The station still has two air raid shelters as a legacy of World War II. The main building is now the oldest surviving masonry railway station in Queensland.

20. Men's Urinal, *Russell Street*

The oldest public toilet in Queensland, this unusual example of Toowoomba's heritage was built in 1919. Possibly designed by the Toowoomba city engineer, the toilet was constructed as part of the move towards improvements in public health. It was designed as part of a rockery garden, of which one palm tree survives.

19 *Toowoomba Railway Station*
20 *Urinal portal*

21. Russell Street Shops

This part of Russell Street, between Victoria and Ruthven streets, developed in the initial years of Toowoomba's settlement. It follows the early teamsters' track to the Downs. A number of buildings in the block were designed by James Marks and Sons, the noted Toowoomba architects whose work made a considerable contribution to the appearance of the town. The buildings were constructed from the mid-1880s, during a period when Toowoomba promoted itself as a resort town, and their flamboyant facades became an architectural feature of the town.

Some buildings now have facades from later periods: for example, Rowes incorporates several early buildings behind a 1959 facade. The area is notable for the long continuity of use as a retail centre and several buildings have continuously housed the same type of business. Number 37, currently True Value Hardware, has been a hardware store since 1886 and number 5, Cossart's, has been a saddlery since 1885.

Russell Street shopping block

Floodwaters in Russell Street, 1906 (John Oxley Library)

Marks and Sons architect's office, Gaydon's Building

Russell Street with the Hotel National (left), c1900s (John Oxley Library)

82

Number 71 Russell Street

Located on the corner of Russell and Victoria streets, this building was constructed about 1906 as three shops with residences above. Built to a design of James Marks and Sons it currently operates as Maies Book Exchange.

Number 55–51 Russell Street

The National Hotel at number 55 was originally named the European Hotel. It was built in 1883, but was greatly altered during renovations in the 1930s. Number 53 was built after 1900. Currently a bookshop, it has been a grocery and a restaurant in the past. Number 51, Russell Street Traders, was built about 1880 and initially housed the business of James Blackburn, one of three saddlers on the block.

Number 41 Russell Street

Ozanam House, currently occupied by St Vincent de Paul, was built about 1906 to a design by James Marks and Sons and was leased by Rowes until about 1927.

Gaydon's Building and Beresfords Shoes, Russell Street

The upper floor of Gaydon's Building, now part of Beresfords Shoes, housed the office of the architects James Marks and Sons between 1903 and 1914. Beresfords Shoes building, on the corner of Russell and Ruthven streets, was built in 1914 to a design by Marks and Sons. It was a pharmacy until its purchase by Beresfords in 1966.

22. Cleary and Lee Solicitors Building, *Russell Street*

The Toowoomba and Permanent Building and Investment Society was formed in 1875 in offices in Margaret Street. The business expanded and larger offices were purchased in Russell Street in 1906. By the 1930s the society had decided to build new offices in Russell Street and commissioned William Hodgen, an architect and a former director of the society, to prepare the plans. The new building was opened in 1934. The current owners, Cleary and Lee Solicitors, purchased it in 1979.

23. Strand Theatre, *Margaret Street*

This three-storey picture theatre was built in 1916 for James Newman, a Toowoomba alderman, and has had a special association with generations of cinema audiences from Toowoomba and the Darling Downs. In 1915 Newman commissioned the Brisbane architect George Addison to design a picture theatre on a site in Margaret Street. On its completion, Newman leased the theatre to Señora Spencer, who named it the Strand. Union Theatres took over the lease in 1918 and from the mid-1920s the theatre was leased by a number of independent exhibitors. The Strand flourished during the 1930s — proudly advertising 'Always first with the latest and the greatest' — and screened features from the big Hollywood studios to large audiences. A wide screen was installed in 1957 and the main foyer was renovated in the 1960s and again in the 1970s. A major redevelopment of the theatre and the adjoining buildings to form a new multi-cinema complex was completed in 1992.

23 *The Strand Theatre*

24. Former Congregational Church, *Margaret Street*

Designed in Romanesque style by the architects Eaton and Bates as a Congregational church, the building was completed in 1903. The first service was held in 1904. Debt and a diminishing congregation forced the sale of the church. The building was occupied by the Trades and Labour Council until its purchase by the Church of Christ in 1929. The building was recently sold by the Church and is presently used as a gallery.

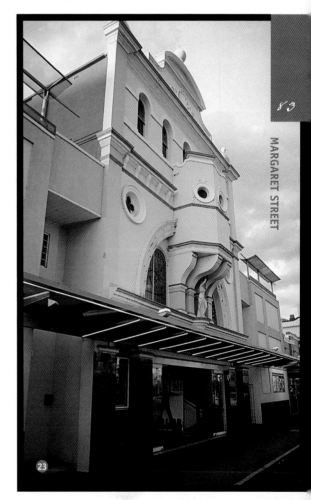

83

MARGARET STREET

23

25. Empire Theatre, *Neil Street*

The Empire Theatre has been an important part of Toowoomba's social life for over 90 years. In 1909 a group of local businessmen formed a company to show silent films in the Austral Hall in Margaret Street. Because of the popularity of the screenings, they decided to build a theatre. The establishment opened in 1911 and was known as the Empire. Disaster struck in 1933, when the Empire was destroyed in one of Toowoomba's most spectacular fires. Architects Hall and Phillips were commissioned to design a new theatre, which was opened later that year. With a seating capacity of 2400, it was the largest provincial theatre in Queensland. Art Deco in style, the Empire Theatre was restored and reopened in 1997.

26. Masonic Hall, *Neil Street*

Designed by the renowned architect F.D.G. Stanley and built in 1886, this hall replaced an earlier building at the corner of Ruthven Street. Freemasonry played an important role in Toowoomba's early cultural and economic development and the members of the lodge were responsible for the ceremony of laying the foundation stone for the school of arts in 1876.

27. St Stephen's Uniting Church, *Neil Street*

Opened in 1884, the bluestone church was built by James Renwick to the design of James Marks. A deliberately lit fire gutted the building in 1989, leaving only the stone walls standing. The fire destroyed the 465-pipe organ, though some of the stained-glass windows were salvaged. The church was rebuilt and reopened in 1993.

28. Toowoomba Police Station, *Neil Street*

The first police barracks on Neil Street were built in 1882, replacing the original police station in Russell Street. The present building, dating from 1936, was one of a number of public buildings constructed in Toowoomba during the 1930s to provide work for the unemployed during the Depression.

25 *The Empire*
26 *The Masonic Hall*
28 *Toowoomba Police Station*

29. Toowoomba Court House, *Margaret Street*

Designed by the Colonial Architect's office in 1876 as the new public offices and law courts, the building was completed by the firm of John Gargett and was occupied in 1878. Constructed of local stone from nearby Highfields, this is a fine example of a Classical Revival building. In 1914 the lower storey was extended along Neil Street, using Helidon stone. It is one of the few remaining early public buildings in Toowoomba and is significant as the focal point of legal administration during the development of the city.

30. Toowoomba General Post Office, *Margaret Street*

Toowoomba's first post office was established in 1858. Three years later the developing settlement had a twice-weekly mail service to Brisbane as well as a telegraph line. The present Toowoomba Post Office was built in 1878. Designed by the Colonial Architect, the post office was constructed by John Gargett after he completed the building of the adjacent law court.

31. Toowoomba Technical College, *Margaret Street*

This site was acquired for a technical college in 1908 and plans for the new college were prepared by the Deputy Government Architect, Thomas Pye. The two-storey brick building, surmounted with a ventilation flèche, the signature of public buildings in this era, was completed in 1911 by builder Alexander Mayes. An extension to the initial block complemented the original design. Technical colleges provided the only public secondary education in Queensland before the introduction of high schools in 1912. As the high schools grew in number, they often shared accommodation with the technical colleges to reduce costs. Toowoomba was no exception to this trend, and it was not until 1962 that the high school moved to its own site.

29 Court House building
30 General Post Office, c1909 (John Oxley Library)
31 Technical College

32. Wesley Uniting Church, *Hume Street*

This is the second oldest church in Toowoomba (St James is older). The foundation stone was laid in 1877. Wesley Methodist Church was designed by Willoughby Powell and constructed by Richard Godsall, a prominent Toowoomba builder. In 1897 the Primitive and Wesleyan Methodist churches amalgamated to form the Methodist Church. Three years later, architect William Hodgen was commissioned to design extensions to the church. His work included a transept and chancel, and a new roof, and the spire was moved.

33. Bishop's House,
Margaret Street

Designed by the architect Henry Marks, Kilallah was constructed in 1911 as the home of a Toowoomba businessman, William Peak. In 1939, after several changes of ownership, the house was purchased by the Roman Catholic Church and became the residence of the Bishop of the recently created Toowoomba Diocese. The various Bishops of Toowoomba lived here until recently, when another residence was constructed adjoining the house. Bishop's House has since been refurbished as offices for the diocesan administration.

34. Toowoomba Grammar School,
Margaret Street

Toowoomba Grammar School was the third school in Queensland established under the Grammar School Act of 1860, under which local citizens had to raise £1000 towards the construction of a grammar school. In 1874 the citizens of Toowoomba raised £2700. With government financial assistance and the granting of a portion of Queen's Park, the project proceeded. An architectural competition was held and the entry of the Toowoomba architect Willoughby Powell was successful. The main building was constructed by John Gargett. Gothic in style, it has gabled end wings, a central spire and a small Gothic chapel with a large western window. The building comprised classrooms as well as boarding accommodation for at least 45 boys and the master's apartments. The school opened in 1876.

33 *Bishop's House*
34 *Toowoomba Grammar School*

35. Queens Park,
Margaret Street

In 1849 most of the land that is now Queens Park was set aside as a reserve for a camping ground and public buildings. The camping reserve was extended in the 1870s and the area was named Queen's Park. Many of the park's trees date from the 1870s, when shade trees for the town were acquired from the Queensland Acclimatisation Society. Landscaping of the park was carried out by unemployed workers under the relief scheme during the Depression. The Boer War memorial gateway in Margaret Street was constructed from bricks salvaged from the demolished Austral Hall.

36. Cobb and Co. Museum,
Lindsay Street

The Cobb and Co. Museum offers an interesting and in-depth insight into the development of transport before railways and motor vehicles. The museum houses Australia's finest collection of horse-drawn vehicles, including the coach that ran the last Cobb and Co. service on the Darling Downs in 1924.

The collection, which was assembled by W.R.F. Bolton, was donated to the Queensland Museum in 1982. The Cobb and Co. Museum was opened in 1987, finally realising Mr Bolton's dream of a horse-drawn vehicle museum on the Darling Downs.

37. George Essex Evans Memorial,
Dudley Street

This monument in Webb Park was erected in memory of the poet George Essex Evans, who died in 1909. During the 1890s Evans became the registrar of births, deaths and marriages in Toowoomba. While still in the public service, he contributed poetry and articles to the local *Darling Downs Gazette* and the *Toowoomba Chronicle*. Evans commemorated the Federation movement in verse and was awarded a prize for a poem celebrating Federation. He took up dairy farming near Toowoomba after his marriage in 1899 and from 1905 published his own weekly paper, *The Rag*. A pilgrimage and a memorial lecture are held annually in his honour.

38. Eagle's Nest Unemployed Camp, *off Warrego Highway*

Although the effects of the 1930s Depression were less severe in Toowoomba than in other parts of Australia, by mid-1930 over 750 local residents and 1900 travellers were drawing unemployment rations in the city. The unemployed demanded public relief work, which was provided in part by the Intermittent Relief Work Scheme. The city council established several camps on the fringes of Toowoomba to cope with the growing numbers of unemployed. One of these, at Eagle's Nest, was famous for its self-help and self-management programs and became well known throughout Australia. Coordinated by Dr T.A. Proce, Toowoomba's enthusiastic public health campaigner, the camp was hygienic, orderly and self-sufficient in vegetables.

39. Tyson Manor, Downlands College, *Ruthven Street*

Now part of Downlands Sacred Heart College, Tyson Manor was built in the 1880s as a single-storey bluestone residence. Originally known as Strathmore, it was renamed by Tyson Doneley, who purchased the home in 1902. In 1915 he added a second storey of brick, its verandahs decorated with iron lace. The house was one of the social centres of the Darling Downs for many years. When the Catholic Diocese of Toowoomba was created in 1929, the first Bishop, the Reverend J. Byrne, saw the need for a Catholic boarding school for boys and approached the Missionaries of the Sacred Heart to establish the school. Tyson Manor was purchased and Downlands College came into existence in 1931. The buildings were taken over as a military hospital during World War II. After the war the school was re-established as a boarding school. It has been coeducational since 1971.

40. Toowoomba Hospital Nurses Quarters, *West Street*

The first hospital in Toowoomba was built in 1865 on the corner of James and Ruthven streets. The building was destroyed by fire in 1867 and plans for a permanent hospital were drawn up by the Colonial Architect, F.D.G. Stanley. The new hospital, opened in 1880, comprised a large two-storey complex with four wards. Separate staff accommodation was built later. Freshney House, named in honour of Dr Freshney, the medical superintendent from 1892 to 1927, was built as a nurses quarters in 1913 to the design of William Hodgen. A Federation-style building, it features wide verandahs on four sides and elaborate brick and terracotta chimneys. New nurses quarters were constructed in 1927. The building was later used as offices by the administration and more recently has been converted for use as a dental clinic and a conference centre. This building was named Cossart House in 1959 in honour of Ethel Cossart, who was the Hospital Matron in the 1940s.

41. Redlands Concordia College, *Stephens Street*

Now the property of the Lutheran Church, Redlands was built in 1889 for Edmund Wilcox and his family. The Wilcox family sold Redlands in 1921 and the house eventually passed to Edward Farmer, a grazier from Gladstone. While the Farmers were in residence the house was often used to host large garden parties and bridge nights; the English cricket team were house guests at one time. On Farmer's death in 1945, the house was acquired by the Lutheran Church for a coeducational boarding college. Since then, Redlands has been used as a headmaster's residence and boarding rooms and today serves as the central administration building for Concordia College. The house is approached by a drive lined with Norfolk Island and bunya pines.

87

39 *Tyson Manor*
40 *Former hospital nurses quarters*
41 *Redlands College*

42. St Matthew's Anglican Church, *Beatrice Street*

Benjamin Glennie first visited Drayton in 1848, when it was part of the Moreton Bay Parish. He was assigned to the parish in 1850 and the first parsonage and church at Drayton were built for his use. The first church was replaced in 1887 by the present church of St Matthew, built of local bluestone and sited on a prominent hill overlooking the town. A small Gothic Revival-style church, it features sandstone buttresses and window frames as well as a Gothic arched entry porch.

43. Royal Bulls Head Inn, *Brisbane Street*

In 1847 William Horton, an ex-convict and former employee of Henry Stewart Russell of Cecil Plains run, established an inn at the new settlement of Drayton to catch the passing trade of people travelling to the Downs. He named it Bull's Head after a champion bull at Cecil Plains. The hotel became an important meeting place for squatters. In 1852 Horton offered the Bull's Head for lease. He leased the Bull's Head to Russell and James Taylor but moved back there in 1858 and expanded the hotel. The new work was completed in time for the visit of Governor Bowen in 1860 and the hotel adopted the name 'Royal Bull's Head Inn'.

After Horton's death in 1864, the hotel was leased by several publicans, but none was as successful. The property was sold in 1875 and ceased trading as a hotel four years later. It became Richard Lynch's family home and was named 'The Terrace'. Members of the Lynch family occupied the home until 1973, when the inn was purchased by the National Trust, which still owns the property.

43 *Royal Bulls Head Inn*

Southern Downs

MAP 5
Southern Downs

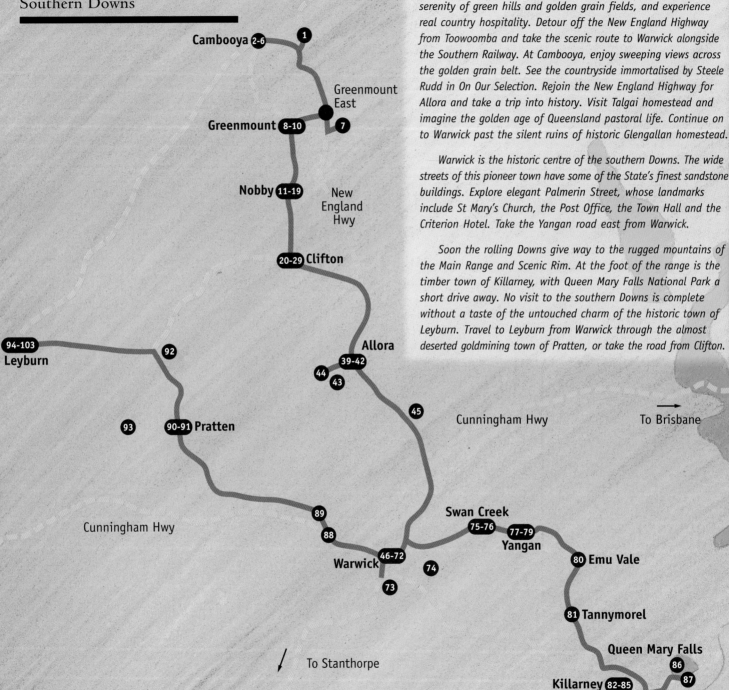

In one of Queensland's most historic areas you'll discover the serenity of green hills and golden grain fields, and experience real country hospitality. Detour off the New England Highway from Toowoomba and take the scenic route to Warwick alongside the Southern Railway. At Cambooya, enjoy sweeping views across the golden grain belt. See the countryside immortalised by Steele Rudd in On Our Selection. Rejoin the New England Highway for Allora and take a trip into history. Visit Talgai homestead and imagine the golden age of Queensland pastoral life. Continue on to Warwick past the silent ruins of historic Glengallan homestead.

Warwick is the historic centre of the southern Downs. The wide streets of this pioneer town have some of the State's finest sandstone buildings. Explore elegant Palmerin Street, whose landmarks include St Mary's Church, the Post Office, the Town Hall and the Criterion Hotel. Take the Yangan road east from Warwick.

Soon the rolling Downs give way to the rugged mountains of the Main Range and Scenic Rim. At the foot of the range is the timber town of Killarney, with Queen Mary Falls National Park a short drive away. No visit to the southern Downs is complete without a taste of the untouched charm of the historic town of Leyburn. Travel to Leyburn from Warwick through the almost deserted goldmining town of Pratten, or take the road from Clifton.

Cambooya 2-6 · 1
Greenmount East
Greenmount 8-10 · 7
Nobby 11-19
New England Hwy
20-29 Clifton
94-103 · 92
Leyburn
Allora
39-42
44
43
45
Cunningham Hwy
To Brisbane
93 · 90-91 Pratten
89
88
Cunningham Hwy
Swan Creek
75-76 · 77-79
Yangan
Warwick 46-72
74
80 Emu Vale
73
81 Tannymorel
Queen Mary Falls
86
87
Killarney 82-85
To Stanthorpe

90

East Talgai Homestead, built in 1868 (John Oxley Library)

Grain shed, Greenmount railway siding

THE SOUTHERN DOWNS

Transportation to Moreton Bay ended in 1840 and squatters began moving to the rich grazing lands of the Darling Downs, in anticipation of the area being opened to free settlers. The Leslie brothers were the first to take up land and other pastoralists followed. The first homesteads on the southern Downs were slab huts on runs such as Canning Downs, Talgai, Eton Vale, Glengallan and Rosenthal. By the 1860s most had been replaced by large, comfortable homesteads.

Despite strong opposition from the squatters, agricultural land on the pastoral runs was opened for closer settlement from the early 1860s. Small settlements were established at river crossings by teamsters carting supplies for the pastoral runs. They became change stations for Cobb and Co. and gathering places, usually with a simple timber hotel and store, for local timberworkers and farming families. Warwick, first surveyed in 1848, became the major town on the southern Downs. Development was slow until the 1850s, when the Spicer's Gap road on the Main Range was opened.

The railway linking Warwick with Toowoomba and Brisbane was completed in 1871 and consolidated the town's pre-eminent position. The line was constructed across the Condamine River to the centre of the town in 1881 and many of Warwick's fine buildings were erected in this period. Gold mined at Talgai and Thanes Creek was responsible for settlements at Clifton and Pratten, but the real growth came with intensive agricultural settlement.

From the early 1870s, hundreds of selectors and their families began farming the district's newly established agricultural reserves. Small towns such as Cambooya and Leyburn were settled along the railway and developed their own commercial and community life.

Wheat became the most important crop, giving rise to the district being described as the 'granary of Queensland'. But it also fostered a population of subsistence farmers whose daily struggles were immortalised in the stories of Arthur Hoey Davis, who wrote under the name Steele Rudd. Wheat growing transformed the landscape and gave rise to loading facilities and storage silos at railway stations. Most of the early homesteads had vineyards and orchards, and a small commercial wine industry flourished, particularly in the years before World War I. The extension of the railway to Wallangarra opened up the border forest areas and supported a timber industry centred on Killarney.

The southern Downs has remained a premier wheat-growing district. The changing economic base of primary industries resulted in a gradual reduction in the town and farming population. This downturn in the region's economy has, until recently, acted to preserve, relatively unchanged, much of the historic rural and urban environment.

1. Eton Vale Homestead

The ruins are all that remains of Eton Vale homestead. Eton Vale run was selected in 1840 by Arthur Hodgson, who had followed the Leslie brothers to the Darling Downs. Originally a grazing property, it was the second run selected in Queensland. Wheat was grown at Eton Vale from 1846 and the run became a sheep stud in 1850. The slab house, erected soon after 1840, formed the core of a larger brick residence, which continued to be extended until the 1880s. Following Hodgson's death in 1902, the estate was broken up. In 1906 the homestead and surrounding freehold property were sold to Christian Barth, a German saddler. The homestead was destroyed by fire in 1912. Eton Vale was sold to Frederick Robotham in 1932; his family still owns the property.

2. Cambooya

Cambooya was surveyed by F. Lord in mid-1867 and the first land was sold in October. The following year the railway arrived, necessitating the construction of a railway station and a hotel. It was not until 1903, when township allotments were resumed from the Eton Vale estate, that the town really developed. By 1908 the town had two hotels, two churches, a school, numerous shops and houses and an aerated water factory. Cambooya's Bull and Barley Inn was built as the Railway Hotel; the name by which it was known until recently.

3. All Saints Anglican Church, *Eton Street*

The second All Saints Anglican Church in Cambooya, consecrated in 1904, was destroyed in a wind storm in 1914. A replacement church was built and dedicated in 1915. The three stained-glass windows depicting St Patrick, St George and St Andrew were donated by Reverend Francis Hodgson to commemorate his father, Sir Arthur Hodgson of Eton Vale station. The windows were imported from England. However, the vessel carrying the first set of windows sank and a replacement set had to be manufactured and shipped.

4. Sacred Heart Catholic Church, *Eton Street*

The first Catholic church in the district was built at Greenmount East in 1884. At Cambooya mass was held in private homes until 1914, when this simple wooden church was built. In 1951 the Cambooya–Greenmount Parish was established, with Father McCormack as the first parish priest. There was no presbytery, however, and the priest relied on the hospitality of his parishioners until 1953, when the brick presbytery was constructed. A larger Sacred Heart Church was built in Cambooya in 1965.

5. Cambooya Community Hall, *Harrow Street*

This building was constructed for the Masonic Lodge in 1909 and was used as a meeting room and dance hall. A splendid timber hall, it was built on a large scale with many decorative architectural features. It was expensive to maintain, however, and its income did not meet the cost of upkeep. In 1917 the local school of arts committee raised funds to purchase the hall, which then became known as the School of Arts Public Hall. The Cambooya Shire Council became the owners of the hall in 1969.

6. Cambooya Railway Station

After the railway from Ipswich reached Toowoomba in 1867, it was extended south towards Warwick, reaching Cambooya in 1868. The line at last provided reliable transport for the squatters' wool to be delivered to the port of Brisbane. The station office and goods shed were built in 1869 and refreshment rooms were added in 1877. The grain siding was completed in 1910; the silos associated with these facilities are a landmark in the township and a testimony to the industry that is now the basis of Cambooya Shire's economy.

1 Eton Vale ruins
2 Bull and Barley Inn, Cambooya
4 Sacred Heart Church, Cambooya

7. Steele Rudd's Hut,
Emu Creek

Subsistence farming on the Darling Downs selections was depicted by Arthur Hoey Davis, who wrote under the pen name 'Steele Rudd'. He was the creator of the Dad and Dave characters who gave comic portrayals of farming life in *On Our Selection* (1899) and *On Emu Creek* (1923). Rudd depicted a generation of farming communities and settlers who acquired small blocks of land following the break-up of the old squatting runs. In Rudd's stories subsistence farming gradually leads to prosperity and the rough slab hut gives way to the neat weatherboard cottage. Much of his writing derived from personal recollections. Arthur Hoey Davis was born at Drayton near Toowoomba in 1868.

He was seven years old when his parents took up a farming selection on Emu Creek near Greenmount East. Davis went to Emu Creek school until 1880, when he obtained work on nearby Pilton station. He entered the public service as a clerk and moved to Brisbane in 1885.

As 'Steele Rudd' he began writing for the *Bulletin* magazine in 1895: his first sketch, titled 'Starting the Selection', was based on his father's experiences. He married a former classmate, Violet Brodie of Greenmount, and in 1909 they purchased a farming property near Nobby. His wife's poor health deteriorated further and the family returned to Brisbane in 1917. In the same year Davis revived his early magazine articles as *Steele Rudd's Annual* (1917–23). He died in 1935.

In the 1970s a small area of the original selection was set aside as a park where a replica of the Davis family's selector's hut was constructed. The old gateposts erected by the Davis family in 1938 still stand there, along with a recent memorial cairn.

An early gate post marks the entrance to the farm

Site of the Davis family's farm selection with a recent re-construction of the 1870s 'Shingle Hut'

THESE ORIGINAL GATE POSTS MARK THE GATEWAY TO "SHINGLE HUT"

Erected by Thomas Davis in 1870, when he pioneered this 160 acre block of land. He called it "Yalcalbah", (Aboriginal for "Tall Grass"). His gifted son, ARTHUR HOEY DAVIS, better known as STEELE RUDD, later depicted scenes surrounding "Shingle Hut" and "The Selection" as part of Australian folk lore in his famous "Selection" stories, synonomous with the early settlement of the Darling Downs of Queensland.

"THE MEMORY OF THE PIONEERS OF AUSTRALIA ,WHO GAVE OUR COUNTRY BIRTH, MUST NEVER FADE."

8. Greenmount

This was once part of the Eton Vale run. It seems that there was initially no intention to form a second township in the area, which officials hoped would be served by Cambooya. However, Cambooya was inconvenient for selectors at Emu Creek and the township known as Greenmount developed. By the early 1900s it had two churches, a hotel, a state school and a post office. The area was opened up for closer selection in 1906. Greenmount continued to grow and in 1915 was declared the administrative centre of Cambooya Shire.

9. Soldiers' Memorial Hall, *Ramsay Street*

This hall was constructed as the school of arts with a library and a dance hall. After World War I the local residents renamed the hall to honour those who had served in the war. Before the advent of television the hall was an entertainment centre, hosting travelling picture shows, vaudeville shows, dances, flower shows, talent quests and more. It still hosts one of the major events on the Greenmount social calendar, the annual Catholic Ball. The war memorial was built near the hall about 1921 in commemoration of World War I.

10. Greenmount Railway Station

Originally named Emu Creek, the station was opened about 1872 and was renamed Greenmount in 1878. For many years the north- and south-bound Sydney mail trains passed at Greenmount Railway Station. The grain shed was constructed by the early 1930s. It survives to show how the Railways Department stored grain for transshipment when wheat was handled in bags. A similar grain shed can be found at nearby Ellinthorp Railway Station.

11. Nobby

The town is situated on King and Sibley's original Kings Creek run, taken up in 1840. A portion of the run was later purchased by Fisher and Davenport to become part of Headington Hill run. Nobby is said to be named after 'Nobby' Carver, a railway worker with a legendary appetite. During construction of the first stage of the Southern Railway from Toowoomba to Warwick, opened in 1869, the area was known as McDonald's Camp. By 1900, the town was officially gazetted as Davenport, in honour of one of the Headington Hill partners, but it has always been known locally as Nobby.

The first wave of selectors arrived in the 1870s, with the resumption of nearby pastoral runs for agricultural settlement. More farmers were drawn to the district in the late 1890s following the resumption of Headington Hill run. Nobby experienced steady growth during these years, but the prolonged drought that followed brought ruin to many and recovery was slow. The town revived by 1920 thanks to the success of grain growing and mixed farming in the district. Despite the decline in rural industries, Nobby retains its place as the centre of the small local community.

9 *Soldiers' Memorial Hall, Greenmount (left)*

11 *Grain for loading at Nobby railway yards, 1921 (John Oxley Library)*

12. Nobby School of Arts, *Sister Kenny Street*

The first school of arts was built in 1909, but was later destroyed by fire. The present building was opened on New Year's Day in 1930. Designed by the Toowoomba architect W. Hodgen, it was equipped with a gas lighting plant. With its lending library and a spacious hall for concerts and dances, the building has been the focus of community events since then.

13. Nobby Railway Station

The Southern Line from Toowoomba was opened in 1869 and parts of the station building may date from soon after this period. In 1900 a waiting shed and ladies room were added. By the 1920s, the Brisbane Milling Company had a grain storage shed at the station and the State Wheat Board had two sheds, the largest of which was often used as a dance hall. The surviving grain shed was not used after the 1960s, when centralised bulk handling of grain was introduced.

14. Holy Trinity Lutheran Church, *Fett Road*

Nobby's Lutheran community held services in private homes and at Headington Hill until St Luke's Church was built at Mount Kent in 1911. The present church at Nobby was built in 1941. A composite of the Mount Kent and Headington Hill buildings, it was constructed by the Schamburg brothers of Toowoomba.

15. Elizabeth Kenny Memorial, *Tooth Street*

The memorial commemorates the work of Elizabeth Kenny, who pioneered an unorthodox treatment for poliomyelitis, or infantile paralysis as it was then known. Born in South Australia in 1886, Kenny was nine years old when her family moved to the Nobby district. After basic nursing training, she opened a hospital at Clifton in 1911 and by 1914 was treating many of the district's children who had contracted the disease. After serving in Europe in World War I with the British Red Cross, she returned to Nobby and her work with polio sufferers. Although Kenny's clinics in Townsville and Brisbane were government-funded, the medical profession did not endorse her treatment methods. She moved to the USA during a polio epidemic; among the people she treated there was President Franklin Roosevelt. Suffering ill health, Kenny returned to Toowoomba where she died in 1952. She was buried in Nobby cemetery, beside her mother.

16. Nobby Newsagency, *Tooth Street*

The building dates from the early 1900s. Opened by Mrs Kane as a billiard room, it was converted for use as a fruit shop before becoming Stapleton's butcher shop. Later Dan Brodie conducted his stock and station agency from the butcher shop for more than 30 years. The shop is now a newsagency.

17. Country Collectables Store, *Tooth Street*

This building was constructed for the Brodie family in 1914. Violet Brodie, widow of pioneer storekeeper Dan Brodie, opened a small timber store on the site in 1898, but by 1914 it had become too small for the thriving business. The size and scope of the new store reflected Nobby's prosperity. It employed seven staff and had several departments of merchandise. When car ownership in the district increased, petrol bowsers were installed in the street outside. The Brodies sold the store in 1942 to the Kuhn brothers, who operated it until 1972. In 1995, new owners set about restoring the shop for the sale of bric-a-brac and collectables.

14 *Holy Trinity Church, Nobby*
15 *Memorial garden to Elizabeth Kenny*

18. Rudd's Pub,
Tooth Street

The Davenport Hotel was one of Nobby's first buildings. It was designed by the Toowoomba architects James Marks and Sons for the owner, Michael Comerford, and completed in 1893. It was originally named after George Davenport, one of the partners of the Headington Hill run. In 1987, however, it was renamed Rudd's Pub to commemorate Arthur Hoey Davis, who wrote under the name Steele Rudd and who lived in the district from 1909 until 1917.

19. Victor Denton Memorial,
Nobby Cemetery

Constructed by Toowoomba stonemasons the Bruce brothers in 1915, this is Queensland's first known World War I memorial. One of the few dedicated to an individual soldier, it honours Private Victor Denton, whose parents owned the Nobby general store. He was killed at the Dardanelles in 1915. The memorial, although erected within the Denton family plot, was funded by the community and marks its recognition of the personal sacrifice associated with the war.

20. Clifton

The town takes its name from the original Clifton sheep run, taken up by Marsh and Forbes in the early 1840s. Clifton was the name of the Marsh family farm near Edinburgh, Scotland. The Southern Line from Toowoomba to Warwick was opened to Clifton in 1869. The town dates from this period, when James Mowen erected a general store beside the line. The town of Clifton was proclaimed in 1875 but development was slow. The land boom during the 1880s was followed by the opening of Headington Hill station for closer settlement in 1898, bringing hundreds of new settlers to the district. Development in Clifton reached a peak between 1898 and 1907.

The town became the centre and terminus for railway branch lines extending to Leyburn in the west and the Main Range to the east. For 50 years the Clifton district was renowned for its wheat production, outstripping even nearby Allora. By the late 1950s, however, many farmers had moved out of wheat production because of increasingly poor harvests and dairying became the mainstay of the district.

21. Clifton Arms Hotel,
King Street

Originally a one-storey premises, this hotel was built by James Mowem and was first located at nearby Spring Creek, with Charles Gillam its licensee. The building was moved to Clifton in 1884 under the licence of Michael O'Sullivan, who later became the first licensee of the nearby Club Hotel. The second storey had been added to the Clifton Arms Hotel by 1897.

18 *Rudd's Pub, once the Davenport Hotel*
19 *Queensland's first World War I memorial*
20 *Fisher Street shops, Clifton*
21 *Clifton Arms Hotel, 1897 (John Oxley Library)*

22. Clifton Railway Station

Clifton and Cambooya were the only intermediate stations on the first section of the new Southern Line from Toowoomba to Warwick when it opened in 1869. The present railway station site was chosen in the 1870s. Clifton station developed over the years in response to local demands. Sheepyards were provided in 1882 and larger stockyards were built in 1909. By then the station complex also included a goods shed, cream shed and crane, as well as a station-master's house. The surviving station office retains some of the early building's features.

22 *Clifton Railway Station*

23. St James and St John's Catholic Church, *Meara Place*

In 1888, a small timber church was erected on land donated by Clifton pioneer James Mowem. The present church was erected alongside it in 1900 in memory of Mowem, who died in 1897. It was designed by the architectural firm James Marks and Sons. A presbytery adjacent to the church was completed in 1911 and the two-storey convent opposite the church was built in 1917. A new presbytery was opened by Bishop Byrne in 1937.

24. Darling Downs Co-operative Dairy Factory, *King Street*

The Clifton Co-operative Dairying Industry Company was floated in 1908 and by November that year the Brisbane firm of Waugh and Josephson had completed construction of the factory. The upper storey where the large butter vats were located had leaded floors and underneath them was the cooling equipment. The factory was sold to the Darling Downs Co-operative Dairy Association in 1912, and in 1933 a new and much-expanded plant was opened. Following the slump in the dairying industry in the late 1950s, the factory was closed in 1966. It has recently been converted into a museum operated by the Clifton Historical Society.

25. Kings Hotel, *Clark Street*

This hotel was built on the site of the old Royal Hotel, which was destroyed by fire in the early 1920s. It was rebuilt as 'The King' for J. Donovan, a Gympie hotelier who also had hotels at Tewantin and Noosa Heads.

26. Clifton Courier Office, *Clark Street*

By the early 1900s, Clifton supported two newspapers, the *Clifton Dispatch* founded in 1896 and the *Clifton Courier*. Both papers were published twice weekly, a testament to the district's thriving economy during that period. The *Clifton Dispatch* had ceased publication by 1920, but the *Clifton Courier* has been published from this small office since 1906.

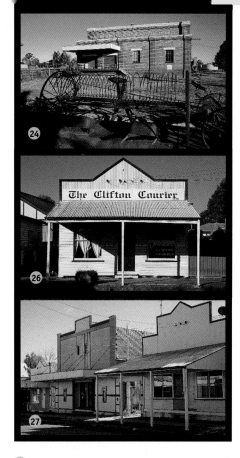

24 *The Downs Dairy Factory is now a museum*
26 *Clifton Courier office*
27 *The Tivoli picture theatre*

27. Tivoli Theatre, *Fisher Street*

The father of the present owner of this theatre conducted travelling picture shows in halls throughout the district. In Clifton he used the school of arts until a group of local businessmen financed the establishment of the first permanent picture theatre. The Tivoli Theatre opened in 1921 in the former Rickert's Hall. The equipment was upgraded to show talking pictures in 1931. Over the years the Tivoli became the venue not only for films but also for many other community and travelling theatre shows, lectures and concerts. The theatre is now closed, but its internal fittings, including the screen, projection room, foyer and canvas seats, are still in place.

28. All Saints Anglican Church, *East Street*

The church was constructed in 1905 by William Leggatt of Allora. The interior fittings, including the pulpit and communion table, are of polished cedar. Clifton's Anglican services were conducted at a small church on Fisher and Davenport's Headington Hill station until 1889, when a church was erected in the town. After the present church was built, the old church was used as a Sunday school until 1929, when it was moved to Monto.

29. St Andrew's Presbyterian Church, *John Street*

Clifton's first Presbyterian Church was dedicated in 1890, but drought and the Depression forced its closure in 1897. By 1906, the economic situation had improved and the congregation had returned. The original property was sold and the present location was selected. In 1909, a larger church with vaulted ceilings of polished timber was built by H.W. Stay of Allora.

29 *Erection of St Andrew's Church, c1909 (John Oxley Library)*

30. Allora

The town of Allora began as a teamsters' camp at a creek crossing on the Goomburra run, which had been taken up in 1844. In 1861, when the first land sales took place, it consisted of a few bark shanties and cottages. These were replaced by permanent buildings as continuing high wool prices brought prosperity to the district. Allora's early public and social institutions reflected the influence of powerful local pastoralists. The 1870s brought intense political activity as the squatters battled to retain their land and their influence. Their runs were subdivided for closer settlement and their influence was gradually lost to the increasing number of agricultural selectors and small business owners.

The Allora Municipal Council was formed in 1869 and by 1915, when the new Shire of Allora was proclaimed, the squatters' influence had virtually disappeared. By 1920 grazing had been replaced by dairying and grain growing and Allora prospered as the business and community centre for the largest wheat-growing area in Queensland. Its importance was gradually eroded by the expansion of Warwick as the principal southern Downs centre. By 1994, when Allora Shire was absorbed into the new Warwick Shire, most of the government and commercial services had been removed to Warwick.

31. St David's Anglican Church, *New England Highway*

The first St David's Church was designed by the noted church architect R.G. Suter and was built on this site in 1868. Previously services had been held in the Dalrymple Hotel and at East Talgai station. In 1876 a new church, the present St David's, was designed by F.D.G. Stanley and erected by a local builder, William Gillam.

30 *Herbert Street, Allora, c1924 (John Oxley Library)*

It had a shingle roof and a single external wall with exposed studs. A second outside chamferboard wall was added in 1897 and the shingles were replaced by roof tiles in 1930. The interior has fine cedar joinery and the cedar altar was a gift of the Clark family of Talgai. The rectory, built in 1901, stands on the site of the original old parsonage.

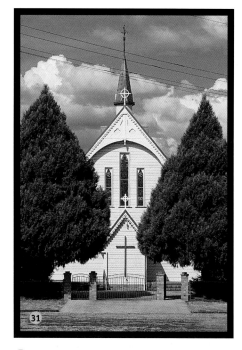

31 *St David's Church, Allora*

32. Boer War Memorial, Warwick Street

This memorial was unveiled in 1904 by Harry Chauvel, later commander of the famous 1st Light Horse Brigade in World War I. It was erected to commemorate those from the district who had fought in the 1899–1902 South African War. The stone was taken from a quarry at Yangan and is inscribed with verse by a local poet, J.K. Cameron. It was the first of only two Boer War memorials to be erected in Queensland. The figure, depicting a soldier in mourning, was the work of Sydney sculptor W.P. McIntosh. Memorials to the dead of World War I and World War II have also been erected in the park, originally named Queen's Park to commemorate Queen Victoria's jubilee.

33. Former Commercial Bank of Sydney, Warwick Street

In 1906, the Commercial Bank of Sydney opened its Allora branch in rented premises in Herbert Street. The bank purchased the present site in 1909 and in the following year commenced business in Allora's first brick building, designed by the Toowoomba architect Harry Marks. Now used as a dental surgery, the building remains largely unaltered, its original cedar bank counters, joinery and pressed-metal ceilings still in place. The front leadlight windows featuring the bank's name in stained glass were probably manufactured in Sydney.

34. Railway Hotel, Herbert Street

The Railway Hotel was built in 1902 by William Leggatt, who was responsible for the construction of many of Allora's early buildings. The O'Callaghan family operated the hotel for many years.

35. Donovan's Building, Herbert Street

This building probably dates from the late 1880s. Originally a private residence, it has been a plumber's shop and a stock and station agency conducted by three generations of the Donovan family. In 1979, it was purchased by the Allora Hospital Board for use as a medical centre.

36. Herbert Street Shops

Dating from the 1890s, the butcher shop was one of the first buildings erected on the western side of Herbert Street. Originally owned by Isaac Holmes, it is one of several shops that survived a fire during the 1920s that destroyed a number of nearby premises, including the post office.

37. Blue Cow Hotel, Herbert Street

The first hotel on this site was the Queens Arms, built in 1866. The present hotel, a much more substantial building, was erected in 1879 and traded for over a century as the Royal Hotel. The name was changed recently.

38. Commercial Hotel, Herbert Street

This hotel has operated since 1882. The railway contractor George Bashford hosted a celebration dinner at the Commercial on the opening of the Allora Branch Railway in 1897.

39. Former Australian Joint Stock Bank, Herbert Street

Built for the Australian Joint Stock Bank some years after the Allora branch first opened in 1880 at the Dalrymple Hotel, the timber building housed a banking chamber, manager's office and residence. It had a brick strongroom on the verandah adjoining the banking chamber and a separate pavilion kitchen at the rear. The bank is now a private residence. Its most famous resident was Pamela Lyndon Travers (her pen name), creator of the Mary Poppins character. She lived here when her father was bank manager from 1905 to 1907.

33 *Commercial Bank, now a dental surgery*
36 *Allora's Herbert Street shops*
38 *Commercial Hotel, Allora*
39 *Former A.J.S. Bank and residence*

40. Former Queensland National Bank, *Drayton Street*

The Queensland National Bank had been operating in Allora for two years before this building, designed by F.D.G. Stanley, was constructed in 1890–91. After a merger in 1948 the bank became a branch of the National Bank of Australasia. The office closed in 1964 when the bank moved to new premises in Herbert Street.

41. Old Allora Shire Chambers, *Warwick Street*

Built in 1907 to replace the first town hall, the Allora Shire Chambers served as the municipal council headquarters until Allora Shire was separated from the former Clifton Divisional Board. The council boardroom occupied the top floor, and weddings and functions were held at the rear of the building. New shire chambers were constructed in 1960 and the building now houses the Allora Historical Society.

42. Allora Railway Station

Allora Station dates from 1897, when the branch line from Hendon was opened. The main Southern Line from Toowoomba to Warwick, opened in 1869, had bypassed Allora in favour of Hendon siding, which was located close to the Clark brothers' East Talgai station. A continuation from Allora to Goomburra operated for the carriage of cream and wheat between 1912 and 1961. As Allora's wheat production increased, grain was stored at the station for transport by rail to mills at Warwick and Toowoomba. The grain shed is of a standard design and was probably erected by the early 1930s.

40 *Q.N. Bank office and residence, c1900s (John Oxley Library)*

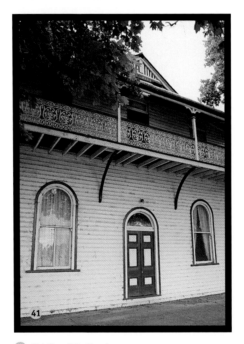

41 *Old Allora Shire Chambers*

43 *East Talgai Homestead*

43. East Talgai Homestead

For nearly 80 years, the Clark family operated a renowned sheep stud on East Talgai, a freehold section of Old Talgai station, which was taken up in 1841 by the Gammie brothers. East Talgai homestead was built in 1868 for George Clark. Designed on a grand scale by the noted architect Richard Suter, it has wide timber verandahs and walls of thick sandstone from the nearby Yangan quarry and was ideal for hot summer conditions. The sandstone cottage in the grounds, built in 1867 as a temporary residence for Suter during construction, was later used as the paymaster's office and store. By the 1880s Talgai was a self-contained settlement with one of the finest gardens in the district, featuring extensive orchards, vineyards, and vegetable and flower gardens. The Clark family connection ended with the death of George Clark in 1942 and the property is now run as a cattle stud and guesthouse.

44. Ellinthorp Railway Station

Originally a siding for loading the cream and pigs produced on West Talgai station, Ellinthorp has had several names. Until 1879 it was known as Clark Crossing, then as Talgai, and in 1912 as Dalrymple, in honour of George Dalrymple, one of the district's first landholders. The following year, when West Talgai was sold, the railway station was renamed Ellinthorp to avoid confusion with Dalrymple station in north Queensland. Ellinthorp was the name of the Clark family property in Tasmania, taken up in the late 1820s. The weighbridge, built in 1916, and the grain shed, built in 1928, reflect the changeover to wheat in the district after 1900. Both are now survivors of the days when wheat was transshipped in bags.

45. Glengallan Homestead

Glengallan was part of the first Darling Downs run taken up by Patrick Leslie in 1840. It was settled and named by the brothers Colin and John Campbell in 1841. In the 1850s the partnership of Charles Marshall and John Deuchar established the famous Glengallan merino stud and extended the property. The two-storey sandstone homestead, built during 1867–68 for Deuchar, was never completed as originally designed. The architect is unknown, but may have been Richard Suter or Charles Balding. At a grand opening ball, guests dined on the timber-louvred front verandahs and danced in the two ground-floor drawing rooms.

The house had cedar fittings throughout, and a pump supplied water to the bathroom and the first flushing toilet on the Darling Downs. Formal gardens and orchards were laid out, a tennis court and cricket oval being added later.

Deuchar had planned to add two wing extensions to the main house, but he was declared bankrupt in 1868 and retired to Warwick. The breeding tradition established by Deuchar was further developed by William Slade who maintained the pre-eminence of the Glengallan stud from 1873 until the property was sold in 1904.

Slade transformed Glengallan from a traditional stud property to one where intensive cultivation of lucerne and other fodder supported not only the stud stock, but also stock bought for fattening from western properties. Further diversification included dairying and a substantial piggery. After 1904 the property was gradually divided for closer settlement. By the late 1970s the grand homestead was in ruinous condition. The main house has been the subject of community concern and plans have been drawn up for reconstruction of the building.

Glengallan house and fields

Glengallan house and grounds, c1870s (John Oxley Library)

102

46. Warwick

Warwick was established in 1847 as an administrative centre on the Darling Downs for the colony of New South Wales. Surveyor J.C. Burnett made an initial survey of the emerging town in 1848 and undertook further survey work in 1850 when the first land sales were held. The first buildings had timber slab walls and shingle roofs. By 1859, the year Queensland separated from New South Wales, the township was a major centre on the Downs. When Queensland's new electoral districts were proclaimed in December of that year, the electorate of the Town of Warwick had its own representative in the new Legislative Assembly. Warwick was declared a municipality in 1861.

In 1871 the Southern Line from Toowoomba reached Mill Hill on the north bank of the Condamine, but another ten years passed before a rail bridge carried the line across the river to Warwick and on to Stanthorpe. Warwick's central business area was relocated to Palmerin Street after the Condamine flooded in 1887. Its role as an administrative centre has left Warwick with a legacy of many fine sandstone buildings. With a population of 10,000 in 1936, the town achieved city status, and was amalgamated with the rural shires of Glengallan, Rosenthal and Allora in 1995.

47. Old St Mary's Catholic Church, *Palmerin Street*

From the 1840s visiting priests from Sydney, Ipswich and Brisbane held Roman Catholic services in Warwick. The first recorded mass was held in 1854. St Mary's Church, designed by Brisbane architect Benjamin Backhouse, was opened in 1865. By 1867 a Catholic school was established in the church. By the 1910s, however, it was decided that the original St Mary's was no longer adequate for the needs of the community, and a larger and more grandiose church was required. After the opening of the new St Mary's Church in 1926 the old church continued to be used as the Catholic primary school.

48. St Mary's Catholic Church, *Palmerin Street*

A Warwick landmark, this is the city's highest and most prominent building. St Mary's, the second Catholic church in Warwick, was constructed between 1920 and 1926. Local architects Dornbusch and Connolly were commissioned to design the new church, which was built on land immediately to the north of the original St Mary's Church. Its foundation stone was laid in 1920 by the Archbishop of Melbourne, Daniel Mannix, assisted by Archbishop James Duhig of Brisbane. The church has been used continually since its opening by Archbishop Duhig in 1926.

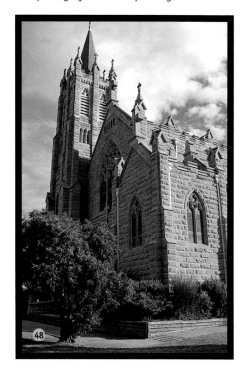

46 *Palmerin Street, Warwick*

48 *St Mary's Church*

49. Catholic Presbytery, *Percy Street*

Father James Horan arrived in Warwick in 1876 to take up duties as the priest. His first residence was in Fitzroy Street before he arranged for the construction of the present presbytery, probably by 1880. Father Horan lived in the building until his death in 1905. The presbytery is still used by the church.

50. Barnes Department Store, *Palmerin Street*

This former store, which now houses a furniture showroom, was constructed in 1911 for Barnes and Company, to the design of Warwick architects Wallace and Gibson. Merchants in Warwick since 1874, the company in 1898 ordered the construction of a stone store several blocks to the north known as the Emporium. The culmination of Barnes and Company's expansion was the opening of their Trade Palace at the corner of Palmerin and King streets. The store was a major addition to Warwick in 1911. The property passed out of the Barnes family in the late 1950s and has been used by various local retailers since then.

51. Australian and New Zealand Bank, *Palmerin Street*

This building was erected in 1912 as the Warwick branch of the British-owned Union Bank of Australia. As an outcome of bank mergers the building is now a branch of the Australian and New Zealand Bank.

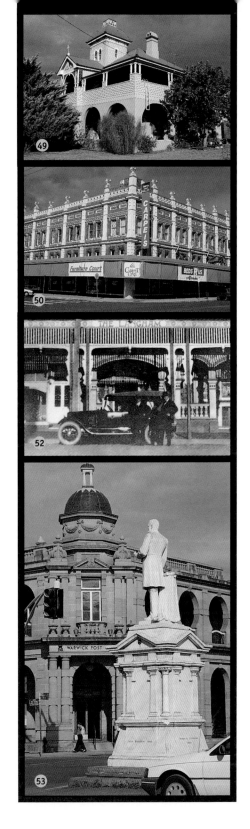

49 *Catholic Presbytery*
50 *Barnes Department Store, Warwick*
52 *The Langham Hotel, c1928 (John Oxley Library)*
53 *Post Office and Thomas Byrne's Memorial*

52. Langham Hotel, *Palmerin Street*

Completed in 1913, the Langham Hotel replaced an earlier hotel known as the Rose Inn. In 1911 the property was transferred to Arthur Cobcroft, a local bank manager, and in 1912 tenders were invited for the erection of the Langham Hotel for Mrs Cobcroft. On its completion in 1913, the owner described the development as 'a progressive move which provided an ornament to the town', a statement reflecting Mrs Cobcroft's optimistic view of Warwick's future. The Langham was transferred to James Roach in 1919 and remained in the Roach family until 1948. The property subsequently passed through a number of hands until the present owners acquired it in 1964. It was recently renamed the Condamine Sports Club.

53. Warwick Post Office and Byrne's Memorial, *Palmerin Street*

This substantial sandstone building was designed by the Government Architect's Office. Construction of a telegraph line from Brisbane to the Downs began in 1859, the line reaching Warwick in 1861. A purpose-built post office was constructed on the government reserve in Albion Street in 1870, but over the next 20 years the site proved extremely flood-prone. In 1897 tenders were called for the erection of a new post and telegraph office at the corner of Palmerin and Grafton streets. The building was completed at the beginning of 1899. A two-storey extension was added in 1941 to accommodate updated telephone exchange equipment, followed by a new brick telephone exchange building in 1962. From the 1970s the post office reverted to providing only postal services.

The statue in front of the post office is one of two in the State erected to the memory of Thomas Byrne, Queensland's first native-born premier, who died in 1898 at the age of 38. The figure of Byrne was carved in Italy and the sculptor is unknown.

54. Criterion Hotel,
Palmerin Street

This two-storey brick hotel, prominently situated in Warwick's main street, was built in 1917 for the Allman family. It replaced a single-storey timber hotel, also known as the Criterion, that had stood on the site from the 1860s. Jeremiah Allman acquired the Criterion Hotel in 1887. Born in Ireland, Allman had arrived in Australia in the mid-1860s, establishing himself on the Darling Downs. From the mid-1880s, he was actively involved in the development of Warwick, serving as mayor in 1895 and 1902. After his death in 1910 ownership of the hotel was transferred to his son Daniel Allman and Patrick Dalton and John Logan. During the early 1900s the Allman family also owned the National Hotel and leased the Langham. In 1917 the original Criterion Hotel was demolished to make way for a more palatial structure.

During the building of the new hotel it was noted that 'the big structure has quite altered the aspect of Palmerin Street'. The hotel remained in the Allman family until 1968.

55. Warwick Town Hall,
Palmerin Street

Warwick's first town hall was established in 1861 in a slab building at the northern end of Albion Street, which had served as the town's first court house. A design competition for the new town hall was held in 1885. The successful architect was Willoughby Powell. It was suggested that the building would be enhanced by the addition of a clock tower, which was subsequently incorporated into the building although not part of Powell's original design.

55 *Warwick Town Hall, 1898 (below) (John Oxley Library)*
55 *Memorial to footballers, Warwick Town Hall (below insert)*

In 1917 the Warwick and District Amateur Rugby Football League initiated a movement 'to honour the Warwick league football heroes, who have given their lives for their King and country'. A tablet unveiled at a ceremony in 1917 reflects the contemporary parallels drawn between sport and war. The memorial was inscribed with names of local footballers who had died on active service. By the late 1960s, the town hall was generally inadequate for the purposes of the council and a new administration centre was built. The last meeting of the council was held in the town hall in 1975. The building remains a venue for community functions.

56. Johnson's Buildings,
Palmerin Street

Thomas Johnson was a well-known local councillor, a mayor of Warwick and subsequently a Member of the State Legislative Council. The two shops adjacent to the town hall were built in 1898 and were converted into premises for the Royal Bank of Queensland in 1900. In 1913 two new shops were built adjacent to the bank and a new facade was constructed to link the existing and new buildings. In 1932 Gertrude Jensen opened a ladies fashion shop. This shop and the adjoining business are still operated by members of the Jensen family. The Royal Bank of Queensland subsequently became the National Bank of Australasia and continued to occupy part of Johnson's Buildings until 1930. In recent years, the premises have been divided into two shops, one of which is the Warwick Newsagency.

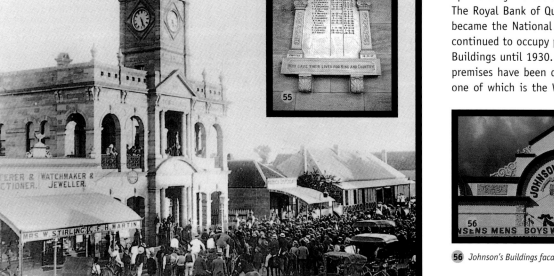

56 *Johnson's Buildings facade, Warwick*

57. Warwick War Memorial Park,
Palmerin Street

The memorial is situated in Leslie Park, which was created as a recreational square during the first surveys in the late 1840s. The foundation stone was laid in 1923 by the Prime Minister, S.M. Bruce. The war memorial, of Helidon sandstone, was unveiled by the State Governor, Sir Matthew Nathan, at a ceremony attended by 3000 people. The memorial gates were erected in 1924. The memorial honours the 122 local men who were killed during World War I and the gates honour the 377 who served and returned.

58. Warwick High School,
Palmerin Street

This building was constructed in 1914 as the Warwick Technical School. The original high school, opened in 1912 in an earlier building, was the first state high school on the Darling Downs.

59. Plumb's Chambers,
Fitzroy Street

Plumb's Chambers comprises two distinct buildings. One is a substantial, two-storey stone building constructed in 1874 for a chemist and seedsman, David Clarke. The second is a small, two-storey brick and timber building. Clarke, a dispensing chemist, arrived in Warwick in 1867. During the next 15 years he played an important role in the development of agriculture in the district by specialising in the importation of seeds and fruit trees likely to succeed there. Clarke's success encouraged him to construct a substantial new stone premises on land opposite the square. His new Medical Hall was completed in early 1875.

The property remained in Clarke's name until 1909, when it was transferred to a retired farmer and grazier, James Wilson. Shortly before his death in 1910, Wilson received council approval to erect the balcony over the footpath in front of his building. Wilson also acquired the title to the brick and timber building next door, which had formerly operated as a drapery store and then as a wholesale spirit store. In 1914, the title to both buildings passed to a Warwick bootmaker, James Plumb, and they became known as Plumb's Chambers.

60. Warwick Police Station and Court House,
Fitzroy Street

When Warwick was gazetted as a town in 1847, a shepherd's hut on Canning Downs is believed to have been used as the police station. A government reserve was set aside in Albion Street and public buildings erected on this land during the 1860s included a court house, police station, post office and telegraph office. The reserve was prone to flooding, however, and by the mid-1880s plans had been prepared for a new court house at the present site. The new building was designed by the Colonial Architect's Office. The court house was erected in 1886, the decision to incorporate a clock tower at the front of the building being made during construction. By the late 1890s, accommodation at the old police station in Albion Street was described as very indifferent.

Plans were prepared for a new police station alongside the court house under Alfred Brady, the Government Architect at the time. Construction of the police station was completed in 1901. The complex survives as an intact and operating example of a late 19th century provincial police station and court house.

59 *Plumb's Chambers, Warwick*
60 *Warwick Court House*

61. St Andrew's Uniting Church,
Guy Street

Opened in 1870, St Andrew's Presbyterian Church was constructed by the local stonemason John McCulloch. The first service was conducted by the Reverend Isaac Mackay, who held services in both English and Gaelic. In 1922 a vestry and choir room were begun and a pipe organ was purchased as a soldiers' memorial. Installation of the organ was completed in 1925. Work on the Protestant Hall, next to St Andrew's, began in 1900. It was opened in 1904 as the Mary Williams Memorial Hall, named in memory of the wife of an early elder. The timber hall incorporates an earlier building on the site.

62. St George's Masonic Lodge, Guy Street

A rare example, in Queensland, of a sandstone masonic lodge, this is considered one of the finest masonic buildings in the State. The foundation stone of St George's Masonic Centre was laid in 1886 and the building, designed by Warwick architect William Wallace, was opened in 1887. The hall was notable for a number of features, including the patent springs under the ballroom floor that had been manufactured specially for this purpose. Ownership was transferred to The Trustees of the St George's Lodge of the Ancient Free and Accepted Masons of Queensland in 1959. The Hebrew inscription on the front of the building reads 'We fear the creator of the universe'.

63. Central State School, Guy Street

Land for Warwick Central School was purchased in 1873 after the town's first school, formerly the National School, was considered badly located. The new school, which opened in 1875 with separate wings for boys and girls, was designed by the prominent architect Richard Suter. It was known as the Warwick West Boys School and Girls and Infants School until 1933.

64. Pringle Cottage Museum, Dragon Street

This two-storey sandstone cottage was built by stonemason John McCulloch as his family home. McCulloch arrived in Warwick about 1862 and was responsible for the stonework of many of the town's finest buildings, including St Andrew's Presbyterian Church (1869), St Mark's Anglican Church (1874), the Central School (1874), the Methodist Church (1875) and Warwick Court House (1885). A Mrs F.S. Pringle and her daughter reportedly ran a private school in the upper floor of the cottage from 1898 until about 1905.

The Warwick and District Historical Society, which gained possession of the building in 1979, chose to name the cottage after the schoolteachers.

65. The Commonage Shop, Dragon Street

This brick cottage, known as the Commonage, was built during the late 1860s or early 1870s for shopkeeper John Leonard. It appears to have served as a residence and store for Leonard. By 1890 the property included the cottage, with a new brick shop with a dry store at the rear. The new store was stocked with drapery, groceries and boots, and advertised as the National Store. Following Leonard's death in 1898 his widow, Annie Leonard, continued to run the business as a general store until about 1914. The shop changed hands a number of times after her death in 1924. The present owners acquired the property in 1977 and have subsequently carried out substantial conservation work on the building.

62 Masonic Lodge building
63 Central State School, c1902 (John Oxley Library)
64 McCulloch's house, now Pringle Cottage Museum

66. Our Lady of the Assumption Convent, *Locke Street*

This building is a fine example of ecclesiastical Victorian architecture, influenced by a revival of interest in the Gothic style and adapted to the Queensland climate. Our Lady of the Assumption Convent was built in 1892 as the second convent of the Sisters of Mercy in Warwick. Additions in 1904 completed the original plans of Brisbane architects Simkin and Ibler. The Sisters of Mercy acquired their first convent in Warwick in 1874, and immediately took over the running of the Catholic school. The foundation stone of the new convent was laid in 1891 by Archbishop Dunne, who also performed the opening ceremony two years later in 1893. The building contract was undertaken by Alexander Mayes of Toowoomba and the stonework was subcontracted to John McCulloch.

The Sisters of Mercy withdrew from Warwick in 1988 and lay Catholics in the town retained Assumption College as a campus for tertiary education. The convent was reopened as Sophia College in 1989. However, in 1994 the building was sold and converted to a reception centre.

67. St Mark's Anglican Church, *Grafton Street*

Warwick's Anglican community has used this church for nearly 130 years. St Mark's was constructed from 1868 to designs of the Brisbane architect Richard Suter. The first Anglican service in Warwick was conducted in 1848. Services were held in the old court house in Alice Street until 1858, when a slab timber church was constructed on the present allotment. The Reverend Benjamin Glennie held services from 1860 until 1872, when he was made Rector of Warwick. During Glennie's time the decision was made to construct a more permanent church building, and the foundation stone of the present sandstone church was laid by Bishop Tufnell in 1868.

John McCulloch was the contractor and the stone used was quarried from Bishop Tufnell's Sidling Quarries. The original section was completed by 1874, when the first additions commenced. Later additions were made in the late 1930s and early 1960s. The early slab timber church was demolished in 1910.

68. Warwick National School, *Fitzroy Street*

The first school in Warwick was established in 1850. It was set up as the result of efforts by the pioneer squatter, George Leslie, who was concerned about the education of his own children. He started making enquiries to the New South Wales Board of National Education in 1848, but the school, with 30 students, was not established until 1850. After Separation in 1859, the Warwick National School came under the jurisdiction of the newly created Board of Education. The present brick building was constructed in 1864 to the design of the early Queensland architect Benjamin Backhouse. This building joined an earlier timber structure, used as a classroom since the school's inception in 1850.

By 1874 the buildings that comprised the Warwick National School were considered inadequate for the growing town and the establishment of a new school, the Warwick Central School, was planned. When this new school opened in 1875, the former Warwick National School became known as the Warwick East State School, a name it still retains.

66 *Our Lady of the Assumption Convent*
67 *St Mark's Church, Warwick*
68 *Warwick National School*
69 *National Hotel*

69. National Hotel, *Lyons Street*

This substantial brick building provides evidence of Warwick's growth during the early years of the 20th century. The town was granted the status of a municipality in 1861 and continued to grow with the introduction of the railway from Toowoomba in 1867. The extension of the line to the Stanthorpe tin field in 1881 contributed to Warwick's becoming the major service and trade centre on the Southern Downs. In 1907 the Allman family, owners of the Criterion Hotel, applied for hotel premises to be erected opposite the Warwick Railway Station. Architects James Marks and Sons of Toowoomba were commissioned to design the hotel, which was opened by early 1908. On the death of Daniel Allman in 1936, Queensland Brewery Limited acquired the National Hotel. Minor alterations to the hotel in 1937 were designed by Addison and Macdonald, an architectural partnership from Brisbane renowned for their work in modernising many early hotels in south-east Queensland during the interwar period. No substantial changes have been made to the hotel since then.

70. Warwick Railway Station,
Lyons Street

This amalgam of buildings dating from the late 1880s includes a sandstone goods shed, passenger station, various staff dwellings and livestock saleyards. The station was catapulted to national significance when an egg was thrown at Prime Minister Billy Hughes while he was visiting Warwick during the World War I conscription referendum. This incident led to the establishment of the Commonwealth Police Force after the local constable refused to intervene. The first rail line in Queensland reached Toowoomba from Ipswich in 1867, and from there a southern extension to Warwick was completed in 1871. The initial terminus was on the northern side of the Condamine River.

The discovery of tin at Stanthorpe prompted the government to make surveys to extend the rail line from Warwick to Stanthorpe in 1873. The extension necessitated the construction of a bridge across the Condamine River. The railway extension was opened in 1881. Tenders were called in 1886 for the construction of a passenger station and goods shed at the new Warwick Station and most of the work was completed in 1887–88.

John McCulloch supervised the stonework construction. From the 1960s the importance of the Warwick Railway Station diminished, due to increased competition from road transport.

71. Warwick Co-operative
Dairy Association Factory,
Victoria Street

The severe drought of the late 1890s demonstrated the need for cooperation among farmers if dairying was to remain a commercial industry. The Warwick Butter and Dairying Company was formed in 1902 to establish the town's first butter factory. The factory was constructed by Waugh and Josephson and production commenced in 1903. The premises were destroyed by fire in 1924, but were rebuilt by the next year and the company went from strength to strength. By 1940 the Co-operative controlled butter factories throughout the southern Downs as the Warwick Co-operative Dairy Association. The factory continues on operation.

70 *Warwick Railway Station, c1911 (John Oxley Library)*
73 *Rosenthal Homestead*

72. Warwick Cemetery,
Wentworth Street

This area, originally known as Evan's Camp, has been used as a burial ground since 1853. It was gazetted as a cemetery in 1868. The Mitchner Memorial, located in the centre of the cemetery, was constructed as a bequest by William Mitchner who died in 1918. The cemetery contains a large Chinese section. During the early years of settlement, because of the difficulties of securing labourers, Chinese shepherds, house servants, cooks and gardeners were recruited from the southern provinces of China. When gold and tin were discovered in the district, numbers of Chinese worked on the diggings. Many of the remains in the cemetery were exhumed and returned to China at the request of relatives.

73. Rosenthal Homestead

Built before 1848, Rosenthal is the earliest homestead on the Darling Downs that remains occupied and intact. Rosenthal run had been taken up by 1843, when it was recorded as the birthplace of the first white baby on the Downs. The explorer Ludwig Leichhardt visited the homestead on several occasions from 1846 and set out from there on his final ill-fated expedition in 1848. Leichhardt's 'L' blaze is said to have been cut on a large old gum tree still standing at the entrance to the homestead. The homestead is not open to visitors.

74. Canning Downs Homestead

One of the earliest homesteads on the Downs, it was established on a run taken up by the Leslie brothers in 1840. Several major additions have been made to the principal timber slab residence, believed to date from 1847–48. The three Leslie brothers arrived in Australia from Scotland in the 1830s, with the intention of establishing a pastoral station. Tales of the fertile Darling Downs region had spread after Cunningham's discovery of the area in 1827. The Leslies were the first squatting expedition to reach the Downs and they quickly claimed a vast tract of country for their run, which Cunningham had named Canning Downs.

By 1842 the Leslie brothers were in dire financial trouble. Continuing financial concerns led Patrick to withdraw from Canning Downs. He purchased land in Brisbane on which he built a cottage, which was to become Newstead House. The discovery of gold in Australia in the 1850s exacerbated the scarcity of labour on stations and in 1854 the remaining brother, George, sold the station and returned to Scotland. The property changed hands a number of times between the 1860s and 1910s. In 1918 the ownership of the station was transferred to John Smith and Sara Barnes. The Barnes family were prominent in horse racing and Canning Downs became an important stud, where many successful racehorses were reared. The homestead is not open to visitors.

75. Swan Creek

The Swan Creek area was part of the Warwick Agricultural Reserve, one of several agricultural reserves to be created on the Darling Downs under the 1860 Land Act. The reserve comprised a tract of farming country wedged between extensive squatting runs.

Offered for selection from the 1860s, it was one of the first areas on the southern Downs to be subdivided for closer settlement. A small settlement grew up to serve the new farming community and by the 1870s it boasted three hotels. The cemetery contains the graves of some of the early pioneering families of the district.

76. White Swan Inn

This small sandstone residence with distinctive attic dormer windows was erected in 1876 as a home for local farmer Edward Malone. Within two years Malone registered his home as the White Swan Inn and became a publican for the expanding Swan Creek agricultural settlement. The White Swan Inn continued trading until 1887, when it was purchased as a private residence. The Tyson family, owners from 1892 until 1989, carried out substantial renovations and added a kitchen and living area to the rear of the house. The original timber shingles remain under the corrugated iron roof.

77. Yangan

In 1840, when the Leslie brothers established Canning Downs run, an outstation was formed at Heifer Creek and the hut and stockyards developed into Yangan township. The settlement served the surrounding industries of the Swanfels Valley — timber-getting, sandstone quarrying, dairying and coalmining. It was, however, the opening of the first stage of the Warwick–Killarney Branch Railway in 1884 that provided the real impetus for further development. The railway became important in the transport of Yangan sandstone.

The line was one of the earliest in the colony, built to transport goods generated by farmers and industry rather than squatters. By 1900 Yangan had become, according to *The Queenslander*, one of the most thriving centres on the line:

74 *The stables, Canning Downs Homestead*

75 *Swan Creek cemetery and the White Swan Inn*

77 *Yangan sandstone quarry, 1908 (John Oxley Library)*

'Here there are two cheese factories which have done an inestimable amount of good for the whole district'. The post-World War II period saw a decline in Yangan's fortunes, further depressed by the closure of the Warwick–Killarney Line in 1964.

78. Yangan School of Arts, *King Street*

The school of arts provided subscribers with a lending library and reading room. Its rooms were regularly rented to other local organisations and provided a social focus for the district. The first Yangan School of Arts was built about 1898. In 1912 it was acquired by the local Masonic Lodge and became the Yangan Masonic Temple. Tenders were called for a new school of arts, land was acquired from the Railways Department and the building was opened in 1912. Despite the decline of the town's fortunes epitomised by the closure of the Warwick–Killarney Railway, the Yangan School of Arts lives on, its facilities used by more than a dozen local groups.

79. Yangan Masonic Lodge, *King Street*

This hall was acquired by the Yangan Lodge in 1912. It had been erected about 1898 as Yangan's first school of arts during the period when the town was developing as one of the Darling Downs' small but prosperous towns. The Yangan Lodge was formed in 1903 and early meetings were held at the Yangan Oddfellows Hall (now the Yangan Hall). After World War I, the Lodge began to expand again; the annual Yangan Masonic Ball was one of the major events of the district. A significant change made to the site in 1957 was the building of a concrete retaining wall with stairs and light pillars at the street entry.

80. Emu Vale

This is the site of the Old Sheep Station, an outstation of Canning Downs run. Early selectors took up farming land just beyond the Canning Downs boundary in the 1860s and maize and potatoes were the main crops. A school had been established by 1882 and the Warwick–Killarney Railway terminated here in 1884. A sawmill was established in the town in the 1890s and Emu Vale survived as a self-sufficient settlement until the decline of the timber industry in recent times. In the late 1940s the local storekeeper, Pat Bolger, persauaded the Council to plant an avenue of pines on the approach to the township in remembrance of those from the area who had died in both World Wars. Emu Vale's Avenue of Honour is a significant feature of the district.

78 *School of Arts, Yangan*
79 *Yangan Masonic Lodge*

81. Tannymorel

The township, originally known as Lower Farm Creek, developed around a sawmill in the 1870s. The first school was built in 1877. Tannymorel coalmine at Mount Colliery commenced production in the 1890s, and a tramway was opened from the colliery to the rail siding at Tannymorel about 1906. The mine was closed in 1920 due to underground fires. However, a second mine was opened at Mount Colliery in 1925 and operated until about 1967. The colliery has since been demolished and no surface structures remain.

82. Killarney

Settlement at Killarney dates from 1857, when George Fitzallen leased Killarney Farm, a portion of Canning Downs. By 1874 a hotel, police station, stores and school had been established on the banks of the Condamine River. In 1878 a town site was surveyed on the south side of the Condamine. The terminus of the 1885 branch railway line from Emu Vale remained on the north side as there were no funds for a bridge. While both towns developed, North Killarney became the principal town once the district was opened up for closer settlement. By the early 20th century it was thriving, its shops and services supporting the local timber and dairying industries. By 1908, two butter factories were in operation and fruit growing was expanding.

Throughout the 1920s, Killarney reflected the economic stability of its farming community. Like other border towns dependent on rural industries, it suffered from the opening of the interstate railway through Kyogle and the continuing rural Depression. A cyclone in 1968 destroyed many of the town's historic buildings. Killarney remains the centre for the district's fruit-growing and specialist dairy products industries and the gateway to the national parks of the border region. The township of Killarney and the nearby countryside is the part-setting for David Malouf's novel *Harland's Half Acre* (1984).

83. Former National Bank of Australasia, *Willow Street*

Built in 1913 as the Queensland National Bank, the building originally contained a banking chamber, manager's office, strongroom and manager's living quarters. Plans for alteration and extension of the building were drawn up in 1928. The Queensland National Bank branch closed in 1943, a result of rationalisation caused by World War II. The National Bank of Australasia reopened the premises in 1947 and operated from here until the branch was officially closed in 1972. The building now serves as the Killarney Heritage Centre.

84. Former Commercial Bank of Sydney, *Willow Street*

This building was constructed in the early 1900s as a two-storey bank building, its wide verandahs on both street frontages adorned with decorative iron panels. In later years the upper storey and verandahs were removed and the building now serves as a real estate office.

85. Killarney Hotel, *Willow Street*

The hotel, dating from about 1884, was one of four hotels trading in Killarney at the end of the 19th century. Since this period the premises has undergone considerable alteration and changes have been made to the building's exterior.

86. Queen Mary Falls National Park

The park was formerly part of the extensive timber reserves in the Queensland border area. A walking track leads to the spectacular 40-metre waterfall on Spring Creek, a tributary of the Condamine River. When first gazetted in August 1908, Queen Mary's Falls became the third national park to be established in south-east Queensland.

87. Smith's Sawmill, *Queen Mary Falls*

This disused sawmill at the entrance to Queen Mary Falls was once operated by Sam Smith. It is typical of the small family-run case mills, of which south-east Queensland once had hundreds. The shed remains intact along with a portable steam engine, belt-drive pulleys and sawbench. The sawmill is on private property.

82 *Bullock team on Willow Street, Killarney (John Oxley Library)*

85 *Killarney Hotel*

86 *Queen Mary Falls National Park (EPA)*

87 *Sawmill, Queen Mary Falls*

86

85

87

82

88. Darling Downs Hotel, *Sandy Creek*

The village of Sandy Creek on the Rosenthal grazing run was already well established when Surveyor Pratten carried out a government land survey in 1861. It was located on the main road from Warwick and its buildings included several hotels catering to the passing coach and teamster trade. Adam Smith erected the Darling Downs Hotel in 1875 and sold it in 1877 to purchase a hotel in Warwick. The Sandy Creek Post Office operated from the hotel from the 1870s. A new Darling Downs Hotel was erected on the same site in the late 1920s, at about the same time as Sandy Creek was renamed Allan. A World War I memorial hall was erected nearby in the 1920s. Known as Allies Hall, it was used jointly with the adjacent hotel to host functions for the Sandy Creek community.

89. Assmanshausen Winery, *Sandy Creek*

By the 1850s, most of the large pastoral properties around Warwick, such as Rosenthal, Talgai and Canning Downs, had well-established orchards and vineyards. In the 1860s Jacob Kircher, who was in charge of the Canning Downs orchard, set up his own vineyard at Sandy Creek, naming it after a celebrated wine-producing district on the Rhine in Germany. By 1873, Assmanshausen red and white wines were winning prizes for their quality. Supplementing his grapes with those of other local growers, Kircher sold to markets not only throughout Australia but also in Great Britain and Europe — the only Queensland winegrower to do so.

Other wineries were established by the 1880s, but Kircher was always acknowledged as the father of the industry. He died in 1903 and until 1915 when it was sold, the vineyard was operated by his nephew, Michael Kircher. The early farmhouse and wine cellar remain, although the original vines have been removed. The property is not open to the public.

90. Pratten

The settlement of Darkey Flat, gazetted in 1862, was surveyed and proclaimed in 1866 as the centre for the booming Talgai goldfield. Although the town continued to be known as Darkey Flat, the Minister for Lands directed that it should be named Pratten after surveyor G.L. Pratten. The town was dependent on the goldfields and its fortunes fluctuated with the level of mining activity. The 1870s were years of growth. The town was the centre for the district's mail runs and Darkey Flat Post Office opened in the school in 1878. By the 1880s, mining had given way to dairying and grain growing as the district's principal industries. A sawmill was in operation and a range of small businesses servicing the carrying industry and the farming community were the basis of the town's survival. The decline of dairying, improvement in road transport and the drift of people to the coast in the 1950s signalled the end of Pratten as a commercial centre. Government services and businesses gradually closed and the buildings were removed or demolished.

90 *Busy scene in White Street, Pratten, c1927 (below) (John Oxley Library)*

90 *Pratten community hall remains (right)*

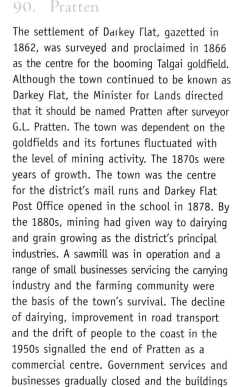

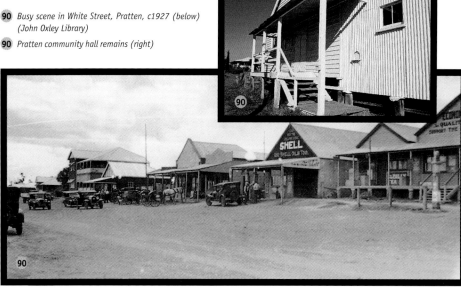

88 *Darling Downs Hotel, Sandy Creek*

89 *Cellar at Assmanshausen Winery*

91. St James Anglican Church, *White Street*

The church was erected in 1882. An elegant timber building with a shingle roof, it may have been designed by James Marks, who was then the Anglican Church Architect. Apart from the new iron roof installed in the early 1990s, the present church is little altered from the original.

92. Old Talgai Woolshed

The date of the woolshed's construction is uncertain. It may have been built about 1862, when the Clark brothers in partnership with Thomas Hanmer purchased the property from Thomas Hood. In 1867 Old Talgai was divided, the homestead remaining with Clark and Hanmer. Almost one-third of the property, including the homestead and the woolshed, was subsequently sold. Old Talgai was further divided for closer settlement after 1900 and the Ramsay family bought the homestead block in 1907. The residence was demolished about 1952 and replaced with a modern house. The woolshed survives, its original shingle roof still visible under the iron roof. The property is not open to the public.

92 *Old Talgai Woolshed*

93. Talgai Goldfield

Small gold finds were made near the present town of Leyburn in 1860 and in 1863 a square mile within the Talgai run was proclaimed as a goldfield. However, the first major discovery of gold in south-east Queensland was made near Talgai washpool in 1864. By 1865 two stamp batteries were in operation, and about 150 miners were working on nine reefs. The Big Hill, also known as Mount Gammie, was the scene of reef mining as early as 1863, when the Queenslander goldmine was being worked. The field underwent a period of development in the early 1890s when the Big Hill open-cut mine started operation. The Monte Christo Reef, south of the Big Hill, was discovered in 1864; it was first worked from about 1869 and on several occasions until the early 1900s.

94. Leyburn

Leyburn began as the settlement of Canal Creek, established around 1850 on the original Canal Creek run taken up in 1844. The early settlement grew up around Leslie's Crossing, the fording place for carriers heading west, and supported several hotels even before the first land sales in 1857. It was renamed Leyburn in 1853. By the 1860s more substantial buildings began to replace the original bark constructions. The town became a centre for the Leyburn Goldfield, proclaimed in 1875. Although the field attracted many miners up to the early 1900s and again during the 1930s, no payable reefs were discovered. The expansion of agricultural settlement and the establishment of dairying and grain growing in the district sustained the town through the 1920s and 1930s. In the postwar years, as the improvement in road conditions ended the isolation of farming communities, commercial services gradually shifted to the larger towns in the region.

95. Police Magistrate's House, *Tummaville Road*

Also known as the Judge's House, this brick residence surrounded by shady verandahs was built in the late 1860s for Police Magistrate George Lukin. Largely unaltered, the house has remained a private residence.

96. Batham's General Store, *McIntyre Street*

Originally owned by Mr O'Halloran, this was one of five general stores trading in Leyburn from the late 1860s.

97. Country Women's Association Hall, *McIntyre Street*

The Leyburn branch of the Queensland Country Women's Association was formed in 1924 and the hall was built in 1928. It stands on land purchased at the first land sales in 1857 by Rebecca Kirby, widow of Leyburn pioneer Henry Kirby. Tennis courts were laid in 1934 and many improvements have been made over the years. The hall was enlarged to its present size in 1954 and remains the centre for community activities.

96 *Batham's General Store, Leyburn*

98. Royal Hotel,
McIntyre Street

Built in 1863 by a Leyburn pioneer, James Murray, this brick hotel is claimed to be the oldest licensed public house in Queensland still operating in the original building.

99. Granall Cottage,
McIntyre Street

This beautifully preserved cottage is among the earliest continuously occupied dwellings in the district. It was built as James Murray's home in 1856. Its foundation of bedlogs, ironbark slab walls and cypress pine floors date from that time. The original shingle roof is intact under the iron roof added in 1911, probably when the calico ceilings were lined with timber. Six sets of double red cedar doors opening to the verandah have an unusual glass panel pattern. The kitchen remains in its original position, separate from the house but linked with it by a covered walkway.

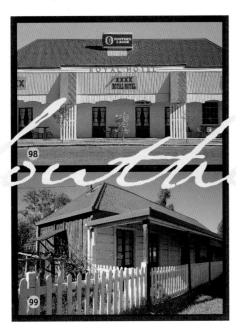

100. Kowitz Brothers' Sawmill

Abundant timber reserves and the demands of the mining and agricultural industries promoted the establishment of several sawmills in the Leyburn district. The Kowitz brothers' mill, opened in 1945, was one of the few still powered by steam until its recent closure. When the smokebox of the Ruston Hornsby steam engine was condemned in 1981, a replacement boiler was acquired from the Dalby Hospital and connected to the steam engine to power the main sawbench.

101. Leyburn State School Play Shed,
Peter Street

This is a typical, but now rare, example of a 19th century Queensland school playshed. It was constructed in 1863 by William Clarke of Toowoomba and the timber floor was added in 1887. The Leyburn Parents and Citizens Association funded the restoration of the original shingle roof in 1973.

102. St Matthew's Catholic Church,
Dove Street

From 1860, when Leyburn was established as part of the Warwick Parish, services were held in the court house and in the Mahony family's home. In 1901, after 40 years of fundraising, St Matthew's Church was consecrated. Designed by architects Wallace and Gibson, the building is of hardwood construction with cypress pine interiors.

103. St Augustine's Anglican Church,
Dove Street

In 1861 the pastoralist Gore family of Yandilla donated land for the building of a church and parsonage at Leyburn, but the small farming community had difficulty raising sufficient funds. The project remained in doubt until Bishop Tufnell directed that money raised by students of St Augustine's theological college in Canterbury, England, be given to Leyburn Parish. Designed by the architect Richard Suter, St Augustine's was dedicated by Bishop Tufnell in 1871. The interior of the church is the work of a local craftsman, Mr Baillie.

98 *Royal Hotel*

99 *Granall Cottage, Leyburn*

100 *Kowitz Brothers' Sawmill, Leyburn*

MAP 6
Granite Belt

The cool high country of the Granite Belt is like no other part of Queensland. It actually has four seasons, while the rest of the State has only summer and winter. In spring the district is carpeted with wildflowers and fruit blossoms; in autumn experience the changing colour of the leaves, the apple harvest and the wine vintage; and in winter, crisp clear days, perfect for bushwalking. From Warwick, take the New England Highway to Stanthorpe. At Cottonvale, take a detour on the 'fruit run', through the former soldier settlements of Pozières, Passchendaele and Amiens, where fruit orchards and vineyards now thrive.

The district's main centre is the charming town of Stanthorpe, surrounded by vineyards and wineries and within easy driving of Girraween National Park. Stanthorpe's main streets boast an interesting mix of architecture. The town's broad ethnic background is reflected in the arts and craft produced by the community. Continue south past historic Ballandean homestead, where the first grapes in the district were planted, and visit the many fine wineries in the area.

Visit Girraween National Park with its awesome landscape of granite domes, large boulders and precariously balanced rocks. The town of Wallangarra, at the southern end of Girraween, marks the State border. This unassuming town, one of the region's most historically significant early settlements, has many interesting remnants of Queensland's colonial past. They include the railway station, with its dual rail gauges for Queensland and New South Wales; the former Customs House, now a cafe; and the blazed stump of the surveyor's tree carved in 1859, defining the State border.

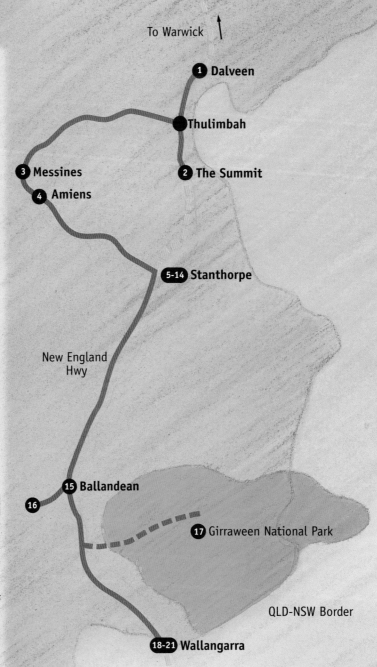

To Warwick

1 Dalveen

Thulimbah

3 Messines

2 The Summit

4 Amiens

5-14 Stanthorpe

New England Hwy

15 Ballandean

16

17 Girraween National Park

QLD-NSW Border

18-21 Wallangarra

THE GRANITE BELT

This trail was one of the early routes followed by pastoralists droving stock over the New England Tableland to the unclaimed lands beyond the limits of settlement. Four extensive grazing runs were stocked by the 1840s; they included Pikedale, Ballandean and Maryvale. The Queensland-New South Wales border was finalised in the early 1860s, placing the district in Queensland. Closer selection of the pastoral runs in the late 1860s led to the establishment of vineyards and fruit orchards on the generally poorer soils. Henry Nichol of Ballandean station imported the first vines from France in the 1850s. Encouraged by an Italian priest, Father Davadi, who planted the first stone fruit in 1873, Italian settlers planted vineyards and orchards throughout the Granite Belt.

Mining provided the impetus for the development of permanent settlement in the district. Gold and copper deposits were discovered on a resumed section of the Pikedale run and a settlement was laid out. The site was abandoned, however, when the discovery of tin at Quart Pot Creek in 1872 started the rush that created Stanthorpe, the only town in south-east Queensland to be founded on tin mining. Although the profitable phase of tin mining was short-lived, the expectation of continuing wealth from tin prompted the government to extend the railway from Warwick to Stanthorpe and the line was completed in 1881.

The railway was the lifeline for the district. Stanthorpe, with its imposing historic buildings, benefited from its role as the railway terminus and the only major town in the Granite Belt. Wallangarra was founded in 1887 when the railway line was extended to the border to capture the lucrative freight trade from the primary industries of the south-west region. The different gauges of the Queensland and New South Wales railways met at the railway station. Stanthorpe's position as the region's principal town was only briefly challenged by Wallangarra. By that time, it was the main loading facility for the Granite Belt's fruit industry. Sawmills turned to the manufacture of fruit boxes.

Soldier settlement blocks, named after significant battles on the Western Front during World War I, were established for fruit growing in the Stanthorpe district from 1919. Although the government assisted the settlements by installing railway sidings, the scheme was a failure here as in other districts. Through the 1920s and 1930s Stanthorpe enjoyed popularity as a mountain holiday resort, several guesthouses being opened. Dairying and fruit growing suffered a long recession until the late 1970s, when Italian farmers revived the wine industry and improved handling methods secured the future of fruit growing.

Wallangarra Railway Station

Washing alluvial tin at Stanthorpe, c1872 (John Oxley Library)

GRANITE BELT HERITAGE TRAIL

1. Dalveen Sawmill

The sawmill in McCosker Drive is on the site of an early brickworks. The Warwick Brick and Tile Company started brick-making in 1912. James Pidgeon, who had formerly worked for the company, purchased the business in 1920. The Pidgeon family built a new brickworks and in the mid-1920s the business was extended to include this sawmill. The small brick building standing within the sawmill property was originally built by Pidgeon's for the Agricultural Bank and Butler's butcher shop. The bank closed during the 1930s Depression and the butcher shop closed some time later.

2. The Summit Railway Station

Built about 1910, The Summit survives as an intact example of a once standard railway office design. It is also significant as one of the highest stations in Queensland, hence the name. The Southern Line from Warwick to Stanthorpe was opened in 1881 in response to tin mining. However it was fruit growing which resulted in the establishment of The Summit and other nearby stations as depots for local orchardists. During the early 1900s the facilities gradually expanded in response to the increasing number of small farms and the growth of the local fruit industry. The Fruitgrowers Co-operative Association sheds formed part of the station by the 1930s.

3. Soldier Settler's Cottage, *Messines*

This cottage is an example of a typical soldier settler home after World War I. Under the government's soldier settlement scheme, 700 returned soldiers took up agricultural blocks on the original Ballandean station. They were expected to engage in mixed farming and fruit growing, but many failed due to the harsh conditions, inexperience in farming and war injuries. Those who survived made an important contribution to the growth of the district's fruit industry. Messines Railway Siding commemorated the battle of Messines Ridge on the Somme. It was one of several sidings constructed in 1920 on the Stanthorpe–Amiens Branch Line and named after major World War I battles in which Australian troops fought.

4. St Denys Anglican Church, *Amiens*

Built in 1923 in the heart of the Stanthorpe soldier settlement district, this is the only Anglican Church in Queensland dedicated to Saint Denys, the patron saint of France, linking the church with the settlers and their World War I memories. The church's cross, altar cloth and candlesticks came from France as gifts, either from the Amiens Cathedral or the military chapel at Le Havre.

1 Dalveen Sawmill and butcher's shop
2 The Summit Railway Station
3 St Denys Church, Amiens
4 Soldier Settler's Cottage, Messines

5.   Stanthorpe

By 1844 squatters had occupied four major pastoral runs in the Quart Pot Creek district including Maryvale and Pikedale. The Land Act of 1868 led to an influx of shepherds and other farm workers intent on acquiring land of their own. The large squatting runs began to be broken up and the settlement of Quart Pot grew to serve local farmers. Tin was first discovered in the area in 1854 but a rush did not occur until 1872, a time when world tin prices were high. W.C. Hume carried out a survey of the settlement in 1873 and named the new town Stanthorpe. The Southern Railway reached Stanthorpe in 1881, ending the necessity to cart ore to the railhead at Warwick.

Many miners turned to farming during the 1890s Depression and the fruit-growing industry began to develop during this period. By the late 1890s, fruit consignments were sent regularly to the Brisbane markets. Stanthorpe reflected the rapid expansion of the industry in the early 1920s as more land was opened for closer settlement and the soldier settlement scheme was expanded. From the mid-1920s Stanthorpe benefited from the popularity of cool mountain areas as holiday destinations. The 1930s Depression and World War II slowed progress until the late 1970s, when winemaking developed into a viable industry and tourists began to return to the district. Advances in growing have stabilised the fruit industry and Stanthorpe has experienced recent success associated with the wine and tourist industries.

6.   Stanthorpe Court House,
Marsh Street

A police magistrate was conducting regular court sittings at Quart Pot by 1874, the earliest sittings being held in a tent. Work on the foundations of the present court house started in 1941 and the building was

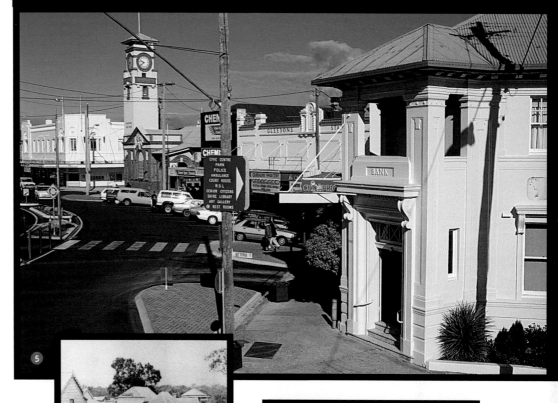

completed by 1942. The court room was located on the top floor. Offices on the ground floor were occupied by the police and other government departments.

7.   Central Hotel,
High Street

The present building is the third hotel to occupy this site. The first was Sheahan's Hotel, a single-storey slab building with a shingle roof, erected in 1872. The second Sheahan's Hotel, also known as the Horse and Jockey, opened in 1908. An imposing two-storey building with verandahs and an ornamental tower, it was Stanthorpe's second brick building. It was known as the Central Hotel by 1927, when it was destroyed in a large fire that also engulfed a number of adjoining shops. The present Central Hotel was subsequently built on the site.

5 *Miners in Maryland Street, c1873 (John Oxley Library)*

5 *Maryland Street and Stanthorpe Post Office (top)*

6 *Stanthorpe Court House*

7 *Central Hotel*

8. Stanthorpe Post Office, *Maryland Street*

This Stanthorpe landmark was built in 1901 when the new Commonwealth Government took over management of postal services. It replaced Stanthorpe's first permanent post and telegraph office, built in 1885. It was designed by J.S. Murdoch, the first Commonwealth Government Architect. The building reflects the influence of the popular Arts and Crafts architectural style. At Federation, the newly constituted Australian Government delegated to each State the responsibility for upgrading or replacing existing post and telegraph offices. The post office stands on the site of Groom's Hotel, which in 1874 housed the telegraph office.

9. Commercial Hotel, *Maryland Street*

This was the site of Kelly's Mining Exchange Hotel, one of the first hotels built during the 1872 tin-mining boom. In 1874, it was taken over by Patrick Tevlin, who rebuilt it as the Commercial Hotel. The premises were destroyed in a large fire that swept through Maryland Street in 1914. The present Commercial Hotel was rebuilt in brick in the same year.

10. Stanthorpe Hospital, *McGregor Terrace*

Following the arrival of large numbers of tin miners, Stanthorpe's first hospital was built in 1873 at another location. The present hospital site was chosen in 1913 and the original ward was moved here. Further accommodation was required to cope with the influx of soldier settlers to the district and new wards were built during the mid-1920s. The present main block was built in 1936 to replace the old hospital.

8 Stanthorpe Post Office
9 Early Commercial Hotel (John Oxley Library)
10 Stanthorpe Hospital

11. El Arish House, *Greenup Street*

This house is associated with the beginning of Stanthorpe's development as a summer holiday centre. In the early 1920s, Major Allan Chauvel and his wife Isabella moved a cottage on to the property, formerly a market garden, and established El Arish as a summer holiday home. It was named after a town on the Sinai Peninsula where Major Chauvel and his famous brother, General Sir Harry Chauvel, served with the Australian Light Horse Brigade during World War I. The garden — designed by Isabella and her son, the renowned filmmaker Charles Chauvel — exhibits many features typical of late 19th century English Arts and Crafts gardens.

The new block was designed by the architect J.P. Donoghue and has since undergone a number of renovations, although its exterior remains intact. The former infectious diseases ward at the rear, built in 1926, is now used as a dental clinic.

12. Stanthorpe Soldiers' Memorial, *Locke Street*

A departure from the conventional design for war memorials, this World War I memorial pavilion was designed by Warwick architects Dornbusch and Connolly. It was officially opened by General Sir William Glasgow in 1926. Honour boards are displayed on the interior walls and the Southern Cross constellation is highlighted in gold on the ceiling. The memorial has a special link with the returned soldiers who settled around Stanthorpe after World War I as part of the soldier settlement scheme.

13. Stanthorpe Railway Station, *Davadi Street*

Erected in 1881, the station was for several years the terminus of the second stage of the Southern Line from Toowoomba and Warwick. Railway contractor John Gargett built the station office and goods shed. After tin mining declined, the railway became important in the development of Stanthorpe's fruit industry, fruit trains regularly loading at the station. By the 1930s additional facilities for the fruit industry included a weighbridge and the Queensland Fruitgrowers' Society shed. The station office displays distinctive features of 19th century railway architecture.

14. Quart Pot Creek Railway Bridge, *near Stanthorpe*

This pin-jointed, double lattice girder bridge was part of the original rail link from Brisbane to Sydney. Despite the difficult mountain terrain, contractor George Bashford completed its construction well within the two-year deadline and it was opened for traffic in 1887. In 1913, the bridge's load capacity was increased by the addition of strengthened centre girders. These dated from the 1880s and were taken from the original Pine Rivers and Bundamba Creek railway bridges near Brisbane.

15. Ballandean

The earliest settlement in the 1840s was known as Severn River. In 1872 land was resumed from Robert MacKenzie's Ballandean run and a new town site was surveyed and named Ballandean. Thomas Fletcher took up a selection in 1872 and erected the Britannia House Hotel. Other businesses clustered around the hotel, catering to the teamsters and carriers, and also to the developing fruit industry. Fletcher established the first commercial orchard in the Granite Belt, probably in the late 1870s. Access to markets was assured after the completion of the Southern Line to Wallangarra in 1888. Despite many setbacks, improvements in quality, new methods of growing, handling and production and the provision of cold storage facilities ensured the stability of the fruit industry and the town. With the recent expansion of local vineyards, Ballandean has enjoyed a revival as a popular tourist centre.

12 *Soldiers' Memorial*
13 *Stanthorpe Railway Station*
15 *Ballandean cherry orchard, 1897 (John Oxley Library)*
16 *Stables at Ballandean Homestead*

16. Ballandean Homestead

The land was taken up as a sheep run by Robert MacKenzie about 1839, when the area was still part of the New England district. In 1844 the property passed to Henry Nichol, who named the run after a small village in the west highlands of Scotland. He established willows and other English trees at Ballandean and imported grapevine cuttings from France to begin the district's wine industry. The first buildings were of vertical timber slab construction with shingle roofs and stone fireplaces. In the 1860s, Nichol sold to Watt and Gilchrist. They were followed by Robert Robertson, who is thought to have constructed the present main house. The original slab living quarters are now in ruins, although several early outbuildings, including the stables and smithy, remain in use. The homestead is not open to visitors.

17. Girraween National Park

Proclaimed in 1932, Bald Rock Creek and Castle Rock national parks were joined in 1966 to form a new park named Girraween. Situated on the northern edge of the New England Tableland, Girraween is noted for its huge granite outcrops and balancing boulders. Its eucalypt forests and heathlands are home to the lyrebird and the rare turquoise parrot. Dr Roberts Waterhole on Bald Rock Creek, near the western boundary of Girraween National Park, is named after Dr Spencer Roberts, a Stanthorpe resident. It was as a result of his representations to the Forestry Department in 1932 that the Department acquired the areas that became Castle Rock and Bald Rock Creek national parks.

18. Wallangarra

The town owes its existence to the Queensland Government's decision in 1884 to compete with New South Wales for the south-west border trade. The plan for a railway extending from Stanthorpe to connect with the railway from Tenterfield required the creation of a new town where the two railways, of different gauges, would meet. Queensland concerns about the collection of intercolonial trade tariffs led to Wallangarra being designated as a border customs post until Federation, when the customs service was discontinued. At the end of the 19th century the high level of trade ensured the rapid development of the town. The opening in 1930 of the more direct Kyogle railway line undermined Wallangarra's position. As road transport became more efficient and recession affected local primary industries, the town gradually declined. Recent renewed interest in the historic significance of the railway as a tourist attraction has led to the restoration of railway buildings and other town buildings.

19. Wallangarra Railway Station

This landmark to intercolonial rivalry was opened in 1888 when the final stage of the Southern Railway from Stanthorpe was completed. The Queensland-New South Wales state border runs through the middle of the railway station, a result of the prolonged dispute between the two governments about the location of the station and the point of break of gauge between the New South Wales and Queensland railway lines. The colonies were unable to agree on a standard railway gauge. Railway contractor George Bashford erected the station buildings comprising the passenger station, engine and goods sheds, and station-master's home. Wallangarra Station remained commercially important until well after World War II despite competition from the Kyogle interstate railway line and road transport. After the Sydney Mail service was discontinued in 1972, rail traffic was considerably reduced and the station was subsequently closed.

17 *Dr Roberts Waterhole, Girraween*
18 *Wallangarra township, c1887 (John Oxley Library)*
20 *The Old Customs House, Wallangarra*

20. Old Customs House, *New England Highway*

Recently reopened as the Customs House Cafe, this building originally housed the Queensland customs office. James Long was customs agent at Wallangarra in 1884. In the following year, he was made the customs officer and his residence became the customs office. Collection of customs duties on goods passing between New South Wales and Queensland was greatly resented by border residents and did much to provoke the move towards Federation. On Federation in 1901, the customs house was closed down. The building was later used as the postmaster's residence before returning to private ownership.

21. Surveyor's Blazed Tree, *New England Highway*

This was one of the trees marked by the government surveyor F.E. Roberts during his survey of the Queensland-New South Wales border, started in 1863. Roberts and his New South Wales counterpart, Rowland, working under extreme conditions, took two years to complete the border survey. The area had not been explored previously and the surveyors faced the task of finding a way through the virtually impenetrable forests of the high border ranges. The stump is now on the State border, overlooking the busy New England Highway.

21 *Border survey tree*

Sunshine Coast
Hinterland

MAP 7
Sunshine Coast Hinterland

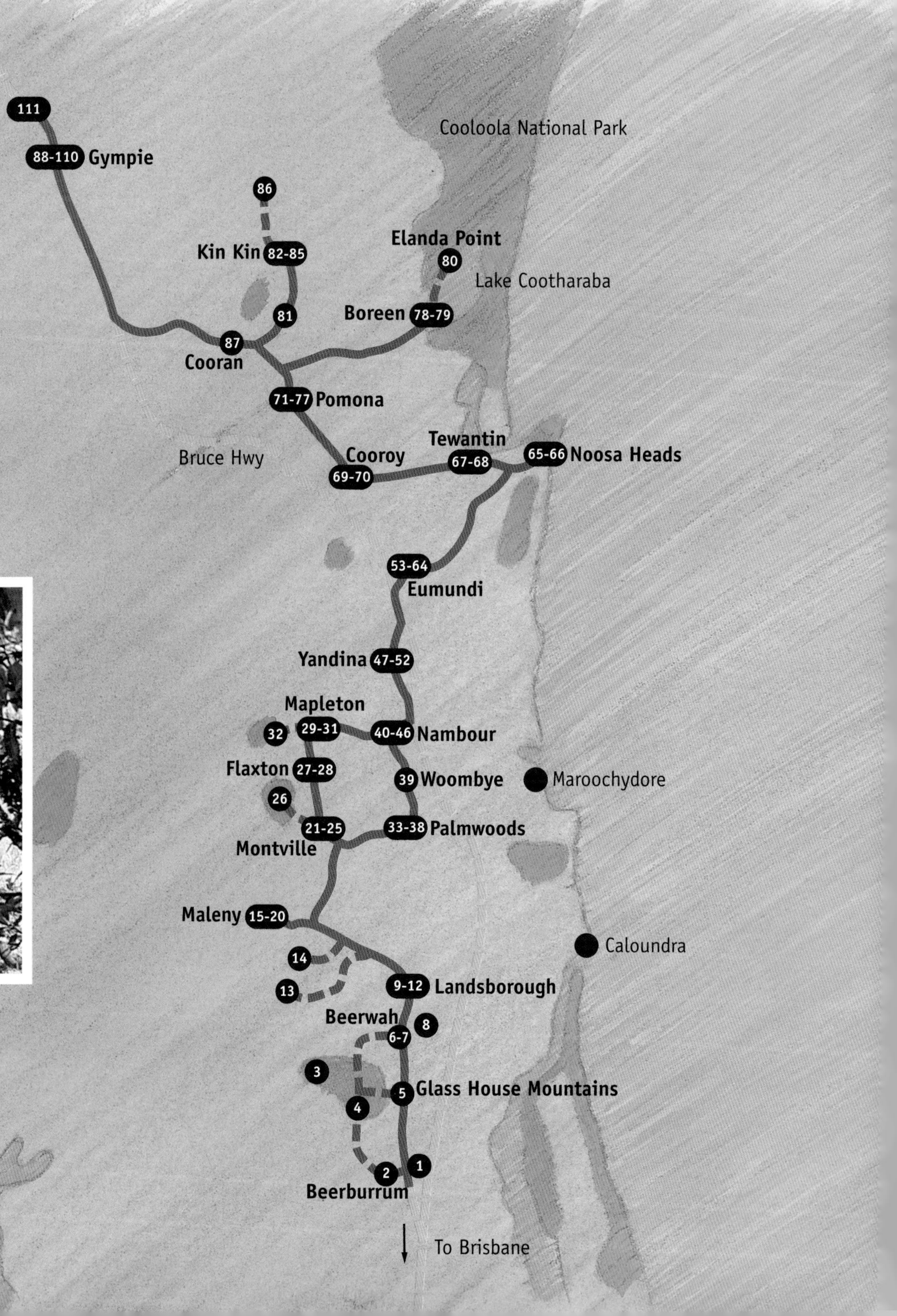

Cooloola National Park

111

88-110 Gympie

86

Kin Kin 82-85

Elanda Point

80

Lake Cootharaba

81

Boreen 78-79

87

Cooran

71-77 Pomona

Bruce Hwy

Tewantin

Cooroy 67-68

69-70

65-66 Noosa Heads

53-64

Eumundi

Yandina 47-52

Mapleton

32 29-31

40-46 Nambour

Flaxton 27-28

26

39 Woombye

Maroochydore

21-25

33-38 Palmwoods

Montville

Maleny 15-20

14

Caloundra

13

9-12 Landsborough

Beerwah 8

6-7

3

5 Glass House Mountains

4

2 1

Beerburrum

To Brisbane

The Sunshine Coast hinterland provides an enjoyable contrast to the sandy beaches of the coast. Surf and sand give way to scattered dairy farms and fields of sugarcane and pineapples. The trail starts on the Old Bruce Highway at the former soldier settlement village of Beerburrum. Travel past the monolithic volcanic peaks of the Glass House Mountains to Landsborough, nestled at the foot of the Blackall Range.

Climb the range to Maleny, a former timber town, and explore its arts and craft markets, restaurants and resorts. Take the ridge road to Montville, a town as close to a Swiss village as you'll find in Australia. Nearby is the quaint hamlet of Flaxton with its Devonshire tearooms and breathtaking coastal views, and Mapleton with its potteries and pub. Much of the area is protected as national park, or reserved as state forest. Take side trips to Kondalilla and Mapleton Falls national parks where remnants of the district's subtropical rainforest can still be enjoyed. From Mapleton, descend the range to the busy sugar-milling centre of Nambour where cane trains rumble along the main street during crushing season. Visit nearby Palmwoods, the district's fruit-growing centre, surrounded by a patchwork of farms set against the backdrop of the Blackall Range.

On leaving Yandina, detour off the highway to Eumundi and stroll down the historic main street with its restored shops and hotels. Mingle with the crowds at the regular Saturday morning market, a long-standing event full of colour, crafts and bargains. Cruise through Noosa, and then on to Tewantin at the southern gateway to Cooloola National Park, which protects part of the largest coastal sand dune and wetlands system in the world. Continue on to Pomona and Kin Kin, hinterland towns popular for their natural scenic backdrops and their rural Queensland atmosphere. See regular showings of early silent movies at the Majestic Theatre at Pomona, or enjoy a counter lunch at Kin Kin's Country Life Hotel.

Gympie is the 'town that saved Queensland' — a once-brash goldfield provincial centre, now an elegant old town whose streets are full of history. Begin your visit at one of Gympie's main tourist attractions, the Gold Mining Museum on Brisbane Road. Opposite are the remains of the old Scottish Gympie Battery, once the greatest gold producer on the field. Historic Gympie Railway Station is the terminus for the 'Mary Valley Rattler', the heritage steam train that goes to Kandanga and Imbil. Nearby on Calton Hill is St Patrick's Church, one of Gympie's best-known landmarks.

Enjoy a heritage walk along Mary Street, Gympie's main street, which follows the original teamsters' track 'as straight as a dog's hind leg'. Its narrow winding path is lined with some impressive heritage buildings including historic pubs, the former stock exchange offices and the Cooloola Shire Council Chambers. Channon Street, on Surface Hill, is the administrative hub, containing the Post Office, the Lands Office and the Court House. Before leaving Gympie, visit WoodWorks Timber and Forestry Museum, on the Bruce Highway north of the town. The museum features a working example of a steam-driven sawmill and demonstrations of early timber-cutting techniques.

Mapleton Falls National Park: view from the lookout

THE SUNSHINE COAST HINTERLAND

The mountainous terrain, dense rainforest and the numerous rivers and creeks of the north coast were major influences on the district's early history. The rivers and creeks were barriers to the establishment of land transport and communication routes. At the same time, they provided the means of access from the sea by which the region was opened up for settlement. The coastal hinterland from Maroochy to Wide Bay was first explored from the sea by Andrew Petrie during several expeditions in the early 1840s. Timber-cutters employed by Petrie were first on the Maroochy River in the 1860s, while others went north to the Noosa River. Sheep runs were taken up in the Upper Mary Valley in the 1840s, but the difficult conditions prevented any permanent occupation.

The catalyst for settlement of the district was the discovery of gold at Gympie in 1867. The rush that followed and the rich deposits mined until the 1920s brought thousands of people to the town. Permanent settlement of the Noosa River area was pioneered in the 1870s. The forests of cedar, beech and pine attracted logging companies that later established sawmills and settlements in the area. Once coastal vessels had access to the Noosa River, Tewantin became the port for the district.

In the 1860s land access from Brisbane was by the Gympie road, along which Cobb and Co. established a coach service in 1868. Hotels, stores and blacksmiths established at the rest stations on the road to serve teamsters and new settlers formed the basis of later settlements and towns. Transport problems and isolation from markets continued until connecting roads between the coast and mountain hinterland and the main Gympie road were slowly constructed. The completion of the Brisbane–Gympie section of the North Coast Railway in 1891 encouraged settlement and agricultural industries and townships emerged at railway sidings.

The Blackall Range settlements above the coastal hinterland relied initially on the district's rich timber resources. Soon dairying and fruit growing became important. Sugarcane growing became a major industry on the coastal hinterland after the opening of the Moreton Central Sugar mill in 1897. Nambour developed around the mill and became established as the administrative and business centre for the north coast. Towns became centres for co-operative associations for processing dairy and fruit products. Queensland's largest soldier settlement scheme was established in the Beerburrum district from 1915. Large tracts of forest were cleared for fruit and pineapple growing but the scheme had failed by the mid-1920s and by the 1950s the cleared land was being replanted as state forest.

Mellum Club Hotel, Landsborough, c1920 (John Oxley Library)

Henderson's Wharf, Tewantin, 1880 (John Oxley Library)

SUNSHINE COAST HINTERLAND HERITAGE TRAIL

1. Beerburrum Soldier Settlement

As early as 1915, the Queensland Government was proposing that land suitable for a 'lighter kind of farming' be set aside for returned servicemen. In 1916 unused Crown land near the Beerburrum Railway Siding was surveyed into 320 portions for pineapple farms. The Governor and the Premier travelled to Beerburrum by train and a ballot for the blocks was drawn by the Governor's wife. By 1921 Beerburrum had become the largest soldier settlement in Australia. Farm life was difficult, however. The land was poor, the returned soldiers were often sick and seldom experienced in farming, and few of the families had any experience of rural life. By 1925 many had abandoned their farms. A hospital, opened in the early 1920s, was closed in 1932 on the failure of the settlement and parts of the building were added to the Maleny Hospital.

2. Beerburrum

Anzac Avenue was the hub of the new soldier settlement township. An avenue of camphor laurel trees was planted in memory of those who fell in World War I. The school of arts, erected about 1918, was one of the first public buildings in the township. By 1921 Anzac Avenue also contained a State store and butcher shop, the Lands Department office, a boarding house, blacksmith, cafe and bakery. At the end of the street stood the railway station. Today only the school of arts and the avenue of trees survive.

3. Glass House Mountains National Park

Four of the ten distinct peaks of the Glass House Mountains – Beerwah, Tibrogargan, Ngungun and Coonowrin – were gazetted as national parks in 1954. The mountains are a series of steep-sided volcanic plugs of trachyte and rhyolite formed during the Tertiary period, 24 million years ago. These volcanic plugs have been exposed by the erosion of enormous volumes of softer surrounding sandstone. The land between the peaks has been given over to agriculture, especially pineapple farming and introduced pine plantations. James Cook described the mountains in 1770 as 'glass houses' as they reminded him of the glass furnaces of his native Yorkshire.

They have been a subject for artists such as Conrad Martens in 1851, Douglas Scott Montagu in 1853, Fred Williams in 1971 and Lawrence Daws in 1980. Musical works such as John Gilfedder's 'Legend of Tibrogargan' (1986) and Robert Davidson's 'Tibrogargan' (1996) further testify to their broad-ranging appeal. The Glass House Mountains are of cultural significance to their traditional owners, the Gubbi Gubbi people, and a native title claim has been lodged for the national park. The Gubbi Gubbi hold that access to the top of the mountains should be restricted as the peaks are spiritual places that should be respected.

1. *Mango trees: Beerburrum soldier settlement*
3. *Glass House Mountains landscape*

4. Bankfoot House, *near Glass House Mountains*

This site on Old Gympie Road was once a coach stop on the original route to Gympie. Bankfoot House was built about 1868 for William and Mary Grigor, who were the only European residents in the locality until 1878. They ran the post office, a store and a butcher shop to supply the miners on their way to the new Gympie Goldfield. Bankfoot House was a horse change and a lunch stop for Cobb and Co. and also an overnight accommodation house. Patronage increased to such an extent that a second dwelling was built in 1878. The 1868 house was constructed of dressed flat logs, laid straight on the ground with no stumps. By 1930 the logs had rotted away and damaged the floor so the house was pulled down and the timber was used to construct extra rooms at the rear of the 1878 dwelling. Bankfoot House is still owned by descendants of William and Mary Grigor.

5. Glass House Mountains

The North Coast Line from Brisbane to Gympie was built to link the capital with the Gympie Goldfield and the timber reserves of the region. This section of the line to Landsborough was opened in 1890. Glass House Mountains Railway Station was originally named Coonowrin after one of the nearby peaks, and was renamed in 1914. A school of arts was established in 1916 and, as soldier settlement increased, a general store was located in the front of the hall. The building is still in use as the Glass House Mountains community hall.

4　*Bankfoot House*

6. Beerwah

William Simpson was logging in the area from the early 1870s. He erected a sawmill at Coochin Creek and opened a hotel nearby in 1881. The settlement became a rest stage for coaches and teamsters travelling between Brisbane and Gympie. James Mawhinney had also taken up land by 1889 and a community based on timber-getting developed. The area was named Beerwah after a siding on the North Coast Railway was established there in 1890.

In 1902 Beerwah became the centre for the first state forest reserves; it continued to play this role throughout the pine and hardwood plantation experiments carried out in the district until the late 1950s. Simpson built a second hotel near the railway station in 1915 and before 1920 Beerwah had a new school, post office, school of arts and church. In 1935 the Simpson estate was subdivided for farms. Pineapples became an important crop and a fruitgrowers co-operative was formed. Between 1949 and 1954, war refugees from Eastern Europe were located in the area as forestry workers. Although some remained to settle in the area, the scheme was not a success. The town continues as a district centre serving the timber and fruit-growing industries.

5　*Greave's store, Glass House Mountains, 1923 (John Oxley Library)*

7　*Mawhinney's Fig, Beerwah*

6　*Simpson's Beerwah Hotel, c1920 (John Oxley Library)*

7. Mawhinney's Fig Tree, *Beerwah Parade*

James Mawhinney planted this fig tree about 1897 near his home on the Old Gympie Road. It is now surrounded by the township of Beerwah, and stands outside the local BP garage.

8. Beerwah–Beerburrum State Forest

The earliest reservations of forest lands in the Beerwah–Beerburrum district occurred in 1902 as the depletion of private timber resources became evident. In 1924, an experimental station was established at Beerwah to trial softwood species from the United States. The first plantings of exotic pine were made in 1931. Unused land set aside for soldier settlements was also made available for pine plantations. The planting program declined during World War II, but continued after the war. In 1947, with the expansion of pine planting at Beerburrum, a new forestry office was built. Between 1949 and 1954, displaced persons from Eastern Europe were sent to work at Beerwah–Beerburrum.

Work continued during the 1950s and the Beerwah–Beerburrum plantations became key areas in the reforestation programs of the State. From 1967, loans from the Commonwealth under a softwood forestry agreement led to even more plantation establishment, resulting in some of the largest private pine plantations in Queensland when Australian Paper Manufacturers commenced planting. By the 1970s, between 800 and 1200 hectares of pine forest were being planted each year in the Beerwah–Beerburrum district.

9. Landsborough

Isaac Burgess, a carrier supplying the Gympie goldfields, selected land on the north side of Mellum Creek in 1871. He built a slab hut that served as the way-station for the Cobb and Co. coach service to Gympie. Five years later, he built a hotel, general store and butcher shop that became a stop for teamsters and settlers opening up the Blackall Ranges and the coastal area around Caloundra.

James Campbell established a sawmill on the creek at Campbellville in 1880. In the late 1880s, Campbell bought Burgess's first block and had it surveyed and sold for town allotments. His firm also built a hotel and a number of houses for mill workers on these allotments.

When the North Coast Railway extension from Caboolture was opened in 1890, a new settlement developed around the railway station at Mellum Creek. It was renamed Landsborough, in honour of the explorer William Landsborough who was farming on his land grant at Caloundra. Improved road and transport facilities and the downturn in local agriculture and dairying contributed to Landsborough's gradual decline as a commercial centre after World War II, and the decline worsened when the new north coast highway bypassed the town in the 1980s. Reminders of Landsborough's pioneering history are still evident in the town, which remains important as the social centre for the district and the gateway to the Blackall Ranges.

10. Mellum Club Hotel, *Cribb Street*

Around 1914, Burgess's hotel, renamed the Mellum Club Hotel, was hauled on skids to a more central location opposite the railway station. It was the first of several buildings relocated within the town over the following years. During this period, the town was the administrative and commercial centre for Landsborough Shire. Its expansion was largely due to its importance as the principal link with Brisbane for the timber, dairying and fruit-growing industries of the Blackall Ranges.

11. Landsborough Railway Station

The North Coast Railway from Caboolture to Landsborough was opened in 1890. Halfway between Brisbane and Gympie, the station became a refreshment stop for passengers. The refreshment room, which stood on the southern side of the station building, remained in use until it was removed in 1971. The reinforced-concrete air raid shelter, built during World War II as the station was a regular refreshment stop, was one of many constructed at important stations at the time. Only a few now survive.

11 *Air raid shelter, Landsborough*

10 *Shifting the Mellum Club Hotel, c1914 (John Oxley Library)*

12. Landsborough Shire Office, *Maleny Street*

Formerly part of Caboolture Shire, Landsborough became a separate shire in 1912. The first council meeting was held in 1913 in a newly constructed shire office and clerk's residence. New chambers built in 1924 provided the council with more spacious office and meeting rooms. In 1968 Landsborough Shire was absorbed into Caloundra City Council and Caloundra became the administrative centre for the district. The building remained empty until the Landsborough Historical Society converted it to a museum in 1976.

13. Inigo Jones House, *Crohamhurst Road*

Inigo Jones arrived in Brisbane with his family in 1874. His interest in meteorology led to his becoming an assistant to the Queensland Government Meteorologist by the mid-1880s. In 1892, Jones's father established a dairy farm in the Blackall Range, which he named Crohamhurst. He was soon joined by his son. Although Inigo Jones preferred long-range weather forecasting to dairy farming, he and his wife continued to run the property as a dairy farm after his father's death. He worked as a meteorologist in Brisbane from 1927 until 1934, when he began planning an observatory at the farm. In 1953 he employed an assistant, Robert Lennox Walker. Although Walker was employed for only 18 months before Jones died in 1954, he subsequently became well known as Queensland's long-range weather forecaster.

Today the observatory is on private land, but the house site is within state forest, marked by a number of large mango trees off Crohamhurst Road. Beneath the undergrowth are the footings of the Jones house, pathways and ornamental plants. The school site nearby is now overgrown by a pine plantation.

14. Mary Cairncross Park

The Blackall Ranges attracted timber-getters as early as the 1860s. Isaac Burgess was the first selector on the range, in 1878 taking up an area that included the present Mary Cairncross Park. Mary Cairncross, the daughter of William Cairncross, after whom Cairncross Dry Dock in Brisbane is named, married A.J. Thynne, a Member of the Legislative Council until 1923 and Minister for Agriculture. The Thynne family became prominent members of the Maleny community.

The area now incorporated in Mary Cairncross Park is said to have been clear-felled during the 1920s. Timber obtained included hoop and bunya pine, cedar, ash, black bean and hickory. Some black bean stumps remain. The last logging in the area is said to have taken place about 1939. Mary Thynne was concerned for the conservation of the area. In 1941, her three daughters arranged for the present reserve to be bequeathed to the Landsborough Shire Council 'for the preservation, conservation and exhibition of the natural flora and fauna' and in memory of their mother. The park was officially opened in 1960.

13 *Crohamhurst school site*

15 *Maleny township, c1922 (John Oxley Library)*

15. Maleny

The town of Maleny officially dates from 1891. The area was first settled in 1878 by the carrier and timber merchant Isaac Burgess, whose original selection now forms part of Mary Cairncross Park. Other settlers followed and in 1880 a track was cut linking Maleny with Landsborough. As timber-getters cleared the rainforest and dairying became established, the town of Maleny took shape. By the early 1900s, private homes and businesses associated with the timber, carrying and dairy industries had been built on the ridge beyond Obi Obi Creek.

In 1904, the Maleny Butter Factory commenced operations in Maple Street, to be followed by a sawmill, the Farmers Co-operative Store, Maleny Hotel and the English, Scottish and Australian Bank. The town was the centre of the local timber industry until the 1950s. In 1914, a second, larger butter factory was opened and access to Landsborough was improved. During the 1920s and 1930s, improved roads attracted new settlers and for many years fruit growing was as important as dairying. In recent years, following the decline of its traditional primary industries, Maleny has enjoyed renewed prosperity from tourism and residential development.

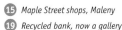 *Maple Street shops, Maleny*

19 *Recycled bank, now a gallery*

16. Naked Vicar Restaurant,
Maple Street

Built in 1935 as the Baptist Church, the building was sold in 1990 when the congregation moved to a larger church. The building was used as an antiques centre before being converted to a restaurant.

17. Maleny Police Station,
Maple Street

Maleny's campaign for a police station began in the 1920s, but it was not until 1952 that permission was granted to convert a private house into the present police station and residence.

18. Maleny Lodge Guesthouse,
Maple Street

The house was built in 1909 for A.C. Cooke and his family of ten children. Cooke started farming at Teutoberg, now Witta, in 1904. He also owned the Maleny Hotel for a time and in 1910 opened an auctioneering business. Constructed of beech and pine and originally named Rosedale, the house was converted into a boarding house, Allawah, in 1924. From the 1930s, it was a highly regarded guesthouse catering for the growing number of visitors to the area. While the original structural elements and appearance have been retained, the interior of the house has been extensively renovated to meet modern accommodation requirements. The landscaped gardens slope down to the creek that once provided the town's water supply.

19. Former English, Scottish and Australian Bank,
Maple Street

In 1908, the English, Scottish and Australian Bank opened its Maleny branch in the Co-operative Store. In 1923, when larger premises were needed, a new bank office with an adjoining manager's residence was erected next to the store. The bank closed in 1959 and the building was occupied by a real estate firm before becoming an art gallery.

20. Maleny Butter Factory,
Fig Street

The difficulties of transporting cream by pack horse down the mountain to the railway at Landsborough led to the construction of the Maleny Co-operative Dairy Association's first butter factory, opened in 1905. Local suppliers and factory production increased and a larger factory with more modern refrigeration and processing equipment was built in 1912. The business expanded to become the largest industry in the district, remaining profitable until the 1970s. The present brick building was constructed in 1940, with extensions added later. A progressive approach to production extended the life of the factory: a plant for the conversion of milk to casein was installed. In 1978, as milk supplies and markets declined, the Maleny factory amalgamated with the Caboolture Co-operative Dairy Association. It ceased production in 1981 and the building is now the Maleny Enterprise Centre.

21. Montville

Timber-getters on the western slopes of the Blackall Range were the first settlers at Montville in the late 1880s. The site was adjacent to Remington's Chute, down which logs were sent before there was a road along the ranges. Henry Smith opened a store at Razorback in the mid-1890s and a provisional school was soon opened for the families of timber-getters. In 1898 residents successfully petitioned for the school's name to be changed to Montville, named for Smith's birthplace in Connecticut, USA. With George Butt, Smith pioneered the fruit industry, which, together with timber, remained Montville's principal industry.

The town became popular as a mountain resort from about 1900. Montville's most prosperous decade was the 1920s, when the fruit industry revived, more farms were taken up and many of the town's present buildings and houses were erected. The road to Palmwoods was completed in 1929 and access to Maleny and Landsborough improved as the use of motor transport became more widespread. In 1959 the town became the setting for Eleanor Dark's novel *Lantana Lane*.

Although Montville has enjoyed a steady popularity with artists and people seeking a beneficial mountain climate, like other towns on the ranges it has experienced a recent revival as a tourist centre.

22. Misty's Restaurant, *Montville–Mapleton Road*

Misty's was originally an observatory. It occupies the site of the first store and post office at Razorback. Alf Smith, a retired sea captain, built the observatory in 1927 to house a telescope. He apparently started by erecting a windmill frame to support the observation room at the top. When that was completed, he filled in the floors below. Very few nails were used in the construction, the timber joints being morticed. Occupied in the early 1970s by an art gallery and craft shop, the ground floor was reconstructed and the walls were lined with slashed pine in preparation for the opening of the restaurant in 1977.

21 *Razorback road coach at Montville store, c1914 (John Oxley Library)*

22 *Misty's Restaurant, Montville*

24 *Montville School of Arts and Memorial Gates*

23. St Mary's Anglican Church, *Montville–Mapleton Road*

The church was constructed in 1914. The bell tower was replaced with a new tower in 1989.

24. Montville School of Arts, *Montville–Mapleton Road*

The hall was completed in 1903 as the Montville School of Arts and in 1920 was dedicated as a memorial hall to commemorate district residents who had taken part in World War I. Their names are inscribed on the honour boards in the hall. The memorial gates were erected in 1921. The weeping figs shading the village park date from the same period.

25. RSL Memorial Hall, *Montville–Mapleton Road*

This was constructed in 1942 by the Montville branch of the RSL, which continued to use the building until the branch was disbanded in 1978. The hall was subsequently transferred to the trusteeship of the neighbouring St Mary's Anglican Church.

26. Kondalilla National Park

The Blackall Range landscape was shaped by volcanic activity that occurred 24 million years ago. Kondalilla's deep gorges, ridges and escarpments were carved from basalt lava that erupted from volcanoes south-west of Maleny. Its outstanding scenic attractions include a deep waterfall gorge, rock pools and creeks, and cool rainforest. The rare, threatened and geographically restricted wildlife species within the subtropical rainforest and tall open forest are of scientific value. Kondalilla National Park protects remnant warm subtropical rainforest, which supports the most easterly surviving stands of emergent bunya pine, and vulnerable plant species including the red lilly pilly and the bopple nut. Kondalilla Falls was protected in 1906 as a recreational area and was declared a national park in 1945. In 1989 Kondalilla was linked to Obi Obi National Park.

27. Flaxton

Flaxton took its name from the farm of an early settler, named after Flaxton Hall Farm in England. Joseph Dixon, who was growing sugarcane at Buderim, is credited with opening up this section of the Blackall Range. A visit in 1882 led to his selecting land there, which he gradually cleared from about 1892 to grow bananas and citrus fruit. Dixon and his family, together with William Skene's family, were the leading developers of Flaxton for many years. The road along the ranges was completed in 1909, opening up more farming land, and fruit farming and dairying were well established by the 1920s.

26 *The falls: Kondalilla National Park*
28 *Tanderra Guesthouse, Flaxton*

To assist local fruit growers, the Flaxton fruit-packing shed was opened in 1931. Modelled on the system used in California, it was the first shed to grade and pack an entire district's harvest. A sawmill built in the early 1930s by Hamilton Sawmills operated until it was burnt down in 1956. Flaxton's growth failed to match that of other towns on the ranges but the pleasant climate, spectacular views and peaceful environment continue to attract artists and holidaymakers.

28. Tanderra Guesthouse, *Montville–Mapleton Road*

This was originally Chermside House, built by Joseph Dixon for his family in 1903 to replace a slab hut erected in 1892. In 1896, Dixon and his family moved to Gympie where he ran the Busy Bee Shoe Shop. Dixon returned to Flaxton in 1903 and built Chermside, named for Lord Chermside, the Governor of Queensland. Originally a timber cottage, the house was extended and altered over the years, its rooms used for different purposes as family numbers and needs changed.

A garden pavilion, now dismantled, was used by the family as a summer living room; apparently of considerable size, it had four large timber entrance doors. Major extensions to the house were carried out in the 1970s and it has been operated as a guesthouse since the late 1980s. Photographs showing the Dixon family at Chermside are on display in the guesthouse.

29. Mapleton

Mapleton was pioneered by fruit growers and the fruit-growing industry was largely responsible for its early prosperity. The Smith brothers of Redland Bay were the first settlers, taking up land near Mapleton Falls to grow bananas. The red cedar and beech they cleared from the land was hauled down the precipitous Dalziel's Pinch track to Nambour. From 1891, as the planting of fruit, vegetables and cereal crops proved successful, more settlers were attracted to the area. The town was referred to by its postal address, Luton Vale, until 1899, when the school was opened and the name was changed to that of a village in England.

The road from the Mary Valley through Mapleton was opened in 1906 and, with improvements to other connecting roads, the timber industry became important. A sawmill was operating by 1909 and, with other mills, produced fruit and butter boxes for local farmers. The mill continued to process timber from nearby forestry reserves until it closed in 1972. In 1914, the Maroochy Shire Council purchased a tramway built by the Moreton Sugar Mill in Nambour and extended it to Mapleton. It brought increasing numbers of visitors from Nambour to enjoy the area's natural beauty and healthy climate. Pineapples, dairying and small crops supported a farming population until the late 1950s. Since then, Mapleton has functioned as the centre of a small farm and residential holiday area for an increasing number of visitors drawn by its scenic beauty.

30. Mapleton Tavern, *Obi Obi Road*

The Mapleton Hotel was built in 1909 by W.H. Rosser, who opened the Mapleton Sawmill the same year. With the increase in holidaymakers visiting the mountain settlements, it became known as one of the finest hotels on the north coast. It survived the fires that destroyed Mapleton's two large guesthouses and has been considerably renovated by successive owners. Despite improvements, many of the exterior and interior Federation features have been preserved.

31. Mapleton Public Hall, *Obi Obi Road*

Public meetings were held at the school until the erection of the first community hall in 1910. The original hall was destroyed in a bushfire and the present building was erected and opened in 1916. The hall was used for regular weekly picture shows during the 1940s and 1950s.

32. Mapleton Falls National Park

The Blackall Ranges were once a focal point for Aboriginal bunya festivals, but were extensively logged following European settlement. About 1840 Tom Petrie accompanied Aboriginal groups to a bunya festival in the Blackall Ranges; as a result of this visit and in recognition of the special relationship that Aborigines had with the bunya pine, Governor Gipps of New South Wales in 1842 passed a decree that reserved for Aboriginal people those places covered by the bunya pine. This effectively prevented the logging of the trees. One of the first actions of the newly separated colony of Queensland was revocation of this decree in 1860. In 1938 Mapleton Falls became a forestry reserve for recreational purposes, before being declared a national park in 1973.

33. Palmwoods

Palmwoods was originally known as Merriman's Flat, the name of the property of the first European settlers, the Kuskopf family, who arrived in 1881. After the arrival of the railway in 1891 the name was changed to Palmwoods, because of the abundance of piccabeen palms in the area. By 1900 Palmwoods had developed into a small township centred on the timber industry. Commercial fruit farming began about 1912. The tramway connection with Buderim, opened in 1914, improved access to the area and encouraged new settlers. The biggest growth was experienced in the post-World War I period. Banana growing was important, but pineapples were the principal crop and Palmwoods became the leading centre for the industry. Many of Palmwoods' present buildings were erected during the 1920s, when economic stability fostered a very active community life. The town itself remains relatively unchanged from that time and is one of the biggest pineapple and citrus loading centres in south-east Queensland.

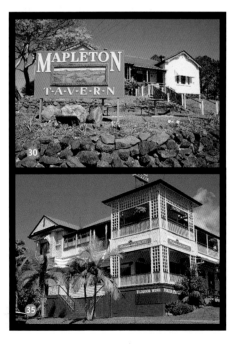

33 *Main Street, Palmwoods, 1917 (John Oxley Library)*

34. St Augustine's Anglican Church, *Hill Street*

This block was purchased by the Anglican Church during the first Palmwoods land sale in Brisbane in 1891. Completed in 1925, the church was dedicated by Bishop Le Fanu of Brisbane in commemoration of St Augustine of Canterbury. The Anglican church is the only original land purchaser still present in the township.

35. Palmwoods Hotel, *Paskins Road*

Built as the Railway Hotel after the tramway from Buderim was constructed in 1914, this hotel was renamed in 1926. The original two-storey timber building had open verandahs and a decorative pavilion on the upper storey. Most of the verandahs are now enclosed, the ground floor interior has been modernised and several brick extensions have been added.

30 *Mapleton Tavern*
35 *Palmwoods Hotel*

36. Palmwoods Railway Station

The North Coast Line from Brisbane to Gympie was built to provide Brisbane merchants with access to Gympie after a line from the port of Maryborough to Gympie was opened in 1881. Construction commenced from Sandgate in 1888 and this section from Landsborough to Yandina, along the foothills of the Blackall Range, was opened in 1891. Brisbane and Gympie were connected during that year.

37. Palmwoods Memorial Hall, *Main Street*

The hall was constructed in 1922 in memory of those from Palmwoods who served and died in World War I. It replaced the old school of arts building, which had become too small for concerts, dances and other community events. The standard of maintenance and the modernised brick entrance emphasise its continuing importance as a community centre for the district.

38. Kolora Park Lagoon

During World War II the freshwater lagoon that now forms the centre of Kolora Park was used to provide water for troops stationed throughout the district. A drinking fountain now marks the site of a pump house and overhead tank from which water was gravity-fed into trucks for distribution to soldiers at gun emplacements and observation points from Noosa to Caloundra.

39. Woombye Cemetery, *Palmwoods—Montville Road*

With its avenue of huge Moreton Bay figs, the cemetery contains the graves of many soldiers who died in the district from accidents and illness during World War II.

39 *Moreton Bay figs at Woombye Cemetery*

40. Nambour

The Nambour district was taken up as grazing land in the 1870s. George Etheridge operated a sawmill for local timber-getters at the earliest settlement, known as Petrie's Creek. In 1891, when the railway was extended from Yandina, the name was changed to Nambour, named after an early grazing run. Sugarcane farming expanded during the 1880s and, as the railhead for the district, Nambour had become the main centre by the mid-1890s. The opening of the Moreton sugar mill in 1897 provided a sound economic base for a growing local workforce.

Public services, business facilities and community associations followed. The town became the administrative, education and commercial centre for the rapidly expanding north coast region. After a devastating fire in 1924, many of the early timber buildings in the main streets were replaced by substantial brick structures. Nambour remained stable through the economic downturn of the 1950s as sugarcane, timber, dairying and fruit growing continued to be productive industries.

The Bruce Highway deviation constructed in 1990 relieved much of the local traffic congestion, but Nambour continues to grow as the centre for the district's residential and tourism development.

37 *Palmwoods Memorial Hall*
40 *Cane train, Nambour, c1939 (John Oxley Library)*

41. Nambour Hospital Nurses Quarters, *Hospital Road*

This building, the earliest surviving section of Nambour Hospital, was completed in 1942. Moves to establish a general hospital at Nambour began in 1922 when the Maroochy Shire Council approached the government for a maternity ward under Labor's commitment to developing better facilities for mothers. The original proposal was for a general hospital ward, administration block and isolation ward. Work on the administration block, which contained the nurses quarters, was not completed until 1928, however. By 1937 the nurses quarters had been found to be inadequate and the Nambour Hospitals Board engaged architects to develop a scheme for a new hospital including new nurses quarters. Before plans could be finalised, the Nambour Hospital was included within the Brisbane and South Coast Hospitals District. The new board reconsidered the plans and increased the provision for nurses. It was not until 1941 that the board was successful in securing funds to carry out the works.

42. Nambour Uniting Church, *Currie Street*

St Andrew's was the first Presbyterian church in the north coast district. Built largely by volunteer labour, it was dedicated in 1910. Later it was removed to the present church site. In 1956, after a new St Andrew's church was built, the original church was converted for use as the church hall. In 1987 the church suffered some damage from a fire that destroyed the early hall.

41 *Nurses quarters, Nambour Hospital*

43. Club Hotel, *Currie Street*

The first Club Hotel was built around 1908. It burnt down in 1938 and was rebuilt soon after. The hotel was extensively improved and extended in 1960.

44. St Joseph's Convent Boarding School, *Currie Street*

Once the only boarding school for Catholic students living in the north coast district, St Joseph's was opened by Archbishop Duhig in 1925. The school was designed by the Brisbane architects Cavanagh and Cavanagh and the builder was a Mr I. Casey who had built the Catholic presbytery at Gympie. The ground floor had reception and music rooms, and a kitchen and separate dining rooms for the nuns and students. A porch with inlaid tiles led to a sweeping staircase to the upper dormitory floor, which was enclosed by verandahs on three sides. St Joseph's Church next door was opened in 1951 to replace an earlier church built in 1921.

44 *St Joseph's Convent School, Nambour*

45. Moreton Sugar Mill, *Mill Street*

Maroochy sugar farmers formed a co-operative association in 1894 to establish a sugar mill in Nambour. The mill was built by H. and W. Smith in 1896 and the first cane was crushed in 1897. Almost immediately, drought affected supplies and production. In 1901 and 1902, tramways were built to district settlements to transport cane to the mill. Horses were used until they were replaced by steam engines in 1906. By 1902 the outlay on these tramways contributed to a financial crisis in the mill's management, which resulted in the mill being taken over by the State Government and restructured as a central mill administered by the Central Sugar Bureau.

Production problems continued through the 1930s, but with more experienced growers and higher yields the mill maintained the highest relative output of any mill south of Mackay. The steam engine that had crushed the cane since 1926 was replaced by a powerful steam turbine in 1981. The mill and the tramway have been popular tourist attractions since the 1920s. The mill was taken over by the British-based Bundaberg Sugar Limited in 1997 and is now known as the Moreton Mill.

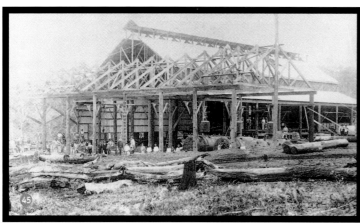

46. Moreton Sugar Mill Manager's House, *Bury Street*

When the mill opened in 1897, accommodation had to be built for the mill staff. A two-storey barracks and workers' cottages were built near the mill gate. Two cottages were also built for the mill manager and the company secretary. As more of the mill's operations became automated, there was less need for management to live at the mill. The original workers' accommodation was demolished in 1979 and the remaining manager's house was converted to provide additional office space.

47. Yandina

Daniel and Zacharias Skyring were the first Europeans to occupy the Maroochy district in 1853. They were granted leases on three cattle runs. Two of the runs, Canando and Yandina, had frontages to the Maroochy and South Maroochy rivers. In 1868 James Low built a hotel at the South Maroochy crossing, naming it Mooroochie House. Low later established a post office on the Yandina boundary and this took the name of the run.

Yandina settlement grew up around the post office. Cattle and cane farming developed during the late 19th century and have remained the economic mainstays of the area. To attract settlers to the district, the government instructed the Surveyor-General to find a suitable site for a new town.

In 1870 Surveyor Fryer suggested the settlement of Yandina as an ideal location for the 'metropolis' of the Maroochy district. The settlement was referred to as Yandina until Low's death in 1883, when it became known locally as Maroochy. In 1891 the post office was transferred to the new railway station, which was named Yandina. Though cedar supplies were exhausted by the 1890s, timber-getting and sawmilling sustained the economy of the district until the 1960s, when the shortage of available timber finally took effect. Low was experimenting with growing sugarcane at the South Maroochy crossing by 1877 and Yandina has now become one of the most productive areas in the Moreton cane district. The Yandina Ginger Factory, established in 1980, is one of the district's major tourist attractions.

45 *Construction of Moreton Central Mill, 1896 (John Oxley Library)*

45 *Moreton sugar mill, Nambour*

48 *John Low's house at Yandina*

48. Koongalba House, *Wharf Street*

This timber house was erected in 1894 for John Low, a prominent member of the Maroochy community and the eldest son of James Low, who was involved in the development of the timber industry in the Maroochy area from the 1860s. John took over the family timber and grazing businesses on his father's death in 1883. He became engaged to Louisa Bury in 1893 and began planning construction of a new house on a portion of the family estate on Wharf Street. The house was completed and occupied by 1894. John Low died in 1914, following a logging accident, and his wife lived in the house until her death in 1957. The house remained vacant until 1970, when it was purchased by a granddaughter of John and Louisa Low. The house was named Koongalba in 1994, to mark the centenary of its construction.

49. Yandina Railway Station

This section of the North Coast Railway was completed in 1891, but the Yandina Station office was built at a later date and demonstrates the railway's gradual completion. The station complex, which includes a goods shed and whip crane, is visually associated with the Yandina Hotel and Memorial Gardens. Railway buildings that have recently been removed include the engine shed and the station-master's house.

50. Yandina Hotel,
Railway Street

In addition to his post office, store and butcher shop, the early settler James Low operated the Mooroochie House hotel until his death in 1883, whereupon the licence lapsed. Yandina was without a hotel for five years until J.G. Sommer built the Australian Hotel on the Gympie road about 1888. With the arrival of the railway in 1891, the hotel was shifted to its present site opposite the railway station. Put on skids and hauled by bullock teams, the hotel continued to trade during the journey, which took several days. The hotel has had many owners since Sommer and has more recently been renamed the Yandina Hotel.

51. Yandina School of Arts,
Farrell Street

At a public meeting of the Yandina Progress Association in 1916 it was voted to establish a school of arts. The building was completed by October that year and was opened by the Home Secretary. By 1936 a billiard saloon and shops beneath the hall had been converted into a supper room. The library was opened in 1917 and remained in use until 1976. The hall has been adapted to meet changing community needs for over 80 years.

52. All Saints Anglican Church,
Farrell Street

Built in 1878, All Saints Church is one of the earliest buildings in the township. A place of worship for over 120 years, it reflects the economy with which early community buildings in developing settlements were erected. The church was built of pit-sawn beech and was opened by the Reverend Bailey of Gympie in 1880. The building was used by the general community until 1919, when the Anglican Diocese of Brisbane bought the property for its exclusive use. All Saints continues to be used for church services.

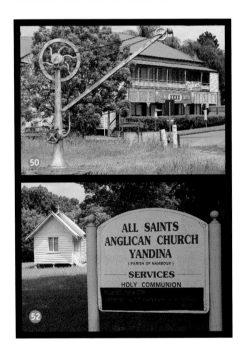

50 Yandina Hotel from the railway station
52 All Saints Church, Yandina

53. Eumundi

The early development of Eumundi, now famous for its Saturday markets and craft stalls, was associated with the extension of the North Coast Railway in 1890–91. Henry Fullagher's original selection was surveyed and sold for town blocks in 1890. Following the closure of the railway Main Camp in 1891, the settlement grew as business premises and public buildings formed the town centre around Cook Street. Eumundi was then known as Eerwah, after Mount Eerwah, but was later renamed to avoid confusion with Beerwah. Once the bridge replaced the railway gates, the town centre moved to Main Street, later renamed Memorial Drive.

Improved roads increased Eumundi's importance as the hub of the district's transport services and, with two sawmills and a butter factory in operation, it enjoyed several decades of prosperity. This prosperity came to an end in the early 1970s, when markets for timber and dairy products declined and the north coast highway was rerouted to bypass the town. A decade later, the successful tourism promotion that began with the Saturday markets had established Eumundi as a fashionable art and crafts centre. Although some changes are evident, the character of Eumundi's townscape has been little altered since the 1920s.

54. Eumundi School of Arts,
Memorial Drive

A school of arts committee was formed in 1904 to raise funds for a hall to replace the barn in which local dances and concerts were held. Completed in 1908, the hall was extended in 1912 to a split-level structure with the public rooms and library installed on the lower level. Silent movies with piano accompaniment were popular in the 1920s and the projector for the 'talkies' installed in the early 1930s is still in place.

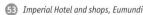
53 *Imperial Hotel and shops, Eumundi*

55. Eumundi Methodist Church, *Memorial Drive*

The Eumundi Methodist Church opened in 1911 on the site of the former Salvation Army hall erected in 1894. Funded by public subscriptions and built by volunteers using timber cut and milled in the town, it served the Methodist congregation until the mid-1970s. In 1996 it was reopened as the Eumundi Historical Museum.

56. Memorial Fig Trees, *Memorial Drive*

Many types of war memorials are found throughout Queensland, but avenues of trees are relatively uncommon. Eighty-seven men from Eumundi and the surrounding district served in World War I and trees were planted to honour the twenty who died. The impetus for the planting of the memorial trees was provided by the Eumundi Women's Patriotic Committee.

The original trees were figs, of which only five survive; the rest have been replaced with other species including camphor laurels, lilly pillies and jacarandas. They remain significant to the community, as shown by the decision made in 1977 to change the name of Main Street to Memorial Drive. The trees are the focal point for remembrance ceremonies on Anzac Day.

57. Country Women's Association Rooms, *Memorial Drive*

The Eumundi branch of the Queensland Country Women's Association was formed in 1927 and opened the rest rooms in 1929. Within twelve months, dedicated local fundraising had paid off the debt on the modest timber and fibro building. Situated close to the railway station, the rooms were available for train travellers, while the Child Welfare Clinic provided services for children travelling alone. Extended several times over the years, the rooms have been used for dances, concerts and church services. They now provide facilities for stallholders at the Saturday markets.

58. Cane Cutters' Barracks, *Memorial Drive*

In the early 1970s, Eumundi suffered a severe economic decline after the timber mill and the butter factory closed down and the highway was diverted to bypass the town. In 1975, concerned residents formed the Eumundi and District Historical Association to preserve the town's historic buildings. In 1983 the Association bought this two-storey building, previously used as cane cutters' barracks in the Maroochy River area. Relocated to the present site, it remains little altered from its original character and structure. It housed the Eumundi Historical Museum displays from 1985 until 1996, when it became the Association's headquarters.

56 *Memorial fig trees, Eumundi*
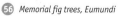
57 *Country Women's Association rooms*

59. Eumundi Antiques Store, *Memorial Drive*

A branch of the Bank of New South Wales was established in this small building in 1909. It was found to be unsuitable for bank business and the branch moved to the former Corner Store. An unusual brick edifice in a street of timber buildings, it was later used as a storeroom for the adjacent Kenilworth Co-operative Association store, opened in 1917, and then as the premises of the Old Bank Pharmacy. It is now an antiques store.

60. Joe's Waterhole Hotel, *Memorial Drive*

Eumundi's first hotel, the Railway, was built on this site in 1890. Soon after, the licence was transferred to the town's leading businessman, E.H. Arundell. His son Sidney took over in 1900 and renamed it the Eumundi Hotel. It became the Commercial Hotel around 1908, when Edgar Jefferies was the licensee. Destroyed in the 1925 fire that started in Arundell's store, the hotel was rebuilt as the Commercial and later underwent several alterations and extensions. In 1988, Ray Whiting renamed the hotel after his father Joe, who had previously owned it.

61. Eumundi Motors, *Memorial Drive*

These premises are important for their association with George Adams, a noted coachbuilder, successful businessman and respected community leader. After leaving Charleville, where he had learnt his craft at Cobb and Co.'s coachbuilding factory, Adams opened a blacksmith and wheelwright's shop in Cook Street in 1913. He gradually extended his business to include a garage servicing the increasing number of cars and trucks in the district. Later he moved the business to the present building, where he also sold cars. Before his death in 1961, he worked for many years as an auctioneer and land valuer. Much of the original internal structure of the garage remains intact.

62. Imperial Hotel, *Memorial Drive*

The first hotel on the site was built about 1910; its licensee was Edgar Jefferies, formerly of Yandina. Destroyed by fire in 1926, the hotel was rebuilt the following year as a first-class hotel boasting the best dining room on the north coast. Profiting from the thriving district and Eumundi's location on the main northern rail and road routes, the Imperial maintained its popularity over several decades. A prominent feature of the town's main street, the hotel enjoyed recent fame as the home of the Eumundi Brewery. Crafts shops now occupy the original brewing and bottling hall.

59 *Bank of N.S.W. and the Commercial Hotel (John Oxley Library)*

60 *Joe's Waterhole Hotel*

62 *Imperial Hotel, c1918 (John Oxley Library)*

63. Old Bakery, *Memorial Drive*

This was the town's first bakery, built in 1909 for a Mr Ulrick. The two-storey timber building housed the bakery and shop on the ground floor and accommodation for the baker and his family on the upper floor. Operated by a succession of bakers, the business finally closed in 1969. Although the timber building has been converted for other uses, the original bakers' ovens remain. The shop's interior timber finishes and decorative pressed-metal ceilings have also been preserved.

64. Eumundi Butter Factory, *Memorial Drive*

Constructed in 1920, the Eumundi Butter Factory operated for more than 50 years. Every Saturday the colourful stalls of the famous Eumundi markets enliven the street scene from the Eumundi Museum to the former butter factory. Evidence remains of a private siding built for the butter factory. The siding was removed in 1974 when the butter factory was closed due to a fall in production, resulting from a declining market for butter and the rising popularity of margarine.

65. Noosa Heads

In the late 1860s Walter Hay of Gympie ran a steamer from Maryborough carrying goods for the Gympie and Kilkivan mineral fields. By 1870, a more direct route was sought for the transportation of goods to Gympie and Hay is credited with successfully finding a route to the Noosa River. Records show that the name 'Nusa' first appeared on a map of Queensland published in 1871. During the 1890s Noosa's popularity as a bathing beach grew and several guesthouses were soon operating. Tourist resort development increased during the 1920s as cafes and accommodation houses were erected along the beachfront.

The rise in car ownership during the 1950s and 1960s meant that Noosa, like other coastal areas in south-east Queensland, continued to grow in popularity. As a consequence of the spiralling pace of development of Noosa as a tourist resort,

the townscape has undergone many changes, including the removal of the timber guesthouses that formerly lined Hastings Street. The largest of these, Laguna House, was demolished in the 1960s. The town provided the setting for Nancy Cato's book *The Noosa Story* (1979), which was prompted by the activities of developers and local authorities, and called for the protection of the foreshore. The town was renamed Noosa Heads in 1988.

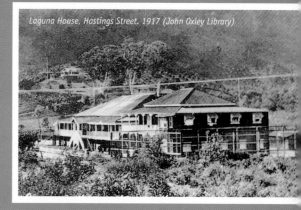

Laguna House, Hastings Street. 1917 (John Oxley Library)

Beach scene at Noosa Heads, c1931 (John Oxley Library)

63 *Smith's Bakery, Eumundi, c1920*

Noosa Heads National Park

Noosa National Park was declared in 1930 on land previously gazetted as a 'Reserve for Natives'. This is the most heavily used park in southern Queensland, its natural setting providing a contrast with recent real estate development in the town and emphasising the importance of the continued conservation of natural habitats. Noosa Heads National Park was established in 1994 to amalgamate five previously separate parks stretching from Coolum to Noosa. This area is the most geologically diverse section of the park, being formed mainly from Quaternary sandstone with some igneous intrusions that, being more resistant to erosion, have developed into rugged, rocky headlands with sheltered beaches in between. Areas of coastal lowland subtropical rainforest, conserved in sheltered gullies, contain the most southerly occurrence of kauri pine. Scenic viewpoints on the rocky headlands provide excellent panoramas of the Sunshine Coast hinterland and the high dunes of Cooloola National Park.

66. Halse Lodge,
Noosa Drive

Originally known as Bayview, then as Hillcrest Guesthouse, Halse Lodge stands on a block that has been occupied by a seaside guesthouse from the early 1880s. In 1882 Walter Hay placed an advertisement in the *Gympie Times* advising that his Bay View House was available for letting. By 1900, Bayview had been converted to a two-storey timber building. It was substantially rebuilt and extended during the 1920s, after which time it was known as Hillcrest Guesthouse. The property was transferred to John Jones in 1929 and the Jones and Hindmarsh families continued to run the guesthouse until the late 1950s. The Anglican Church acquired Hillcrest in 1959 and renamed it Halse Lodge, after Archbishop Halse. For the next three decades the lodge was used mainly for group accommodation. Substantial renovations were undertaken in 1988 and the lodge was leased to managers, now operating as a popular backpackers' hostel.

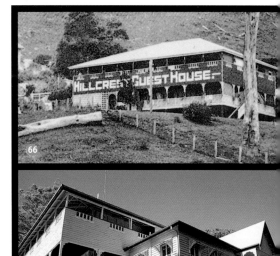

66 *Hillcrest Guesthouse, c1928 (top) (John Oxley Library)*
66 *Halse Lodge guesthouse, Noosa Heads*

Noosa Heads National Park (EPA)

67. Tewantin

After 1869, when trading vessels were first able to navigate the Noosa bar, Tewantin became the river port for the Noosa area and for Gympie. The settlement was the starting point for the track cut by pioneer Walter Hay that offered a shorter route to the Gympie goldfields than through Maryborough. In 1871 Surveyor Clarendon Stuart surveyed a town site. Tewantin's importance as a port and transport centre was heightened when plans for a railway extension from Eumundi were abandoned in 1891. It was the principal outlet for the gold, timber and fishing industries and also for the fruit orchards and cattle runs later established in the district. Tewantin businessmen were behind the early development of Noosa and until the 1930s Tewantin provided the only access to the beaches for a rapidly increasing number of visitors. Surviving on the river trade and as an access point for visitors to the unspoiled northern beaches and forests, Tewantin retained a quiet, unchanging character until the new development wave of the 1980s.

67 *Tewantin War Memorial*

68. Royal Mail Hotel, *Poinciana Street*

The first hotel on the present site overlooking the Noosa River was built around 1882 by Edward Murdoch, a driver for Cobb and Co. In 1883 Jim Wordsworth, a bullock driver, assisted Murdoch with extensions including additional bedrooms. Cobb and Co.'s coach run from Brisbane to Gympie was extended to Tewantin from 1880 to 1891, when it ceased in anticipation of a proposed branch railway from Eumundi. The railway was not built and in 1892 John Myles took over the hotel and established the Royal Mail coach line, carrying goods and passengers to and from the railway at Cooran and Cooroy. Visitors to Noosa stayed at the Royal Mail before being ferried across the river and the hotel developed a steady trade as a holiday centre.

In the 1920s, the sprawling, single-storey hotel burnt down and was replaced by the present two-storey masonry building in the late 1930s. The hotel remains a landmark in the town and a reminder of Tewantin's importance to trade and transport in the area.

69. Cooroy

Cooroy began as a staging camp for timber-getters after the sawmiller William Pettigrew explored the area in 1863. Construction of the North Coast Line from Gympie began in 1889 to meet up at Cooroy with the main line approaching from the south. When the Cooroy Railway Station opened in 1891, a post office was established at the station and homes were built for railway staff. A rail siding was built for the timber merchants Dath Henderson and Company. Henderson held the land around the siding until 1907, when it was surveyed for a township.

68 *Royal Mail Hotel*
69 *Cooroy Railway Station, c1910 (John Oxley Library)*

Within a few years, the sale of town allotments resulted in a main street lined with shops and homes. The timber previously hauled by bullock teams to Tewantin was now delivered to Cooroy for transport by rail to Brisbane. The town remained an important timber centre even as land was gradually cleared for dairying and fruit growing. With two sawmills operating and its butter factory opened in 1915, Cooroy became prosperous during the 1920s. Like other hinterland towns, Cooroy suffered from depressed markets in the dairying and fruit-growing industries in the 1970s. In the 1980s, the town benefited from rural residential development and the increased popularity of the coastal beaches.

70. Cooroy Arts Centre, *Maple Street*

The Cooroy Butter Factory opened in 1915 as a branch factory of the Wide Bay Co-operative Dairy Company. The factory closed in 1975, a victim of declining markets for butter and the centralisation of milk-processing facilities. The building remained empty until 1985, when it was reopened as an arts centre. During renovations, the original terracotta floor was discovered intact, along with evidence of the spur line from the railway to the factory.

71. Pomona

Timber-getters were the first to settle around Pomona in the late 1880s. Construction of the railway from Cooran to Cooroy in 1891 opened up the land around Pomona for farming. Pinbarren siding developed as an important stop on the railway line for the timber industry and for an increasing number of small crop farmers. In 1906, local farmers petitioned to have the name changed to Pomona, after the goddess of fruit and orchards in Roman mythology. When it became the administrative centre for the new Noosa Shire in 1909, the town was thriving as the business and transport centre for the district. Several sawmills were operating and dairying became important. Another industry was the Pomona Potteries, started in 1919. After fires devastated the main streets in 1939 and again in 1942, many buildings were rebuilt in brick. The move from dairy to beef cattle production and the recent boost from tourism and small acreage farming have consolidated the town's future.

72. Majestic Theatre and Cafe, *Factory Street*

The Majestic was built in 1921 as Pomona's public hall. In 1923 it was licensed to operate as a movie theatre when Mr Page, the travelling picture show man, applied to show silent movies at the hall on a regular basis. The movies proved enduringly popular, ensuring that the theatre stayed open even during the Depression years. Talking pictures were introduced by Ernest Bazzo, who purchased the theatre in 1933. After his death in 1970, the theatre closed and remained empty until Ron and Mandy West purchased it from the Bazzo family in 1984. The Wests have gradually restored the building and the cafe as a silent movie theatre. The 1920s Wurlitzer organ that plays accompanying music for the movies was originally from Melbourne's De Luxe Theatre. The projector was installed by Mr Page in 1923. Using a range of period materials and furniture, the Wests have succeeded in recreating in the Majestic Theatre the setting and atmosphere of the silent movie era.

70 Cooroy Arts Centre, formerly a butter factory
72 Majestic Theatre, Pomona

71 Pomona township, c1920 (John Oxley Library)

COOROY — POMONA

144

73. Pomona School of Arts, *Reserve Street*

The school of arts was built in 1919 as a memorial to district residents who died in World War I. In addition to the library and the dance hall, the building provided temporary offices for the police and the Court of Petty Sessions until a separate police building was erected in 1934.
After World War II, the Pomona RSL branch planned to erect a new memorial hall. The branch successfully tendered for the recreation hut at Brisbane's Gaythorne military camp and had it dismantled and railed to Pomona. Reconstructed as an addition to the existing hall, it had a spacious ballroom, raised stage with lighting installed and a supper room underneath. The new complex was officially opened with a grand ball in 1947. The honour board from the original Memorial School of Arts was transferred to the hall.

74. Australian and New Zealand Bank, *Reserve Street*

A branch of the English, Scottish and Australian Bank was established in Pomona in 1909. This new office was erected for the bank in 1936. The building is now occupied by the Australian and New Zealand Bank.

75. Pomona Ambulance Station, *Reserve Street*

The Pomona Ambulance Brigade was operating in the town by 1912 and in 1917 the local service was incorporated into the Queensland Ambulance Transport Board. The station was relocated to the Reserve Street site during the 1940s and the present station office was opened in 1951.

76. Pomona Hotel, *Station Street*

C.J. Walters opened Pomona's first hotel in 1905. A long, lowset building with a wide verandah, it occupied a central position in the main street. It was burnt down in 1911 and the present two-storey hotel was built. Constructed on spacious lines, it still displays the fine timber and craftsmanship for which the Pomona district was known.

77. Noosa Shire Office, *Factory Street*

The Noosa Shire Council was formed in 1909, from divisions wishing to establish independence from Widgee Shire. Of the three principal towns in the new shire — Cooroy, Cooran and Pomona — Pomona won the referendum conducted among ratepayers and became the shire council's headquarters. Constructed in 1910, the building was converted to a historical museum in 1985 following the transfer of the Noosa Shire Council offices to Tewantin.

78. Boreen

In the 1870s, resumptions of the pastoral runs taken up in the 1850s fostered farming in the district to supply produce to Gympie and other Mary Valley mining communities. The small settlement was named after Jim Breen, or Boreen, the first permanent settler on the point. He was the nominee selector for the sawmilling firm of McGhie, Luya, Goodchap and Woodburn, which owned most of the land around Lake Coothamba by the 1890s. Timber-getting was the most important industry at the end of the 19th century, when over 100 workers and their families lived around the point. Remnants of the loading ramps used to transfer logs to paddle steamers for transporting to the Elandra Point mill are still visible.

After the land was opened for selection, it was developed for dairying and agriculture.

 Pomona Hotel
 Apollonian Hotel, re-located at Boreen

Although it benefited from the extensive reforestation programs begun in the area in 1946, Boreen remained a quiet boating and fishing centre. Rapid population growth throughout the north coast has spurred recent residential and tourism development.

89. Apollonian Hotel, *Laguna Street*

The hotel was originally located on the Apollonian Vale Road in Gympie, the scene of a thriving mining community throughout the 1870s and 1880s. It was moved to its present location in 1981. Known as Barlow's Music Hall in 1868, it was renamed the Apollonian by William Taylor around 1870. Richard Cox took it over in 1889. The music hall hotel became famous for the shows featuring Richard's daughter, the singer Mabel Cox. She died in 1980, at the age of 90. As mining declined and the local community moved away, trade also declined and the hotel finally closed in 1949. The last musical event held there was for the Gympie eisteddfod in 1958. The Apollonian was the only survivor of the many music hall hotels that flourished during Gympie's mining boom.

Lake Cootharaba shoreline (EPA)

A donkey boiler marks the sawmill site

80. Lake Cootharaba,
Cooloola National Park

Located in Cooloola National Park, Lake Cootharaba is well known as a challenging sailing course but its chief attraction lies in the beauty and diversity of the surrounding natural landscapes and the abundance of native plants and animals. Early European settlement around Lake Cootharaba dates from the late 1860s, with the exploration of the area's timber resources. It was not until the 1870s, however, that permanent settlement was established as timber-getters worked the forests to supply timber for the mill at Elanda Point. Dairy farms and beef cattle studs have been established over the years, but the future of Lake Cootharaba lies in its use as a recreational facility and as the centre of a unique natural environment.

Elanda Point Sawmill

Cedar-getters were working in the Noosa River area by the mid-1860s and in 1869 Charles Russell lodged an application to select land that included Elanda Point. Russell formed a partnership with a group of Gympie mining investors, headed by Abraham Luya, to establish the Cootharaba sawmill. The sawmill was built on a swampy area on the edge of Lake Cootharaba and the swamp was progressively filled in with sawdust to create, and extend, the timber yard. To overcome the problems associated with the transport of logs across the swamp, a tramway system was constructed to allow logs to be drawn to the sawmill on wagons pulled by draughthorses. Flat-bottomed paddle-wheelers towed barges of sawn timber through Lakes Cootharaba and Cooroibah to Tewantin, where the cargo was loaded onto the firm's steamer, the *Culgoa*, and shipped to Brisbane.

By the early 1890s the softwood resources in southern Cooloola were nearing exhaustion, having been exploited for nearly 20 years, and completion of the Brisbane–Gympie railway link in 1891 ended the need for ship and coach services. Just two months before the opening of the railway, the *Culgoa* was wrecked on the Noosa Bar. The sawmill finally closed in 1892. Dairy farmers moved into the area in the early 20th century, but farming was never particularly successful. Elanda Point was acquired by the Queensland Government in 1983 and became part of Cooloola National Park in 1985.

Mill Point Settlement

The small settlement of Mill Point flourished for the 20 years that Luya and Company's sawmill operated. Governor Normanby's account of a visit in 1873 records: 'Leaving the works and passing to the rear we found a regular little township of workmen's houses and others directly connected with the establishment, a good store, well-equipped, conducted by the owners, a butcher shop, and there seemed nothing wanting to complete the comfort of all connected with the establishment'. A school established at the settlement about 1874 was the first school opened in the district. A hotel appears to have operated from 1876 until 1878, when it was destroyed by fire. The cemetery was used during the years 1873–91, the first burials being four of the five victims of a boiler explosion at the sawmill in 1873. The cemetery is marked by a stone memorial placed by the National Trust in 1993.

Tankstand remnants at Mill Point settlement

Mill Point settlement ruins

81. Pomona School Memorial Forestry Plot, *Pinbarren Creek*

In the early 1930s the Forestry Department began providing free tree seedlings to state schools to plant forestry plots. After the closure of the Pinbarren Creek State School north of Pomona, students at the Pomona State School began a tree-growing project at Pinbarren Creek. The fenced area of the Pinbarren Creek School reserve was cleared and planted with pine seedlings in 1939. In 1942, during the darkest period of World War II, the plot was named the Pinbarren Victory Plot. In 1944, with the end of the war in sight, it was renamed the Pomona District School Memorial Forestry Plot in memory of local servicemen who had lost their lives. Arbor Day was celebrated at the forestry plot from 1942 until 1951. A row of camphor laurels extends along the edge of the plot, which contains hoop pines.

81 *Memorial forestry plot on Pinbarren Creek*

82. Kin Kin

Kin Kin is named after a small black ant found locally. One of the places established by timber-getters around Lake Cootharaba from the late 1870s, it grew into a permanent settlement as a camp for bullock drivers hauling logs to the sawmill at Elanda Point. The high quality of Kin Kin timber, particularly the kauri pines, was recognised throughout Australia. By the early 1900s, progressive scrub clearing saw the start of dairying and banana growing.

In 1908, the Risden group of dairy farmers from Richmond, New South Wales, followed by the Moran group, moved to Kin Kin. Their skills and systematic approach to pasture improvement established dairying as a viable industry. Construction of the Wolvi Range road in 1912 improved access to the town and resulted in the opening of the Kin Kin Butter Factory, which operated until 1937. In the 1950s, Kin Kin suffered the decline of towns dependent on the timber and dairying industries, but it received support from the local reforestation programs undertaken in that decade. Today it is a centre for recreational activities associated with Lake Cootharaba and Cooloola National Park.

83. Country Life Hotel, *Main Street*

The Kin Kin Hotel was built by the first licensee, William Rohan, in 1918. In 1914 Rohan built the town's first general store, which he then sold to Thomas Waddell of Gympie. The store was moved up the hill and Rohan built the hotel on the present corner site. This is a typical rural hotel, constructed of timber with wide verandahs on the ground and first floors, its size and location indicative of its central role in the commercial and social life of both the town and the district.

83 *Country Life Hotel, Kin Kin*
84 *Kin Kin School of Arts*

84. Kin Kin School of Arts, *Main Street*

In 1909 a local committee was formed to raise funds for a school of arts. The hall was opened in 1911 and, with tennis courts laid out at the rear, became the centre for Kin Kin's social and sporting events. The township school was located there in 1916.

85. St Luke's Anglican Church, *Main Street*

The church was dedicated by Archbishop Sharp in 1926.

86. Bell's Tree Reserve, *near Kin Kin*

One of the largest kauri pines in the Gympie district once stood on this site, at the former junction of the Kin Kin and Gympie–Cootharaba roads. The Kin Kin district enjoyed a reputation for its native softwoods including kauri pine, whose distribution was confined to an area extending from Tewantin to Maryborough and Fraser Island. In 1907, as the impact of logging in the district became noticeable, a move was made to preserve a large kauri pine growing at this location. The Secretary for Public Lands, Joshua Bell, lent his support to local calls for the protection of the tree. A reserve was proclaimed in 1912, known as Bell's Tree Reserve.

In 1918, Bell's Tree was uprooted during a storm. Although the trunk was cut into five sections for transport to Brisbane for milling, the logs would not fit through the railway tunnels on the line to Brisbane, and were subsequently sent north to a sawmill at Gundiah. Bell's Tree Reserve was revoked in 1938, but in 1989 a group of residents located the site of the reserve and planted a replacement kauri pine. Since then a 'Back to Bell's Tree' gathering has been held each year.

86 *Bell's Tree Reserve*

87. Cooran

Before the completion of the North Coast Railway at Cooroy, most seaborne goods passing through Tewantin were transported by road to Cooran, which became the railhead station for Gympie in 1889. Cobb and Co. coaches ran between Yandina and Cooran until the final railway link was completed in 1891, and Royal Mail coaches and teamsters operated to Tewantin. With the opening up of the Pinbarren scrub lands for farm selection and timber-getting, Cooran became a very busy station. Huge logs were hauled in to be placed on rail trucks for transport to sawmills at Gympie and Maryborough. At this time, Cooran's growth was also influenced by land selection and settlement occurring in the Mary Valley, to the west of the township. Besides dairying and timber, banana growing became an important activity during the 1920s and 1930s. Pineapples were grown extensively for some years after World War II. Cooran has survived, though its population and economic base have continued to decline since the 1890s.

88. Gympie

The town of Gympie was established after James Nash discovered gold in the area in 1867. The Gympie bonanza saved the Colony of Queensland from bankruptcy. Almost immediately, Gympie had a population of several thousand. It developed so rapidly that a substantial part of the town had already been established by the time the official surveyors arrived in 1868. This resulted in the streets being laid out in an irregular pattern, following the topography of the land and the mining sites, rather than the grid pattern familiar to most Queensland towns. The three stages of mining — alluvial gold to the early 1870s, shallow reef mining to 1880 and then the years of sustained underground production until the 1920s — were reflected in the range and style of buildings.

Most of the original slab constructions were gradually replaced by substantial timber or brick and masonry buildings designed by Gympie architects, an unprecedented amount of construction being carried out during the 1880s mining boom.

Gympie was officially declared a town in 1903 and became the administrative centre for the Widgee Shire. Even after the prosperity of the mining era declined, Gympie remained important as the principal town for the rich Mary Valley district. The North Coast Railway from Brisbane, completed in 1891, opened up the district to more intensive settlement. The hardwood, pine and plantation timbers of the Gympie forestry district sustained the local timber industry and a large-scale powdered milk factory established in 1953 provided a further economic boost. The construction of Borumba Dam brought a range of benefits to Gympie and, more recently, the City Council inaugurated a beautification scheme that included the presentation of the town's historic buildings.

89. Scottish Gympie Battery and Retort House, *Brisbane Road*

This was the richest and most productive mine on the Gympie Goldfield from 1867 to 1923. Now significant as the most intact surviving example of early mining on the Gympie field, with the foundations of the largest gold battery in south-east Queensland. In the 1890s, after more than 20 years of operation, the mine went through a number of changes of ownership. Gympie Gold Mines was subsequently formed and in 1895 was sold to Scottish investors, becoming the Scottish Gympie Gold Mines Limited, with its head office in Glasgow. Development in the No.1 Scottish Gympie Mine proceeded, and by the following year the main shaft was the deepest on the field. By 1904 the battery was reported to have 125 head of stamps and 394 men employed, and to be raising 7000 tons of ore for crushing each year, with an estimated ore reserve for another ten years.

Scottish Gympie Gold Mines Limited closed the mine in 1923. Cyanide treatment of the tailings continued from 1927, when Runge and Alexander took over the mine and battery site. The leases were held by the Runge family until their recent acquisition by the Gympie City Council. Features of the site include the brick assay office, constructed about 1897, and a light four-head prospecting stamp battery installed after the original plant had been removed.

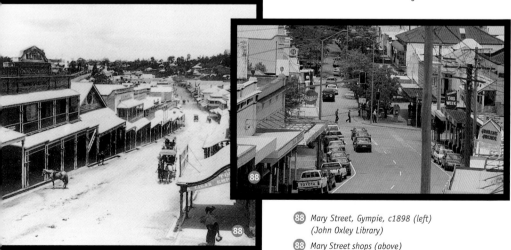

88 *Mary Street, Gympie, c1898 (left)*
(John Oxley Library)
88 *Mary Street shops (above)*

89 *Scottish Gympie Mine and battery, 1908 (top)*
(John Oxley Library)
89 *Scottish Gympie retort house and assay office (above)*

90. Gympie Mining Museum, *Brisbane Road*

The Gympie and District Historical and Mining Museum was established in 1967 on the site of one of the richest mines on the Gympie Goldfield, the No.2 South Great Eastern Mine. A former tailings dam, disused since the closure of the mine in 1918, has been landscaped and now forms an attractive pond within the surrounding picnic grounds. Focal point of the museum is the reconstructed headframe with its associated steam boiler house and winding engine. From small beginnings the Gympie Gold Mining Museum has developed into a fascinating complex of attractions, where visitors can experience almost every facet of Gympie's colourful past.

91. Phoenix Hotel, *Red Hill Road*

Opened in 1882, the hotel was designed for Richard Alcock by the Gympie architect Hugo Durietz. It was named after the nearby No.2 North Phoenix Mine, one of several goldmines on the Phoenix Reef, which proved to be one of the most profitable on the Gympie Goldfield.

92. Railway Hotel, *Tozer Street*

Dating from 1883, when Mary-Ann McCowan was the licensee, this two-storey timber hotel was one of several built in Gympie at the height of the 1880s mining boom. The hotel, with its wide upper verandah defined by a decorative timber balustrade, retains much of its original style.

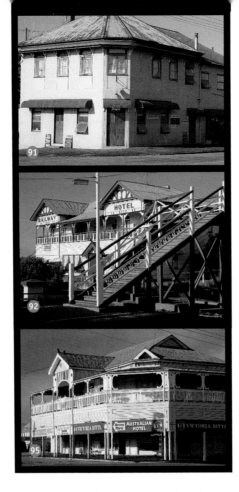

93. Gympie Railway Station, *Tozer Street*

A railway line from Maryborough to Gympie was opened in 1881, providing direct access to port facilities for miners on the Gympie Goldfield. Gympie was a dead-end station for ten years, until the arrival of the North Coast Line from Brisbane in 1891. A contract for moving and re-erecting the station buildings was awarded in 1888. The station took its present form after major changes beginning in 1911, involving conversion of the platform into an island with tracks each side and construction of a new station building with a subway street entrance. The present station building was completed in 1912.

With the growth of traffic on the North Coast Line, the station was progressively extended. By 1940 Gympie functioned as a terminus for the Mary Valley Line and as a refreshment stop for the Brisbane and Maryborough passenger services. The importance of Gympie Station has diminished since the 1960s. The station now serves as the terminus for the 'Mary Valley Rattler' heritage steam train to Imbil.

94. Mary Valley Heritage Railway, *Tozer Street*

The historic Mary Valley Line is easily one of Queensland's most scenic railway lines. Construction commenced in 1911 and was completed in 1915. Cream, timber and pineapples were the main goods carried. When the line was closed by Queensland Rail in 1996 the Mary Valley Heritage Railway Association was formed to preserve the line and to establish a heritage tourism railway service using an original C17 class steam loco and diesel rail motors. The 'Mary Valley Rattler' heritage steam service to Imbil began in 1998. The service operates from the Association's museum at Gympie Railway Station.

95. Australian Hotel, *Bligh Street*

Built in 1873 on Caledonian Hill, the hotel was associated with the early rich workings of the nearby Caledonian and Lady Mary mines. Mary Catherwood was the first licensee, followed by Thomas Findlay, who stayed until the end of the 1880s boom period. Its original character still in evidence, the hotel remains a significant Gympie landmark.

91 *Phoenix Hotel, Gympie*
92 *Railway Hotel*
95 *Australian Hotel*

96. Gympie Fire Brigade Station, *Bligh Street*

Gympie's fire brigade was established in 1900. The impressive timber building featuring decorative latticework on the upper-storey verandah was extended in the 1920s to accommodate the fire trucks that replaced the original horse-drawn units. In 1940 the early fire brigade station was replaced by the present brick building, with its modern architectural character.

97. St Patrick's Catholic Church, *Church Street*

This church has been a landmark in Gympie since its completion in 1887. The first Catholic mass in the town was celebrated in 1868, at the Brisbane Hotel. Later that year Father Matthew Horan arrived on the new goldfield as the parish priest, a position he held until his death in 1923. On arrival, Father Horan pitched his tent on Calton Hill, beginning the long Catholic domination of the site. A timber church was soon erected, but survived only four years due to the effects of weather and white ants. A second timber church was opened in 1872. A Catholic school was established on land nearby in 1879, when the Sisters of Mercy arrived in Gympie.

Plans for a new church were prepared by the renowned Brisbane architect F.D.G. Stanley. The foundation stone was laid in 1883 and St Patrick's Church was opened in 1887. In 1929 Archbishop Duhig dedicated newly installed stained-glass windows in remembrance of the Catholic emancipation. He also laid the foundation stone for the new convent, commemorating the centenary of the Sisters of Mercy and the jubilee of their arrival in Gympie.

96 Gympie Fire Station   97 St Patrick's Church and convent school

98. Gympie City Hall, *Caledonian Hill Road*

Gympie's first local government, the Widgee Divisional Board, held its inaugural meeting in 1880. When Widgee Shire was proclaimed in 1903, Gympie was declared a town and in 1905 it became a municipality with its own City Council. The Gympie Town Hall was constructed in 1910, reputedly adjacent to the site where James Nash had first found gold. The two-storey masonry building was half the size originally planned, the severity of its design relieved by the magnificent clock tower topped by an ornate observatory platform. The hall was remodelled and extended in 1938. The upper floor was largely taken up with a panelled reception hall with a decorative balcony overlooking the main street. The extended ground floor contained a war memorial alcove, reception rooms and a branch post office. An imposing leadlight window and elaborate timber staircase were also installed. Further alterations were carried out in 1982. Since 1993 the former City Hall has been used as offices for Cooloola Shire Council after the amalgamation of Widgee Shire and Gympie City councils.

99 Gympie and Widgee War Memorial Gates

99. Gympie and Widgee War Memorial Gates, *Mary Street*

Unveiled in 1920 by the Prince of Wales, the gates were designed by George Rae of Brisbane. The monumental masonry firm of Andrew Petrie and Son of Toowong undertook the stonework, while a local blacksmith produced the ironwork. The memorial honours two Boer War victims and 167 local men who were killed in World War I.

100. Royal Hotel, *Mary Street*

The first Royal Hotel was opened in 1871. The single-storey timber building was replaced in 1881 by a more elaborate two-storey hotel with verandahs on both levels. The present Royal Hotel was built in 1935.

101. Gympie Stock Exchange Offices, *Mary Street*

With nearly 30 members and 60 companies listed at the height of the speculative share trading boom of the 1880s, the Gympie Stock Exchange operated its public trading room in a timber call room at the rear of this site. This imposing building, with its classic design features, was constructed for the Australian Joint Stock Bank in front of the Stock Exchange call room in 1888. When the bank failed in the 1893 Depression it was taken over by the stockbrokers as a private club from which they had easy access to the nightly share calls in the adjoining Exchange building. The Stock Exchange ceased trading in 1923 when company mining came to an end and the club was bought for solicitors' offices. The call room building was removed in 1946. In recent years solicitors Neilson, Stanton and Parkinson have occupied the building.

102. Cooloola Shire Council Chambers, *Mary St*

The first Widgee Divisional Board was elected in 1880. In 1897, the board purchased the Masonic Hall for its headquarters, having previously occupied offices in the school of arts. Taking over from the board in 1903, Widgee Shire Council continued to occupy the same offices until 1940, when it purchased the Bank of New South Wales building for new headquarters. The bank was designed by the Brisbane architect Richard Gailey in the early 1890s. The offices and residential accommodation on the first floor were retained by the council and the later brick extensions were built to house the shire engineer and his staff. Further additions were made in 1985. The building became the Cooloola Shire Office after Widgee Shire was absorbed into the new Cooloola Shire in 1993.

103. Commercial Hotel,
Mary Street

The first Commercial Hotel on this site was erected in 1871. In 1892, P. Talty opened a new Commercial Hotel, designed by Brisbane architect Richard Gailey, who had recently designed the adjacent Bank of New South Wales building.

103 *Commercial Hotel*

104. Surface Hill Uniting Church,
Channon Street

Located on one of the first sections to be settled in the town, this church has dominated the townscape since it was built for the Wesleyan congregation in 1890. At the time, it demonstrated the improved financial situation of Gympie's miners. The first church established on the site in 1868 had been constructed of bark. It was replaced in 1869 by a timber building that was later used as the church hall. The 1890 church, designed by Hugo Durietz, was of brick overlaid inside and out with a rendered cement mixture that has gradually taken on the appearance of mellowed stone. The arched doors, clerestory windows and twin spires forming the front entrance and facade serve to lighten the church's otherwise solid lines. The rock wall at street level was built during 1937 under the unemployed relief work program of the Depression.

105. Gympie Post Office,
Channon Street

Completed in 1880, the Gympie Post Office is the third to have been established in the town since the discovery of gold. It was designed by the Colonial Architect, F.D.G. Stanley. The first unofficial post office was opened in 1867 from a shop in Mary Street, following complaints about the lack of postal facilities. In 1868, an official postmaster was appointed and postal services were conducted from Gympie's second post office building. The gold rush continued to bring an influx of people and postal services increased accordingly, soon rendering the second post office inadequate.

Tenders for a new building were called in 1878. The building was finally completed in 1880 and included space for the post office, the Land Commissioner, the telegraph office and accommodation for the postmaster and his family. The building underwent further alterations in 1901 when a telephone exchange opened, and in 1954 when the postmaster's residence was transformed into a new telephone trunk exchange. In 1975, the present post office in Mary Street was opened, and the former office was closed. The building is now controlled by the Cooloola Shire Council.

106. Lands Department Office,
Channon Street

A Land Commissioner was appointed to Gympie in 1868 when the first official survey of the town was carried out. He worked in a temporary slab hut that also served as the court house. In 1876, both the Land Office and the court moved to this substantial masonry building erected as a permanent court house. After 1902, when the court moved to the newly constructed court house, this building became known as the Lands Office.

104 *Surface Hill Uniting Church*
105 *Gympie Post Office (John Oxley Library)*
106 *Lands Department office*

The various branches of the Lands Department operated from the building until they were transferred to a new building in 1998. Forming a precinct of government buildings with the old post office and the court house, the former lands office is a reminder of the importance of land administration in Gympie's history.

107. Gympie Court House, *Channon Street*

The first court proceedings in Gympie were held by the Gold Commissioner in tents and temporary accommodation, in the wake of the gold rush of 1867. A more permanent court house, a timber slab building, was erected in the late 1860s on what was known as Commissioner's Hill. In 1876 a substantial masonry court house building was erected in Channon Street on land reserved for police purposes. This building served the town until the mid-1890s, when there was pressure for construction of a new court house, primarily from a local Labor politician Andrew Fisher, who was later to become Prime Minister of Australia. The 1876 court house building, which still stands, was later used as the lands office.

Although the Colonial Architect was asked to prepare plans for a new court house in 1898, none were prepared until 1900. The new court house was designed by John Murdoch, an architect in the Public Works Department. Tenders were called in 1900 and the building was completed in 1902. The clock tower became a landmark and was once a popular place from which to view and take photographs of the town.

108. Gympie School of Arts, *Nash Street*

Gympie School of Arts was established in 1870 and a temporary reading room was obtained in an existing building until a hall could be constructed in 1874. As early as 1890 it was decided that a replacement building was required. In 1904 the school of arts committee asked a local architect, Hugo Durietz, who had previously served on the committee, to draw up plans for a new building. The design was of a functional nature with few decorative features. Constructed of brick, it was of two storeys, with verandahs on the upper floor. The ground floor had a central entrance, with a library and four classrooms. The upper floor contained rooms for billiard tables and a reading room.

The new building was opened in 1905 as the School of Arts and Technical College. It offered classes in practical subjects, which were also provided for state school students from 1909. As was the case with most schools of arts, the 1920s saw the beginning of the demise of the institute. The Gympie City Council took over the administration of the library at the end of 1975. The building now serves as the Cooloola Shire Public Gallery.

109. Gympie Hospital, *Henry Street*

A new hospital consisting of a two-storey brick ward block with a detached kitchen was designed and built in 1888. The complex was expanded during the 1920s. In the 1930s a maternity ward, new nurses quarters and a new ward block were added. In 1951 a large new nurses quarters was opened, as was a ward block for intermediate patients. The hospital has continued to be redeveloped and the original 1888 general ward was demolished and replaced with a new ward block in 1985. A 1939 ward block near the main entrance to the hospital, which originally contained private rooms on the upper floors, is now used for stores. The former medical superintendent's residence nearby, designed by the architect Charles Griffin in 1936, is of an English Bungalow style, similar to that of many of the Brisbane houses Griffin designed during the interwar period.

110. Gympie Cemetery, *Shields Street*

Gympie's first cemetery was located on the corner of King and Alfred streets. The present cemetery dates from 1886. Among the graves of Gympie residents of all ages and from all walks of life is that of James Nash, the discoverer of the Gympie Goldfield. Nash died in 1913, aged 77 years. His last years were spent in comparative poverty. To provide Nash with a living in his later life, the government appointed him keeper of the Gympie powder magazine.

Also in the cemetery is a memorial to John Flood. Transported to Australia for his role as a leader of the Irish revolutionary movement in 1867, Flood elected to remain when many of the Irish political transportees were pardoned in 1869. He worked as a journalist before becoming a miner on the Palmer River. In 1888 he was the principal owner of the *Gympie Miner* newspaper. He died in 1909. The memorial erected in 1911 commemorates his life's work for 'Irish Nationality'.

111. WoodWorks Forestry and Timber Museum, *Bruce Highway*

Opened in 1984, WoodWorks is dedicated to the early pioneers of the timber industry. Visitors can see working demonstrations of a steam-driven sawmill and enjoy the landscaped grounds and shady trees, which provide a relaxing place for a picnic lunch. Stop at the blacksmith's shop to watch the repair and maintenance of wagon tyres, bullock chains and other items of ironwork used in the early timber industry. The museum contains a unique collection of timber jinkers, bobtails, log trolleys and early motor trucks of the types used in south-east Queensland's timber industry until the 1930s.

109 *Gympie Hospital, 1930s ward block*
110 *John Flood's Memorial, Gympie Cemetery*

Chapter 8

FORESTRY RANGES

MAP 8
Forestry Ranges

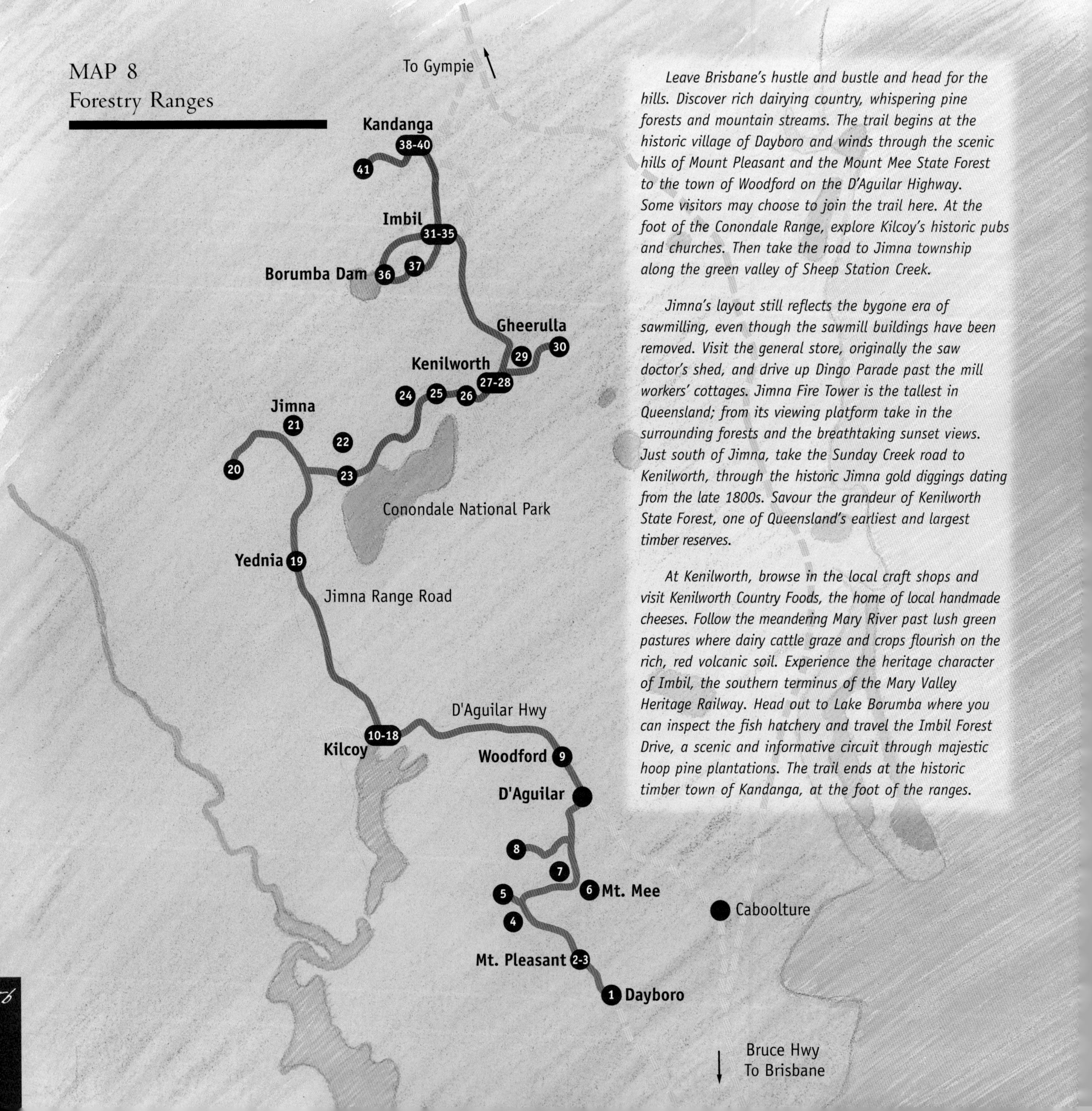

To Gympie

Kandanga
38-40
41

Imbil
31-35

Borumba Dam   36   37

Gheerulla
29   30

Kenilworth
27-28
24   25   26

Jimna
21
22
20   23

Conondale National Park

Yednia   19

Jimna Range Road

Kilcoy   10-18

D'Aguilar Hwy

Woodford   9

D'Aguilar

8
7
5   6   Mt. Mee
4

Caboolture

Mt. Pleasant   2-3

1   Dayboro

Bruce Hwy
To Brisbane

Leave Brisbane's hustle and bustle and head for the hills. Discover rich dairying country, whispering pine forests and mountain streams. The trail begins at the historic village of Dayboro and winds through the scenic hills of Mount Pleasant and the Mount Mee State Forest to the town of Woodford on the D'Aguilar Highway. Some visitors may choose to join the trail here. At the foot of the Conondale Range, explore Kilcoy's historic pubs and churches. Then take the road to Jimna township along the green valley of Sheep Station Creek.

Jimna's layout still reflects the bygone era of sawmilling, even though the sawmill buildings have been removed. Visit the general store, originally the saw doctor's shed, and drive up Dingo Parade past the mill workers' cottages. Jimna Fire Tower is the tallest in Queensland; from its viewing platform take in the surrounding forests and the breathtaking sunset views. Just south of Jimna, take the Sunday Creek road to Kenilworth, through the historic Jimna gold diggings dating from the late 1800s. Savour the grandeur of Kenilworth State Forest, one of Queensland's earliest and largest timber reserves.

At Kenilworth, browse in the local craft shops and visit Kenilworth Country Foods, the home of local handmade cheeses. Follow the meandering Mary River past lush green pastures where dairy cattle graze and crops flourish on the rich, red volcanic soil. Experience the heritage character of Imbil, the southern terminus of the Mary Valley Heritage Railway. Head out to Lake Borumba where you can inspect the fish hatchery and travel the Imbil Forest Drive, a scenic and informative circuit through majestic hoop pine plantations. The trail ends at the historic timber town of Kandanga, at the foot of the ranges.

FORESTRY RANGES

The district is dominated by the great forests of the Conondale and Jimna ranges that provide a complex pattern of introduced softwood plantations, eucalypt forest and subtropical rainforest. Much of the district is now covered by State Forest reserves. Established to control the exploitation of the timber resources, the reserves have ultimately contributed to the preservation of a unique and extensive forest environment. Gold, agriculture, dairying, fruit growing and cattle have all been important, but the history of the district has been predominantly the history of timber: its exploitation and conservation, the towns and settlements it fostered and the people whose livelihood depended on it.

During the 1840s and 1850s, squatters overcame difficult conditions to establish the first European occupation of the upper Mary Valley. Gold was discovered at Imbil in 1861, but it was the discovery of gold at Gympie in 1867 that brought thousands of people to the district and paved the way for settlement and the exploitation of its timber resources. Although land became available for selection from the 1870s, the lack of transport, the marginal living conditions and the availability of more accessible timber stands elsewhere meant that early settlement was confined. The long absence of adequate roads meant bullock teams were relied upon to transport timber and dairy products. These limitations fostered a way of life that did not entirely disappear until the 1920s, when roads were constructed over the ranges and the use of motor transport increased.

The timber industry expanded rapidly after the completion of the railway from Brisbane to Gympie in 1891 and the construction by 1914 of a branch line to the upper Mary Valley. Towns such as Imbil and Kandanga grew up around sawmills located near the railway. After World War II, plantation pine was cut for commercial use and reforestation programs began in earnest. Numerous camps were built for forestry workers and their families, and for displaced persons who came from Europe after the war. The network of roads and tracks constructed over the years by the Forestry Department now form scenic drives throughout the district.

Hoop pine plantation on the Jimna Range

Burt Brothers Transport, Kilcoy, c1923 (John Oxley Library)

FORESTRY RANGES HERITAGE TRAIL

1. Dayboro

The town of Dayboro began as Terror's Creek, identified in 1854 as a coach stop on the old north road from Brisbane to the North Pine River. By 1866 a pit sawmill had been established. Timber operations expanded throughout the 1870s as loggers harvested the timbers of the D'Aguilar Range: these included hoop pine, cedar, silky oak and black bean. The logs were hauled to the rafting grounds for transport by steamer to Brisbane. For some years, W.H. Day had a sugar plantation on the creek, where he used German and Melanesian labour.

Settlers arrived in the area throughout the 1870s and 1880s and schools were established at Terror's Creek and upper North Pine. The town grew around the sawmill, the blacksmith's forge and James Berry's Crown Hotel. The hotel was built in 1892 of bricks taken from an abandoned sugar mill operated by Berry in the 1870s. When the Enoggera Branch Railway was extended from Samsonvale to Terror's Creek in 1920, the name was changed to Dayboro to commemorate pioneer W.H. Day. Banana growing, started under the government's unemployment relief scheme in the 1930s, achieved some success but pineapples became the area's main fruit crop.

2. Mount Pleasant

First settled in the 1870s, Mount Pleasant was a centre for local dairy farming, pineapple growing and sawmilling by the early 1900s. In 1910 the growing number of new selectors in the area prompted the building of a school of arts as a community centre. Renovated and added to over the years, the hall continues to be used for community activities.

3. Mount Pleasant Sawmill

A mango tree is all that remains to mark the site of the Mount Pleasant Sawmill. Controlled by Charlie Rose and his sons, Edwin and Athol, the sawmill began operations in 1930. It was eventually sold to the Brett brothers, who relocated it at nearby Byron Creek.

4. Mount Mee State Forest

Mount Mee State Forest was gazetted in 1907 to regulate the logging of the surviving stands of timber in the district. The forest is on the western rim of the Mount Mee Plateau, at the headwaters of the North Pine River. Logs from the forest were taken to various centres for milling, being hauled by wagon or truck to Mount Mee West, Kilcoy or Gatton, or milled at one of several sawmills established in the state forest.

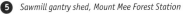

1 *Crown Hotel, Daybro*
5 *Sawmill gantry shed, Mount Mee Forest Station*

5. Hancock's Sawmill, *Mount Mee Forest Station*

Hancock's sawmill operated on this site during the 1930s, using a steam-driven plant and bullock teams. It later became known as Simpson's mill. This large shed was added to the sawmill in the 1950s to house the overhead gantry crane. The original sawmill has been removed, but the gantry shed has survived and has recently been restored as an interpretive feature at Mount Mee Forest Station.

6. Mount Mee

Located in the D'Aguilar Range, Mount Mee — or, as it was originally known, Dahmongah — was first selected in 1860 by Benjamin Franz, the son of a German missionary from the Nundah district. The size of the community grew to such an extent that a provisional school was opened in 1884. Timber-getting was the main activity for the first European settlers who, with their bullock teams, blazed trails from Caboolture and Terror's Creek (now Dayboro). Many of today's roads in the district follow the path of these pioneer tracks.

7. Avenue of Honour,
Robinson Road

Almost 50 men from the Mount Mee community enlisted for service in World War II and a number were killed in action. The 1939–45 roll of honour is displayed in the Mount Mee hall alongside that of World War I. The avenue of hoop pines was planted as a memorial soon after the end of the war.

8. Mount Mee Banana Blocks,
Settlement Road

A Depression relief scheme was introduced in Queensland during the early 1930s to increase land productivity and decentralise unemployed families. Areas of state forest were set aside for banana growing. From 1934 two settlements were established adjoining the Mount Mee State Forest, one near Mount Mee and the other near Mount Pleasant. The settlements struggled for survival as families became disillusioned with the poor returns, and when the Depression eased most made their way back to their previous environments and occupations.

As early as 1935 the Forestry Department was concerned that many blocks had been abandoned, necessitating urgent action to combat lantana and weed outbreaks. The Mount Mee banana settlement was short-lived and was mostly abandoned by 1939. The land currently supports hoop pine stands, and some fence posts and wire are the only remaining evidence of the banana blocks. Of the 30 or more huts that formed the settlement, only a few survive; they are now used as sheds.

9. Woodford

Named after H.C. Wood, a partner in the firm of McConnel and Wood, owners of Durundur station, the town was settled in 1878 when part of Durundur was resumed for farm selection. The town replaced an earlier settlement named Yatesville, located on the other side of the Stanley River. The surrounding forests ensured the long-term importance of the timber industry to the town. With closer settlement, dairying was successfully established and a co-operative dairy factory was opened in 1904.

The railway branch line from Caboolture, reaching Woodford in 1909, assisted primary producers. Still the centre for the district's timber and agricultural industries, Woodford has experienced recent growth as the service town for new rural subdivisions and as home to the famous Woodford Folk Festival. The Woodford Hotel, built shortly after the railway was completed, dates from around 1910. During the 1920s, when George Carney was the licensee, it was a popular venue for boxing events.

7 Robinson Road Avenue of Honour, Mount Mee

8 Banana settlement huts, Mount Mee, c1934 (John Oxley Library)

9 Woodford Hotel

10. Kilcoy Homestead,
near Kilcoy

This homestead was constructed about 1857 for Louis Hope, a British aristocrat, Queensland grazier, sugar plantation owner and politician. The Kilcoy run had been taken up as a sheep station by brothers Evan and Colin Mackenzie, of Kilcoy, Scotland, in 1841. The first Kilcoy head station was a simple slab hut. In 1844 it was replaced by a brick dwelling. Kilcoy run was transferred to Charles Atherton in 1849, then to Louis Hope and Robert Ramsay in 1853. Hope purchased Ramsey's interest in Kilcoy in 1863. Hope had arrived in New South Wales in 1843, and was an active participant in early Queensland economic and political life. In the 1850s he acquired extensive landholdings in the Moreton region, including Kilcoy station, Shafston House at Kangaroo Point, and Ormiston House at Cleveland. Hope died in Geneva, Switzerland, in 1894, but Kilcoy homestead remained the property of his heirs until 1908, when William Butler purchased the house. Local grazier Jeremiah Kennedy of Monte Cassino acquired the homestead in 1922. The homestead is not open to the public.

11. Kilcoy

Kilcoy takes its name from Kilcoy run, taken up in 1841. The first settlers arrived in the area after part of the station was resumed for closer settlement in 1876. A new town was surveyed in the early 1890s after floods had devastated the earlier settlement at Hazeldean, south of the Stanley River. The new settlement was named Hopetoun, after the sugar pioneer Louis Hope, the owner of Kilcoy station. The growth of dairying and the timber industry saw the town develop, schools, churches, hotels and stores being established by the early 1900s.

The district's population increased substantially in 1902 when the blocks offered for sale from the resumed Durundur Station were taken up for farming. This was followed in 1906 by the equally successful sale of land after the resumption of Kilcoy station. In the following year the town was renamed Kilcoy, to avoid confusion with Hopetoun in Victoria.

Kilcoy became the headquarters of the new Shire of Kilcoy in 1912. Local industries were assisted by the completion of the railway branch line from Caboolture, which operated from 1914 until 1962. Kilcoy became the major service town for the Somerset Dam construction works begun in 1935, gaining road improvements and access to electricity ahead of other rural towns. Although the district's population declined in the 1960s, the town has benefited from diversification into new rural industries.

10 *Kilcoy Homestead, c1890s (John Oxley Library)*

11 *Mary Street Kilcoy with the Stanley Hotel, 1939 (John Oxley Library)*

12. Stanley Hotel, *Mary Street*

In 1916, Elizabeth Elliott transferred the licence of the Hopetoun Hotel, operated since 1901 by her husband Tom Elliott, to the new Stanley Hotel. The impressive two-storey timber hotel burnt down in 1935 and was replaced by the present building. The first-floor verandahs were later enclosed, but the interior of the hotel retains much of the original decor.

13. Exchange Hotel, *William Street*

Built in the early 1900s, the Exchange Hotel had been considerably altered and extended by the mid-1920s, when it assumed its present layout.

14. Memorial Clock, *William Street*

The clock was erected by Kilcoy residents in 1916 as a memorial to William Butler, the manager of Kilcoy station after its purchase by Louis Hope in 1854. In 1907, when Kilcoy was resumed for selection, Butler purchased the homestead estate. The imposing stone monument, its four clock faces framed in decorative carvings, commemorates Butler's contribution to the early growth of Kilcoy.

15. Burt's Transport Garage, *William Street*

In 1922, brothers Frank and George Burt started a motor transport business offering services across the district. One of their major contracts was to transport the timber cut at Jimna, using trucks to haul logs down the mountain range to the loading depot at Yednia. The present garage and workshop was built in 1936. Burt's Transport still operates from Kilcoy and is one of the earliest continuously operating road haulage companies in Queensland.

16. Kilcoy Uniting Church and Hall, *William Street*

Kilcoy became a Methodist home mission station in 1902. The first missionary was the Reverend James Moorhouse. His successor, the Reverend Watkinson, expanded the mission services that were held in homes and local halls. The church was built in 1905 on donated land. The parsonage was erected for a permanent minister in 1924.

17. St Michael's Catholic Church, *William Street*

Kilcoy's Catholic Church was built in 1909.

18. St Mary's Anglican Church and Rectory, *William Street*

In a picturesque location, the church was designed by J.H. Buckeridge and was dedicated by Bishop Webber in 1898. Lack of funds resulted in a smaller and less ornate building than Buckeridge had originally envisaged. The intended expansion of the nave to the west was never carried out, although the west baptistry was completed in 1947. Buckeridge's typical design features have been largely preserved and the church complex, including the rectory built in 1911, the timber bell tower and arched gateway, remains a notable Kilcoy landmark.

13 *Exchange Hotel, Kilcoy*
14 *Butler's Memorial Clock*
15 *Burt's Transport Garage*
18 *St Mary's Rectory, Kilcoy*

19. Yednia Sawmill

This abandoned sawmill once processed much of the hardwood timber cut in the Jimna area during the 1960s and 1970s, but the reduced output is now hauled to mills nearer the coast. The empty sawmill shed, the former Yednia State School and a few houses remain.

20. Monsildale Sawmill

Hancock and Gore's Monsildale sawmill operated from 1912 until 1922, when the mill and the settlement were removed to Jimna. Brown and Broad's Louisavale mill was relocated to Monsildale in the early 1930s. The sawmilling plant was acquired by the United States Army during World War II and shipped to New Guinea. However, the ship carrying it is reputed to have been torpedoed and all the cargo lost. A new sawmill and settlement were established at Monsildale after World War II, but have since been demolished. Abandoned garden plots and the stumps of the mill workers' cottages can still be seen.

21. Jimna

Commercial logging was being undertaken on the Jimna Range by the 1890s. In 1922 Hancock and Gore decided to move their Monsildale mill to nearby Foxlowe, an area named by George Byrne who selected land along Yabba Creek in 1878. The sawmill and the buildings at Monsildale were pulled down and moved to the new site, which was renamed Jimna in 1926. The Forestry Department established a presence in the town from the mid 1930s with the development of a hoop pine nursery. After World War II displaced persons from Europe were assigned to work in the new pine plantations and barracks, married quarters and cottages were erected during a period of great activity between 1947 and 1960. The end of sawmilling in the mid-1970s saw a rapid decline in the town's population.

The township of Jimna had been established on forestry land, but Hancock and Gore owned the sawmill and most of the buildings. The mill site is evident as a large clearing in the middle of the township. Still standing are the saw doctor's shed (now the general store), the Jimna hall (opened in 1934) and the mill office, store and post office (all in the same building dating from 1944). Other buildings include the original school (now a private house) and the present school (opened in 1934). A row of mill workers' cottages remain along Dingo Parade and the single men's barracks still stands near the old tennis court. In 1984 the Forestry Department offered freehold title to remaining residents for the purchase of their properties and the Jimna Progress and Historical Association was formed in the same year.

Jimna sawmill office, store and post office

Mill worker's cottage, Dingo Parade

Jimna sawmill engine foundation

Bullock team at the Jimna sawmill, 1937 (John Oxley Library)

 Yednia sawmill shed
 Monsildale sawmill settlement site

Jimna Fire Tower

Jimna Sawmill

Hancock and Gore's Jimna sawmill processed native hoop pine from 1922 until 1947, when it was destroyed by fire. Two mills operated in the town from 1943, when the company added a hardwood mill, but this mill was soon destroyed by fire. When softwood mill burnt down in 1947, it was immediately rebuilt and by the 1960s it was processing hardwood. The largest hardwood log sawn during this period was a blackbutt over 2.2 metres in diameter. All 50 pupils at the school were photographed standing on this huge log. Hancock and Gore closed their Jimna sawmill in the mid-1970s. The sawmill complex at the centre of the township was demolished and all that remains are the concrete engine foundations.

Jimna Fire Tower

Jimna boasts the tallest fire tower in Queensland: its 241 steps climb 47 metres to a platform that offers a 360° view of the state forest. Supported on three ironbark legs 44 metres in length, the tower was completed in 1977 to replace an earlier tower on the site. The builder, Arthur Leis, was responsible for the erection of over 20 fire towers in Queensland; he developed his innovative tripod-leg design for greater rigidity and strength. Consideration had been given to the need for effective protection from fires in forest reserves as early as 1911 and various methods of fire control including firelines and firebreaks were applied in subsequent years. Fire protection procedures were reviewed in the mid-1920s, following a number of severe outbreaks in native hoop pine forests. Construction of towers for fire-spotting started during the mid-1930s.

22. Jimna State Forest

Land was resumed from Yabba station in 1868 and gazetted for alluvial gold diggings. Officially named the Yabba Goldfield, at the junction of Yabba and Jimna creeks, the area became known as the Jimna Gold Diggings. Early prospectors concentrated on the easier alluvial gold, although several underground shafts were also sunk in the late 1890s. Timber-cutters began working the forest during this period. Logs were hauled out by bullocks and, when floods permitted, floated down the Mary River.

The Jimna district was an area rich in native timbers. Rainforest softwoods such as hoop pine and cedar were in greatest demand by early loggers and merchants and were also the easiest to cut and mill; hardwood logs from the eucalypt forests were exploited later. The Forestry Department's interest in the Jimna district began in 1935, when a hoop pine nursery was established in the township. Scrub clearing and the planting of hoop pine began at Jimna in 1938. Today Jimna State Forest is 33,000 hectares in area, and includes about 3000 hectares of native hoop pine plantations.

22 Gold mine on the Jimna Diggings, c1900 (John Oxley Library)

JIMNA

23. Sunday Creek Environmental Education Centre, *Jimna State Forest*

A steam-driven sawmill owned by Queensland Soft and Hard Woods of Nundah operated here between 1948 and 1963. The remains of the old Sunday Creek sawmill were demolished in 1984 so that the area could be used for organised educational activities. Of the five cottages in use at the time of the sawmill's operation, one remains. The Forestry Department took over the barracks in 1964 and a forest station operated at the site until 1976, when the Education Department purchased the buildings and leased the land to establish a field study centre. Sunday Creek Field Study Centre was one of a group of centres opened in 1978. Education Queensland now operates 27 environmental education centres throughout the State.

24. Kenilworth State Forest

Kenilworth State Forest 135 was gazetted in 1907. The reserve covers a large area of the Conondale Range, from the Jimna district north to Imbil, where the forestry headquarters and nursery were established in 1918. Following several years of experimentation with various native softwood species, the first state plantations were established in Queensland in 1920 in three regions, the Mary Valley, the Atherton Tableland and Fraser Island. Hoop and bunya pines made up most of the plantings. During the Depression years in the 1930s government employment schemes enabled many more men to be employed in the State's forests on plantation establishment work. Planting of hoop pine started at Kenilworth in 1938. Kenilworth State Forest now covers an area of about 20,000 hectares, including 1800 hectares of native hoop pine plantation.

25. Charlie Moreland Forest Park, *Kenilworth State Forest*

The Charlie Moreland camping area was dedicated in 1974 to the memory of a forestry ranger who had been based at the nearby Kenilworth Forest Station from 1939 until his retirement in 1966. Moreland died in 1971 and in 1972 a picnic area on Little Yabba Creek was selected for placement of a plaque in his memory. The development of the Charlie Moreland State Forest Park occurred during the early stages of establishment of state forest camping areas as recreational alternatives to reduce visitor pressures at popular national parks near Brisbane.

26. Kenilworth Forest Station

A committee of inquiry established in 1932 to look into the resumption of forest land for farming on Little Yabba Creek reported that the area around the junction of Little Yabba Creek and the Mary River provided a logical administration site for a forestry office and nursery to serve three forest reserves in the district, Kenilworth, Cambroon and Maleny. A nursery was established at Kenilworth in 1938 and surveys for plantation areas commenced. The first hoop pine plantation was begun alongside the nursery in 1939. Workers were accommodated in tents until the early 1950s, when the first barracks were built. Refugees from war-torn Europe were engaged for work at the forestry station during this period. Kenilworth Forest Station is now a centre for the management of the surrounding state forests and associated camping and picnic areas. A visitor information centre was established at the station in the mid-1990s.

27. Kenilworth

Selectors who took up land on the Mary River flats in the 1870s and 1880s formed the small settlement of Kenilworth, which became the base for the Kenilworth Farmers Association established in 1902. The Mary Valley Branch Railway extension to Brooloo in 1915 made the area more accessible for farming and in 1920, after Kenilworth station was subdivided, a section of the station was surveyed for the new town of Kenilworth. Over the next decade, as the district's population doubled, the town developed to provide shops, a school and public hall, and services for the expanding timber, dairying and fruit-growing industries. Kenilworth weathered the Depression years and during World War II Italian prisoners of war worked on the district's farms. The town gradually declined in the postwar period as its supporting industries contracted.

25 *Charlie Moreland picnic area, Kenilworth State Forest*
27 *Kenilworth garage and hotel*

28. Kenilworth Cheese Factory

The cheese factory opened in 1952. Using a reconditioned steam boiler and hand-operated presses, the factory began producing the distinctive Red Malling cheddar cheese, developed especially for Australian conditions. Faced with the factory's closure, a group of former employees purchased the plant in 1990 to continue producing a range of specialist handmade cheeses.

29. Kenilworth Homestead

Taken up as a sheep run by Richard Smith in 1850, Kenilworth was initially referred to as the Obi Obi run. Although it was probably named Kenilworth after Sir Walter Scott's novel, it is unclear when the name was first used. Successive owners extended the station. In 1875 Isaac Moore sold Kenilworth to the successful Gympie miner and businessman Patrick Lillis. The homestead dates from this period. Built in Colonial style, the lowset house had wide verandahs and an iron roof, which was brought out in ballast from England. All the timber, including the red cedar used for walls and fittings, was cut on the property.

29 *Kenilworth Homestead*

Lillis built up a beef cattle herd and made huge profits from the station's cedar stands. When Lillis's investments failed in 1888, Isaac Moore, who then owned nearby Jimna station, repossessed Kenilworth. The station was subdivided for farming settlement in 1921 and the present owners, the Rowe family, purchased the homestead block in 1925. The detached kitchen and stables were remodelled in 1987 to provide visitor accommodation and the barn was converted into a large hall.

30. St Matthew's Anglican Church, *Gheerulla*

This church was built about 1926 and named after St Matthew's Anglican Church at Grovely, near Brisbane, whence many of the early settlers of Gheerulla had come. Services are still held here on one Sunday every month.

31. Imbil

Settlement at Imbil dates from the 1868 gold rush. Imbil, with shops for miners' supplies and Chinese market gardens, enjoyed a brief period as a boom town until the alluvial gold ran out. Farming selections were slowly taken up in the following decades and the subdivision of Imbil station for farming blocks in the years 1908–14 brought in more settlers. Lack of roads and impenetrable scrub kept the area relatively isolated until the Mary Valley Railway opened in 1914. The first town allotments were sold the same year. In 1916 a forest station and nursery were opened at Imbil, which became a centre for one of the earliest experimental timber plantations in Queensland.

The town remained small, but by 1920 was well established, having a school, bank, public hall and general stores. Rail and commercial facilities developed to serve the district's expanding fruit-growing and dairying industries. Imbil's growth was reduced as the timber industry was cut back in the 1960s, although the town continued to benefit from forestry programs. The town's dependence on the timber industry and its fluctuating fortunes is reflected in the streetscape.

32. Railway Hotel, *Yabba Road*

As the name suggests, the hotel was expected to open in 1914 to take advantage of the trade from the newly constructed railway. The original licensing application was turned down, however, and not until 1917 was James Larney able to proceed with building the hotel.

30 *St Matthews's Church, Gheerulla*
31 *Imbil Station on the Mary Valley Railway (John Oxley Library)*
32 *Railway Hotel, Imbil*

33. Imbil Railway Station

The Imbil section of the Mary Valley Railway between Kandanga and Brooloo opened in 1915. A bridge was required over Yabba Creek. The structure is now a dominant landmark in the town and was a feature of the approach to the railway office. The restored station is now the terminus of the Mary Valley Heritage Railway.

34. Imbil Forest Station

Reservation of forested land in the Imbil district began in the 1880s. In 1906 over 16,000 hectares were reserved at Brooloo to form the first state forest in the district. After early nursery experiments at Sterlings Crossing in 1913 and the development of an experimental area in Brooloo State Forest in 1916, an office, staff housing and a nursery were established at the present Imbil Forest Station site in 1920. The nursery operated continuously until 1977.

In 1917 a hectare of scrub near the nursery was felled and planted with both hoop and bunya pine. This was the earliest plantation at Imbil. Today it is the oldest surviving hoop and bunya pine plantation in south-east Queensland. By the 1920s, Imbil was the centrepiece of forestry operations in south-east Queensland and during the 1930s and 1940s it was developed as one of the most important forest stations in Queensland. By the 1990s, over 12,000 hectares of hoop pine plantations had been established in the district, managed from the Imbil Forest Station.

🏵 *WWII hut used as a store shed, Imbil Forest Station*
🏵 *Hoop pine avenue, Imbil Forest Station*

35. Hoop Pine Avenue, *Imbil Forest Station*

In 1918, two years after its establishment, Imbil Forest Station was chosen for a visit by a viceregal entourage led by the Governor of Queensland. The visitors planted six hoop pines on what now forms the main entrance driveway to the station. Further trees were planted between then and 1932. The trees now form an impressive avenue of mature hoop pines leading to the administration office and workshops.

36. Borumba Dam, *near Imbil*

In 1960 approval was given for the construction of Borumba Dam to supplement Gympie's water supply and to provide for farm irrigation in the Mary Valley. The dam, which cost over $2 million, was officially opened in 1964. It has a rock-filled wall rising to 45 metres above the bed of Yabba Creek. A major project was begun to develop recreational facilities at Lake Borumba in the early 1980s. The State Government established a fish hatchery in 1980. Operated by the Cooloola Shire Council since 1986, the breeding program includes golden perch (yellowbelly) and silver perch (black bream); the emphasis is on the production of fingerlings for release into public waters.

37. Imbil Forest Drive

Imbil Forest Drive uses forestry tracks to provide a scenic and informative drive through the state forest pine plantations between Imbil township and Borumba Dam. A number of stops along the way interpret the forest's natural and historic values.

Forestry Camp Sites

By 1949 newly arrived refugees from Eastern European were being allocated work in Imbil State Forest at three main camps, Sterlings Crossing, Araucaria Camp and Derrier Camp. Derrier was known as the 'Foreign Legion Camp'. Until the mid-1950s, the workers were generally accommodated in tents. It is not clear at what period the Derrier and Araucaria camps ceased operation. The Araucaria Camp comprised barracks for single men; today nothing remains of the camp apart from mango, persimmon, peach, orange and loquat trees. Both sites are significant for their association with the postwar migration to Australia and the subsequent employment of migrants for forestry work. The Sterlings Crossing Camp was in use until the 1970s.

Relict Cedar Tree

This giant is one of the few native cedar trees surviving in the Imbil district, and is also one of the largest.

38. Kandanga

Upper Kandanga Creek experienced a minor gold rush soon after gold was found at Imbil in 1868. Land in the Mary Valley became available for selection after 1869 and farm blocks were taken up for cattle and small crops during the 1870s. The first settler on Bunya Creek, the original name for Kandanga, was William Chippendall. By the 1890s, his holding had been subdivided, along with the other large blocks. Floods, redwater fever and fruit pests hindered progress, however, and Kandanga was not declared a town until 1912.

It consisted of a store and hotel for the workers on the Mary Valley Railway, which reached the town in 1914. Timber, with dairy farming along the river flats and some fruit growing, supported a growing population and brought prosperity in the 1920s. With the backing of an active progress association, new stores, churches, a bank and a public hall were opened, the school was extended and local businessmen built the picture theatre. Today Kandanga serves a small farming community and activities associated with the logging of state forests in the area.

39. Kandanga Hotel

The hotel, built for its owner, Charles Boyling, was opened in 1914, two months after the railway reached Kandanga. Even before the later extensions, it was a substantial building, with spacious bar rooms, a billiard saloon and accommodation for travellers. With its wide verandah, the hotel has retained its Queenslander style and the restored barber chair on display was used for many years in the hotel barbershop.

40. Kandanga Railway Station

The first section of the Mary Valley Branch Railway from Gympie to Kandanga Station was opened in 1914. Kandanga Creek Railway Bridge, on the approach to the station, is an unusual example of a rail bridge placed over a road bridge. Both bridges cross Kandanga Creek.

37 *Relict cedar tree, Imbil Forest Drive*
38 *Q.N. Bank at Kandanga, 1921 (John Oxley Library)*
39 *Kandanga Hotel*
40 *Kandanga Railway Station*
41 *Upper Kandanga sawmill shed*

41. Upper Kandanga Sawmill

The valuable hardwood stands of the Upper Kandanga area were first developed in the early 1930s as part of a Queensland Government employment scheme for forestry workers during the Depression. The timber was milled at John Doyle's Upper Kandanga sawmill. By the 1940s Doyle's son-in-law, Bill Sterling, had taken over the mill. During the late 1950s, the timber quota allotted to the Upper Kandanga sawmill was only enough to provide a month's work in a year; consequently, the mill was forced to close in 1961 and the Sterling family turned to dairying. The plant was sold, but the sawmill shed remains, a reminder of early milling at Upper Kandanga.

GENERAL BIBLIOGRAPHY FOR FURTHER READING

Burrows, Robyn 1989, *Dairies and Daydreams: The Mudgeeraba Story*, Boolarong Press, Brisbane.

Charlton, Peter 1991, *South Queensland WWII 1941–1945*, Boolarong Press, Brisbane.

Cohen, Kay: Wiltshire, Kenneth [eds] 1995, *People, places and policies: aspects of Queensland government administration 1859-1920*, University of Queensland Press, St Lucia, Qld.

Curtis, Eve 1990, *The Turning Years: A Tamborine Mountain History*, Beaudesert Times Ltd, Beaudesert, Qld.

Dornan, Dimity 1992, *The Petrie family: building colonial Brisbane*, University of Queensland Press, St Lucia, Qld.

Fitzgerald, Ross 1982, *From the Dreaming to 1915: A History of Queensland*, University of Queensland Press, St Lucia, Qld.

French, Maurice 1990, *A Pastoral Romance: The Tribulation and Triumph of Squatterdom* [A history of the Darling Downs frontier], University of Southern Queensland Press, Toowoomba, Qld.

French, Maurice 1994, *Pubs, Ploughs and Peculiar People: Towns, Farms and Social Life* [A history of the Darling Downs frontier], University of Southern Queensland Press, Toowoomba, Qld.

French, Maurice and Waterson, Duncan 1982, *The Darling Downs: A Pictorial History 1850–1950*, Darling Downs Institute Press, Toowoomba, Qld.

Gill, J.C.H. 1981, *Spicers Peak Road: A New Way to the Downs*, Library Board of Queensland, Brisbane.

Gregory, Helen 1991, *Making Maroochy: A History of the Land, the People and the Shire*, Boolarong Press, Brisbane.

Gregory, Helen 1996, *The Brisbane River Story: Meanders Through Time*, Australian Marine Conservation Society, Brisbane.

Horton, Helen 1988, *Brisbane's Back Door: The Story of the D'Aguilar Range*, Boolarong Press, Brisbane.

Johnston, W. Ross 1982, *The Call of the Land: A History of Queensland to the Present Day*, Jacaranda Press, Milton, Qld.

Johnston, W. Ross [ed] 1988, *A documentary history of Queensland*, University of Queensland Press, St Lucia, Qld.

Kerr, J.D. 1990, *Triumph of Narrow Gauge: A History of Queensland Railways*, Boolarong Press, Brisbane.

Kerr, R.S. 1988, *Confidence and Tradition: A History of the Esk Shire*, Council of the Shire of Esk, Esk, Qld.

Longhurst, Robert 1992, *Taming a Plateau: A History of the Beechmont District*, Beechmont Centenary Association Inc., Beechmont, Qld.

McIvor, S. and T. 1994, *Salute the Brave: A Pictorial Record of Queensland War Memorials*, University of Southern Queensland Press, Toowoomba, Qld.

Pullar, Margaret 1995, *Historic routes of Queensland*, National Trust of Queensland, Brisbane.

Reynolds, Henry 1981, *The other side of the frontier: Aboriginal resistance to the European invasion of Australia*, Penguin, Ringwood, Vic.

Reynolds, Henry 1987, *Frontier; Aborigines, settlers and land*, Allen and Unwin, Sydney.

Steele, J.G. 1972, *The Explorers of the Moreton bay District 1770–1830*, University of Queensland Press, St Lucia, Qld.

Steele, J.G. 1978, *Conrad Martens in Queensland: The Frontier Travels of a Colonial Artist*, University of Queensland Press, St Lucia, Qld.

Steele, J.G. 1984, *Aboriginal Pathways in Southeast Queensland and the Richmond River*, University of Queensland Press, St Lucia, Qld.

Tranter, Deborah 1990, *Cobb & Co.: Coaching in Queensland*, Queensland Museum, Brisbane.

Ward-Brown, Jan 1988, *Rosenthal — Historic Shire*, Rosenthal Shire Council, Warwick, Qld.

Whitmore, R.L. 1985, *Coal in Queensland: The Late Nineteenth Century 1875 to 1900*, University of Queensland Press, St Lucia, Qld.

Whitmore, R.L. 1991, *Coal in Queensland: From Federation to the Twenties 1900 to 1925*, University of Queensland Press, St Lucia, Qld.